Exterminating Poverty

The true story of the eugenic plan to get rid of the poor,
and the Scottish doctor who fought against it.

Mark H. Sutherland
in conjunction with Neil Sutherland

Front cover design: Mark H. Sutherland.

Cover photograph: Little Collingwood Street, Bethnal Green, London circa 1900. Photographer: John Galt.

Mark Sutherland's dedication: For Anna and Benedict.

Neil Sutherland's dedication: For Fiona, Olivia and Jamie.

Celebrating the life and work of
Dr Halliday Sutherland (1882-1960):

hallidaysutherland.com

Contents

Preface

I was born in the year my grandfather died and was named Halliday in his memory. At some point (I forget when), I learned that he had been the defendant in a libel trial in the High Court in London, and that the plaintiff was Dr Marie Stopes.

As I learned about the trial, I found information readily available in the biographies of Stopes. From this I was able to ascertain the accepted view of the trial, summarised here in the BBC's online biography:

> "In 1921, Stopes opened a family planning clinic in Holloway, north London, the first in the country. It offered a free service to married women... The Catholic church was Stopes's fiercest critic. In 1923, Stopes sued Catholic doctor Halliday Sutherland for libel."[1]

I used to believe this version because, firstly, it was labelled "history" and, secondly, because no one, family or otherwise, told me differently. I now know the accepted view is false and, given the uniformity and settled scholarship of Stopes' biographers in relation to Dr Sutherland, I have written this book to correct the historical record.

Of course, being Dr Sutherland's grandson will create a perception of bias in his favour. For this reason, I have cited the sources for the assertions I make. These include biographies of Marie Stopes, her papers at the Wellcome and British Libraries, the archive of the Archdiocese of Westminster and, uniquely, Dr Sutherland's personal papers. This book also draws on the transcript of the Stopes *v* Sutherland libel trial, a document commissioned by Dr Stopes herself to record the proceedings of the High Court.

There are many people that I must thank. My brother and collaborator, Neil Sutherland, bridged the gap between my Sydney home and the archival materials in Britain. I have benefitted greatly from his suggestions, ideas, support, and research.

When I became stuck with the magnitude of the task, Larry Lucas listened patiently and generously gave his time and sound advice. Bill Martin read an early draft of this book, and not only did he tell me how to improve it, but he did so with characteristic kindness and tact. My son Benedict read a later draft and suggested structural changes that improved the work.

Ann Farmer's books (*Prophets and Priests* and *By Their Fruits*) provided insights about Dr Sutherland, and I will always be grateful for her encouragement. I would also like to thank Charles Coulombe (author of *Puritan's Empire* and *Star-Spangled Crown*) for his support as well.

Thank you to my mother, Pamela Sutherland, who gave me unfettered access to Dr Sutherland's papers. Thank you too to Julian and Christine Bowman, Paul Gabrielli, Simon Horton, Margaret Horton, Paul and Sarah Ivens, Lesley Moore (author of *Turn Right, Good Moon*), Andrew Nunn, Kevin O'Doherty, Philip Sutherland and Karen Wakefield.

Thank you to the staff at the Wellcome Institute, the British Library, the Westminster Archdiocese Archive, and to Louise Williams of the Lothian Health Services Archive who was so helpful in finding Dr Sutherland's 1911 film *The Story of John M'Neil*.

Most of all, a huge thank you to my wife, Anna and son, Benedict. The fact that the book was finished was a result of your love, support and patience. I thank you from the bottom of my heart.

Any errors and mistakes are my own.

Mark Halliday Sutherland,
Annandale, New South Wales.
August 2020.

---

[1] See: British Broadcasting Corporation. (2018, December 28). History. Marie Stopes (1880-1958). Retrieved from:
http://www.bbc.co.uk/history/historic_figures/stopes_marie_carmichael.shtml.

Introduction

The Stopes *v* Sutherland legal dispute of 1923-4 arose from a passage in a 1922 book: *Birth Control: A Statement of Christian Doctrine Against the Neo-Malthusians*. Dr Marie Stopes brought an action for libel against the author, Dr Halliday Sutherland, complaining that in it, he had accused her of performing experiments on the poor.

As an historical conflict it is special because, during the course of the battle itself, the protagonists revealed their motives and the factors which influenced them in the fight. The fact that statements were sworn under oath adds to their veracity or, where a false statement was made, highlights the significance of that lie.

Given that much of what took place was recorded in the Court documents and in the transcript of the trial, the work of the historian becomes easier, at least in some ways. Certainly, it ensures that there is much less room for leeway in the historical interpretation of events.

Despite this, there are significant gaps in the biographies of Dr Marie Stopes in relation to the trial. These gaps have been addressed and are presented in this book for the first time.

These include the fact that no biography has connected Sutherland's work as a doctor specialising in tuberculosis to his opposition of eugenics, and subsequently to Stopes' birth control clinic. Again, biographies tell a story of Stopes visiting Dr Louise McIlroy in disguise after the trial, and use it to portray McIlroy as a shameless hypocrite. While it is a good story, the key points that make it so were fabricated (see Appendix 4).

In their enthusiasm to impose a modern framework on Stopes' work and show her as giving women access to contraceptives, the biographers gloss over or otherwise obfuscate her eugenic aims. As this book will show, eugenics was fundamental to that work; you cannot have the one without the other.

Likewise, in the biographies of Stopes, you will not find the statement of her aims to the High Court:[1]

"Not reduction in the total birth rate, but reduction of the birth rate at the wrong part and increase of the birth rate at the right end of the social scale."[2]

"The object of the Society is, if possible, to counteract the steady evil which has been growing for a good many years of the reduction of the birth rate just on the part of the thrifty, wise, well-contented, and the generally sound members of our community, and the reckless breeding from the C3 end, and the semi-feebleminded, the careless, who are proportionately increasing in our community because of the slowing of the birth rate at the other end of the social scale. Statistics show that every year the birth rate from the worst end of our community is increasing in proportion to the birth rate at the better end, and it was in order to try to right that grave social danger that I embarked upon this work."[3]

In addition, the biographies ignore Stopes' commercial dealings with Lambert of Dalston (a manufacturer of contraceptive devices), or her falsification of the statistics showing how effective her contraceptives were, or the significant dangers of the Gold Pin. And when biographers state that Stopes aimed to give women "choice", they don't mention that in the case of so-called "C3" mothers, the choice would have been made by the State had the compulsory sterilisation laws Stopes campaigned for been enacted.

In its time, the Stopes *v* Sutherland libel trial was known as "The Birth Control Libel Trial". This book aims to show that, more than just a spat about contraceptives, the conflict was part of a wider and longer-running struggle between those who advocated population control, and those who opposed it. It is a conflict that continues to this day.

In the context of this book, the ideas of the population controllers were manifested in Malthusianism, neo-Malthusianism, eugenics, contraceptives, voluntary sterilisation, compulsory sterilisation of the unfit and even infanticide. In our times, their repertoire has expanded to include full-term abortion, eutelegenesis, genetic screening and euthanasia. And while infanticide has not been formally implemented, the moral justification[4] and legal precedents continue as a gradual work in progress.

While Dr Stopes' complaint was that Sutherland accused her of performing experiments on the poor, he countered that hers was a social experiment, namely:

> "The indiscriminate distribution of knowledge of contraceptives amongst the poor for the purpose of attempting to redistribute the birth rate by means of artificial contraceptives and contrary to the law of nature."

During the trial, Sutherland's advocates stated that the results of the experiment would not be known for many years and indeed, they were right; the results are still coming in today.

These include contemporary reports of the collapse in fertility rates in Britain and other Western nations. A statement that the fall was a "huge surprise"[5] contrasts with Dr Sutherland's 1922 prediction:

> "Our declining birth-rate is a fact of the utmost gravity, and a more serious position has never confronted the British people. Here in the midst of a great nation, at the end of a victorious war, the law of decline is working, and by that law the greatest empires in the world have perished. In comparison with that single fact all other dangers, be they war, of politics, or of disease, are of little moment… "Let us have children, children at any price," will be the cry of tomorrow."

This then is the true story of the eugenic plan to get rid of the poor, and of Dr Halliday Sutherland's fight against it.

◆   ◆   ◆

The following points will enhance your enjoyment of this book. Firstly, there is a glossary at the back in which the medical and legal terms used in the book are explained.

Secondly, please also note that superscript letters indicate who a barrister is acting for, or on whose behalf the witness is testifying. The key is as follows:

P — acting for the plaintiff;
D — acting for the defendants;
S — indicates appearing under subpoena.

Thirdly, the proceedings of the High Court trial have been quoted verbatim from the transcript of Mr William Rogers, the stenographer appointed by Dr Stopes. At various times, the stenographer appears to have garbled what was said, not unlikely given the pace of the trial and the poor acoustics in the Court. For instance, one speaker refers to the "Society for Constructional Birth Control" whereas the correct name was the "Society for Constructive Birth Control". Given that it is not possible to identify if this was the speaker's or the stenographer's mistake, and given that any amendments I made might have altered the meaning of what was said, I have left these apparent errors uncorrected.

Finally, please note that in the course of the book, all street names should be assumed to be in London, unless otherwise stated.

---

[1] To those who would point out that the second of these statements is quoted in Stopes' Wikipedia biography, this author would say "I know, but only because I placed it there".

[2] Femina Books. (1967). *The Trial of Marie Stopes*. (M. Box, Ed.) London: Femina Books Ltd. Page 50.

[3] *Ibid.*

[4] For instance see: After birth abortion: why should the baby live? https://jme.bmj.com/content/39/5/261 accessed 26 July 2020.

[5] For instance see: 'Remarkable' decline in fertility rates by James Gallagher https://www.bbc.com/news/health-46118103 accessed 26 July 2020.

PART 1

PRELUDE

"The cataclysm which may end the eighth known epoch in civilisation may be a lack of European children."
— Dr Halliday Sutherland (1882-1960)

Chapter 1

An Extraordinary Speech

On Tuesday, 4th September 1917, Dr Halliday Sutherland addressed the National Council of the Young Men's Christian Association in King George's Hall, London. His subject was Consumption: Its Cause and Cure.[1]

Consumption had a different meaning then to how we understand it today. Back then, it was a disease whose name described what happened to you if you were infected. A cough, gentle at first, increased until you could do little else. The harsh, hacking cough that followed ripped the fabric of your weakened lungs, and coughing up blood was not unusual. As your debilitated body wasted away — consumed from within — you gave off a foul corporeal smell. Death followed shortly afterwards. Today we call Consumption "tuberculosis" and we know that it occurs when the bacillus tuberculosis infects the lungs.

At the time of the speech, around 50,000 Britons died each year from Consumption, 20,000 from other forms of tuberculosis and 150,000 were disabled.[2] Consumption was three times more likely to affect the poor than the better-off and when the breadwinner became ill, whole families became destitute. It was the cause of around 10% of pauperism in Britain.[3] It was for good reason that tuberculosis was described as a plague.

Sutherland was an acknowledged expert in the disease. At around the time that he had graduated at Edinburgh University, he had come under the influence of Dr (later Sir) Robert Phillip,[4] a pupil of Robert Koch, the brilliant German physician who identified the *tubercle bacillus* as the cause of the disease. Phillip had created the "Edinburgh System" for the prevention, treatment and cure of Consumption.[5]

Sutherland became a protégé of Dr Phillip and implemented many of his ideas and schemes. In 1910, he became Medical Officer at the St Marylebone Dispensary for the Prevention of Consumption. From its premises at 15 Allsop Place,[6] he set up an "Open-Air" school for tuberculous children in a bandstand in Regent's Park. He edited and contributed to *The Control and Eradication of Tuberculosis*, a book of essays by 32 international experts. He dedicated the book to Phillip and, when it came to the attention of Prime Minister Asquith, it led to a knighthood for Phillip.[7] In 1911, Sutherland produced Britain's first public health cinema film, *The Story of John M'Neil* which was shown in the newly-popular "picture palaces" across the country.[8]

A key message of Sutherland's speech was that Consumption could be prevented and, if treated early enough, cured. Yet his speech was not good news amidst the slaughter of the First World War, so much as a declamation that Britain had failed to prevent and cure this disease.

He cited the 10,000 children who died each year from drinking tuberculous milk. It caused, he said, "an amount of child sickness, suffering and sorrow so widespread as to be incomprehensible to a finite mind", yet the contamination of milk was "no more natural than if their food had been poisoned with arsenic".[9]

In the United States at that time, cattle were tested for tuberculosis. Milk was assessed and graded so that its purity could be matched to the vulnerability of the end-user and tuberculous milk was rendered harmless by pasteurisation. Such measures could have been implemented in Britain – indeed, more than twenty years had passed since a Royal Commission had recommended that milk be tested – yet nothing had been done.

Sutherland singled out "self-styled eugenists" for blame and he described them as "race breeders with the souls of cattle-breeders".[10]

"They say the efficiency of the State is based upon what they call 'the survival of the fittest.' This war has smashed their rhetorical phrase. Who talks now about survival of the fittest, or thinks himself fit because he survives? I don't know what they mean. I do know that in preventing disease you are not preserving the weak, but conserving the strong. And I do know that those evil conditions which will kill a weakly child within a few months of birth, and slay another when he reaches the teens, will destroy yet another when he comes to adult life."[11]

A eugenist[12] listening to the speech might have protested that eugenics aimed for more than the efficiency of the State, and might even have suggested that among the benefits of eugenic science was the elimination of tuberculosis itself. For this reason, it is to the eugenists to whom we will now turn.

---

[1] Sutherland, H. (1917). *Consumption: Its Cause and Cure*. London: Red Triangle Press.

[2] *Ibid.*

[3] Sutherland, H. (Editor). (1911). *The Control and Eradication of Tuberculosis*. London and Edinburgh: William Green and Son. Page 5.

[4] British Medical Journal. (1960, April 30). *Obituary Dr Halliday Sutherland*. British Medical Journal, 1368-1369.

[5] Sutherland, H. (1936). *In My Path*. Geoffrey Bles.

[6] Allsop Place is a few hundred metres from Madame Tussauds in London. Today a bus depot stands where the dispensary once stood.

[7] British Medical Journal. (1960, April 30). *Obituary Dr Halliday Sutherland*. British Medical Journal, 1368-1369.

[8] *The Story of John M'Neil* can be viewed on the website of the British Film Institute. See: https://player.bfi.org.uk/free/film/watch-the-story-of-john-mneil-1911-online.

[9] Sutherland, H. (1917). *Consumption: Its Cause and Cure*. London: Red Triangle Press.

[10] *Ibid.*

[11] *Ibid.*

[12] The adherents of eugenics can be described as "eugenists" or "eugenicists". In this book, I have used "eugenist" in keeping with the form used by Dr Sutherland and the Professor of Eugenics at London University, Karl Pearson.

Chapter 2

"Race Breeders with the Souls of Cattle Breeders"

Francis Galton had seen how selective breeding could be used by farmers to improve their livestock, and he wondered: "Could not the race of men be similarly improved? Could not the undesirables be got rid of and the desirables multiplied?"[1]

Galton's ideas had been stimulated by his cousin Charles Darwin's book, *Origin of Species*. He envisaged that man might control his own evolution and he wondered how the relative influence of heredity and environment could be accurately determined. While caught in a rainstorm, he realised that biometrics and statistics could reveal the transmission of hereditary traits between successive generations in a family and quantify the relative influence of nature and nurture.

Galton founded a new scientific discipline which involved the "study of agencies under social control that may improve or impair the racial qualities of future generations either physically or mentally."[2] He called it "Eugenics", derived from the Greek words for "good" and "breeding".[3] While the word was new, the essential idea was not. G.K. Chesterton described it as "one of the most ancient follies of the earth,"[4] which aligned with the "modern craze for scientific officialism and strict social organisation".[5]

In 1873, Galton had predicted that as the population increased, inferior humans would come to compete for resources with their more gifted counterparts and that, as a result, they would "decay out of the land."[6] As the Nineteenth Century wore on, however, it became clear that the inferior had not decayed so much as decamped to Britain's industrial cities. Here, despite squalid living conditions and overcrowding, their numbers proliferated.

Eugenists were acutely aware of the problem they called the "differential birth rate". It meant that while the overall birth rate in Britain was falling — it had peaked at 36.3 births per thousand in 1876 and fell by 21% by 1901 and by around 34% by 1914[7] — the fall was more pronounced among the well-to-do than among the lower classes. If, as eugenists suspected, heredity was more significant than environment in shaping the person,[8] Britain was doomed because "… [one-] half of each succeeding generation was produced by no more than a quarter of its married predecessor, and that the prolific quarter was disproportionately located among the dregs of society."[9]

It was self-evident that a livestock farmer who bred his herd from the worst specimens would lose his farm and it seemed that an analogous process was taking place at the heart of the British Empire. Eugenists spoke gloomily of "degeneration", "national deterioration" and even "race suicide".

The signs of decline were apparent to those who were looking for it. Britain's economic growth had faltered in the face of increased commercial rivalry from Germany and the United States.[10] The men who presented themselves at military recruiting stations for the Boer War revealed the poor condition of Britain's working-classes, and between 40 and 60 percent of recruits were rejected as physically unfit to serve.[11] It was around this time that the jargon of military recruitment entered the national lexicon: "A1", meaning the best recruits and "C3", meaning those rejected on mental and physical grounds.[12]

These circumstances created the conditions to pique interest in Eugenics as a possible solution to the decline of British "racial stocks". In 1907 the Eugenics Education Society (EES) was formed with a membership that included: "leading townspeople… distinguished scientists and social scientists, prominent lawyers, clerics, physicians, schoolmasters, intellectuals and… several knights of the realm".[13]

Biometric research began in earnest. In 1904, Galton donated £500 to University College London for a Research Fellowship in National Eugenics.[14] Galton's protégé and later biographer, Karl Pearson, headed the Department of Applied Statistics at the Biometric Laboratory there, and it produced three hundred biometric studies. These investigated, amongst other things, "the relationship of physique to intelligence; the resemblance of first cousins; the effect of parental occupation upon children's welfare or the birth rate; and the role of heredity in alcoholism, tuberculosis, and defective sight."[15]

Large projects were undertaken: *The Treasury of Human Inheritance* which registered "the facts of Family Inheritance" (to prevent them from being "irrevocably lost") was published in 1912.[16] Dr Charles Goring's *The English Convict: A Statistical Study* was published the following year.[17]

Ethel Elderton, the researcher in Pearson's Laboratory who did much of the work for *The Treasury of Human Inheritance*, summarised the purpose of their work: "in the present state of our knowledge the calculus of correlation is the sole rational method available for attacking these urgent social problems."[18]

On his death in 1911, Sir Francis Galton (as he had become) bequeathed £45,000 to establish the Professorship of Eugenics at University College London, and Pearson was appointed to the role.[19] The EES established a Parliamentary Committee for "the task of watching all bills going through Parliament that were of concern to eugenists",[20] in other words, to determine whether they were eugenic or dysgenic. When the *Mental Deficiency Act* was passed in 1913, the *Eugenics Review* boasted that it was the first piece of social legislation in which the influence of heredity had been practically applied.[21]

Given that eugenists had examined so many aspects of British life, it was inevitable that they would study tuberculosis, to see if it was caused by heredity or environment.

---

[1] Kevles, D. J. (2004). *In The Name of Eugenics: Genetics and the Uses of Human Heredity* (5th Printing ed.). Cambridge, Massachusetts: Harvard University Press. Page 3.

[2] Searle, G. (1976). *Eugenics and Politics in Britain 1900-1914*. Leyden: Noordhoff International Publishing. Page 1.

[3] Galton, F. (1904). *Eugenics: Its Definition, Scope and Aims*. The American Journal of Sociology (Volume X, Number 1).

[4] Searle, G. (1976). *Eugenics and Politics in Britain 1900-1914*. Leyden: Noordhoff International Publishing. Page 3.

[5] Chesterton, G. (1922). *Eugenics and Other Evils*. London, New York, Toronto and Melbourne: Cassell and Company, Limited.

[6] Galton, F. (1873). *Hereditary Improvement*. Fraser's Magazine, January 1873. Page 129.

[7] Soloway, R. A. (1990). *Demography and Degeneration: Eugenics and the Declining Birthrate in Twentieth Century Britain* (Digital Edition). Chapel Hill: University of North Carolina Press.

[8] Pearson, K. (1910, April 28,). *"Nature and Nurture: The Problem of the Future"*. A Presidential Address at the Annual General Meeting of the Social and Political Education League. Pearson thought that environmental influences were between ten and 20 percent of heredity. In a 1910 speech, he said: "Now I will not dogmatically assert that environment matters not at all; phases of it may be discovered which produce more effect than any we have yet been able to deal with. But I think it is safe to say that the influence of environment is not one-fifth of heredity, and quite possibly not one-tenth of it. There is no real comparison between nature and nurture; it is essentially the man who makes his environment; and not the environment that makes the man."

[9] Kevles, D. J. (2004). *In The Name of Eugenics: Genetics and the Uses of Human Heredity* (5th Printing ed.). Cambridge, Massachusetts: Harvard University Press. Page 74.

[10] Soloway, R. A. (1990). *Demography and Degeneration: Eugenics and the Declining Birthrate in Twentieth Century Britain* (Digital Edition). Chapel Hill: University of North Carolina Press.

[11] Winter, J. (1980, April). *Military Fitness and Civilian Health in Britain during the First World War*. Journal of Contemporary History, 15(2), 211-244. Page 211.

[12] *Ibid.* According to Winter, 'A' meant fit for general service, 'B' meant fit for service abroad in a support capacity, and 'C' meant fit for service at home only. There were three gradations of 'B' and 'C' fitness, which related to the recruits' aptitude for specific types of work in the Army, as well as two categories of unfitness: temporary and permanent.

[13] Kevles, D. J. (2004). *In The Name of Eugenics: Genetics and the Uses of Human Heredity* (5th Printing ed.). Cambridge, Massachusetts: Harvard University Press. Pages 59-60.

[14] *Ibid.*, page 37.

[15] *Ibid.*, page 39.

[16] Pearson, K. (1912). *Treasury of Human Inheritance (Vol. 1)*. London: Dulau and Co. Ltd. Retrieved January 7, 2019, from https://archive.org/details/treasuryofhumani01bull/page/n5.

[17] Goring, C. (1913). *The English Convict: A Statistical Study*. London: His Majesty's Stationery Office. Retrieved January 7, 2019, from https://archive.org/details/englishconvictst00goriuoft/page/n3.

[18] Elderton, E. (1915). *The Relative Strength of Nurture and Nature*. London: Cambridge University Press. Retrieved August 20, 2019, from https://archive.org/stream/relativestrength00eldeiala#page/n1/mode/2up.

[19] Kevles, D. J. (2004). *In The Name of Eugenics: Genetics and the Uses of Human Heredity* (5th Printing ed.). Cambridge, Massachusetts: Harvard University Press. Page 38.

[20] Searle, G. (1976). *Eugenics and Politics in Britain 1900-1914*. Leyden: Noordhoff International Publishing. Page 72.
[21] *Ibid.*, page 111.

.

Chapter 3

Tuberculosis: Heredity or Environment?

Tuberculosis is one of the oldest known diseases and its cause has been debated throughout history:[1] was it caused by an inherited susceptibility to the disease or by infection? If it was caused by a combination of both, how significant was heredity compared to infection?

Various metaphors were used to describe the issue: was tuberculosis inherent in a person's nature, or did it arise from their nurture? Was the disease present in the seed or was it a contaminant from the soil?

Dr John Haycraft was one expert who came down firmly on the side of nature. In 1894, he delivered three Milroy Lectures to the Royal College of Physicians. These were published in *The Lancet* and in a book, *Darwinism and Race Progress*. According to Haycraft, "a certain type of individual is readily attacked by this microbe" and the *tubercle bacillus* could not "gain access to, or multiply in, the tissues of a healthy and vigorous man or woman".[2] The "certain type of individual" was "one who comes of a family liable to fall a prey to this microbe… Sufferers… are prone to other diseases, such as pulmonary and bronchial attacks, so that… they are to be looked upon as unsuited not only for the battle of life, but especially for parentage and for the multiplication of the conditions from which they themselves suffer."[3]

He concluded: "If we stamp out the Infectious Diseases we perpetuate Poor Types. It is a hard saying, but none the less a true one, that the *bacillus tuberculosis* is a friend of the race, for it attacks no healthy man or woman, but only the feeble."[4]

The research of the Department of Applied Statistics at the Biometric Laboratory of University College London concurred. In 1907, the *First Study of the Statistics of Pulmonary Tuberculosis* was published,[5] followed by the second in 1908.[6] In total, seven studies into tuberculosis were published between 1907 and 1913.[7]

The transmission of infection between family members could be statistically measured. According to Pearson, "on the pure infection theory it would be expected that husband and wife would be at least as likely to infect one another as parent would be to infect a child." If consumption were caused by heredity, on the other hand, it would be transmitted to the child but not to the spouse. When the Laboratory found a higher correlation of consumption "... between parent and child than between husband and wife [it] was a strong argument in favour of the hereditary factor."[8]

The Biometric Laboratory's findings were not universally accepted, and even Pearson himself admitted that he had formed his view when he had "between 200 and 300 fairly complete histories, [whereas] 2,000 or 3,000 are necessary".[9] His study was criticised by Dr (later Sir) Arthur Newsholme, formerly the Medical Officer of Health in Brighton, on the grounds that he had gone beyond his data.[10]

In retaliation, Pearson mocked Newsholme's own work in this field. He lamented that there had not been "adequate scientific inquiry into the relative importance of the hereditary factor... the environment factor [nor] of the liability to infection." Further, Newsholme had made "the classic statistical error of confusing correlation with causation". He pointed out that had Newsholme linked deaths from tuberculosis to expenditure on the Royal Navy, exports to Canada, or even the price of bananas, his conclusions would have been unchanged.[11]

This was not merely an academic spat, because if tuberculosis was inherited, then efforts to control infection were futile and, as Pearson pointed out, the best way to reduce the death rate was to aid what he called "Nature's method":

> "... the bulk of the tuberculous belong to stocks which we want *ab initio* to discourage. Everything which tends to check the multiplication of the unfit, to emphasize that the fertility of the physically and mentally healthy,

will *pro tanto* aid Nature's method of reducing the phthisical death-rate. That is what the Eugenist proclaims as the 'better thing to do…'"[12]

Dr Sutherland's view was expressed in the opening caption of his 1911 public health film, *The Story of John M'Neil*: "Before you see the picture it is necessary for all to realise that not only is tuberculosis CURABLE in its earlier stages, but above all it is PREVENTABLE."[13]

Not all doctors agreed with him, including the President of the Liverpool Branch of the EES, Sir James Barr, MD who wrote:

"… for many years medical men have been neglecting heredity and devoting their attention solely to environment. This has chiefly occurred since the discovery of the *tubercle bacillus*, and in the present day you may hear the blatant proclamation of many medical men that consumption is not hereditary, but is entirely due to the *tubercle bacillus*. They make so much noise over the matter that you might almost think they had made a new discovery. Everyone knows that the *tubercle bacillus* is not, except perhaps on extremely rare occasions, transmitted in the germ plasm, but in the long narrow flat chest and delicate lungs [that] are undoubtedly inherited, and so the soil is laid and only wants fertilising."[14]

Barr's eminence gave weight to his views. In July 1912, he served on the General Committee of the First International Eugenics Congress[15] and shortly afterwards addressed the annual conference of the British Medical Association (BMA) as President.

Professing that the medical profession was at a crossroads, he asked: "What are we? What are we doing here? Whence do we come and whither do we go?"[16] He challenged delegates to show their "… value to individuals and to the State to justify our continued existence as a profession. Is the world any happier for our presence? Are we really an advantage to the higher evolution of the race?"[17]

In Barr's opinion, doctors had "successfully interfered with the selective death-rate which Nature employed in eliminating the unfit, but, on the other hand, we have made no serious attempt to establish a selective birth-rate so as to prevent the race being carried on by the least worthy citizens."[18]

Barr thought that doctors should change their focus from the health of the individual to the larger organism: the nation. They should, he said, raise "up a vigorous, intelligent, enterprising, self-reliant and healthy race" and, while they would still "deal with the prevention and treatment of disease", Barr urged them to "also ascend to a higher platform and raise the banner of health with all the fervour of a new religion."[19]

"The race must be renewed from the mentally and physically fit, the moral and physical degenerates should not be allowed to take any part in adding to the race. Above all, we must breed for intelligence. The laws of heredity should be widely taught, so that those with hereditary blemishes may consider their moral responsibility in bringing children into the world. It is a question of quality rather than quantity."[20]

He then turned to tuberculosis:

"If we could only abolish the *tubercle bacillus* in these islands we would get rid of tuberculous disease, but we should at the same time raise up a race peculiarly susceptible to this infection — a race of hothouse plants which would not flourish in any other environment. We would thus increase at an even greater rate than we are doing at present, nervous instability, the numbers of insane and feeble-minded. Nature, on the other hand, weeds out those who have not got the innate power of recovery from disease, and by means of the *tubercle bacillus* and other pathogenic organisms she frequently does this before the reproductive age, so that a check is put on the multiplication of idiots and the feeble-minded. Nature's methods are thus of advantage to the race rather than to the individual."[21]

In November 1912, four months after Barr's Presidential Address, Dr Sutherland's rebuttal appeared in the *British Medical Journal*.[22] In *The Soil and the Seed in Tuberculosis*, Sutherland wrote that he understood why some physicians believed that consumption was an inherited disposition, given that it appeared in the children of a tuberculous parent more frequently than in the spouse. He even confessed that he had once held similar views, but now he said that such views were fallacious. Setting out data he had collected while working at the St Marylebone Dispensary for the Prevention of Consumption, he said that a child's increased susceptibility to infection from a consumptive parent was not from heredity, but because the child's immune system was not fully developed.

He summarised his findings in five points:

"1. There is more tuberculosis among the children of consumptives than among the children of healthy parents.

"2. This may be due to their exposure to infection, to their lowered general health, or to their heredity.

"3. There is more tuberculosis among the children of infectious consumptives than among the children of non-infectious consumptives.

"4. This must be due to exposure to infection plus lowered general health, inseparable from it as the result of the stage of the disease in the parents.

"5. Therefore it is not heredity which determines whether the children of consumptives will develop the disease, but the existence of certain immediate factors which are under our control."[23]

He concluded by looking forward to the eradication of tuberculosis:

"Owing to the rapidly increasing number of tuberculosis dispensaries in this country, the data on which these deductions are based may be tested on an unprecedented scale. If they be corroborated, it means that the influence of heredity is disproved once and for all. Of greater import, it will imply that if our present activity against tuberculosis be augmented we may look with confidence to the total eradication of this disease."[24]

The following edition of the *British Medical Journal* included a letter from a friend of Barr's, Dr D.W. Hunter, which attacked Sutherland's article on the grounds that the data was "hardly sufficient" and that it had not been proved "that there is no such thing as hereditary predisposition to tuberculosis."[25]

Hunter's remarks were disingenuous, because Sutherland had stated that his hypothesis would need to be tested. Further, he had not said that there were no hereditary factors at play, merely that infection played a more significant role than heredity.

◆   ◆   ◆

At this point, our story is — and the lives of its protagonists were — interrupted by the First World War. Sutherland joined the Royal Navy, serving on an armed cruiser, with the Royal Marines at Deal and, at the end of the war, with the newly-formed Royal Air Force. It was not until 1917 that we find him again speaking out against eugenics, as mentioned in Chapter 1.

The war did little to assuage fears of national deterioration and there were fears that it was dysgenic because, while Britain's finest were being slaughtered in the trenches, the C3s were far from the fighting.

At the end of the war, eugenists began to propagate their views once more. The first example was Prime Minister Lloyd George who, in 1918, gave a speech in which he said that Britain had achieved great things in the war, but had been hampered by the poor health of its people:

"A war, like sickness, lays bare the weakness of a constitution. What has been our weakness? Let us talk quite frankly. We have had a Ministry of National Service and carefully compiled statistics of the health of the people between the ages of 18 and 42. Now, that is the age of fitness, the age of strength. You have these grades, I, II, and III, and all I can tell you is the results of these examinations are startling, and I do not mind to use the word appalling. I hardly dare tell you the results. The number of Grade II and Grade III men throughout the country is prodigious. So much so that we half suspected the doctors; but there were re-examinations which did not make very much difference, and I apologise to the doctors here for the first time.

"What does it mean? It means that we have used our human material in this country prodigally, foolishly, cruelly. I asked the Minister of National Service how many more men we could have put into the fighting ranks if the health of the country had been properly looked after. I staggered at the reply. It was a considered reply, and it was 'at least one million'. If we had only had that million this war would have been ended triumphantly."[26]

To loud cheers, George promised action, and said: "… you cannot maintain an A1 Empire with a C3 population."[27]

The second example was Sir James Barr who in September 1918 spoke on *The Future of the Medical Profession*. His views on tuberculosis had not changed and he quoted Dr D.W. Hunter "whose name I deeply regretted to see in a recent casualty list":

"The death-rate among idiots is about ten times that of the normal population at the same age. Further, of deaths of idiots about 80 per cent are due to tuberculosis. Now an idiot has not even the resisting power necessary to die of phthisis; he dies of acute tuberculosis, death taking place in from three to six weeks from the onset of the illness. Surely here there is some inherited lowering of the soil. There are some 150,000 (estimated) of these defectives in England and Wales, and for every defective there are from six to a dozen of his relatives only a shade better than himself. Practically the same holds for insanity, yet we are asked to believe that a man cannot inherit a soil which will remain during his lifetime permanently below the average in resisting power. Until we have some restriction in the marriage of undesirables the elimination of the *tubercle bacillus* is not worth aiming at. It forms a rough, but on the whole very serviceable check, on the survival and propagation of the unfit. This world is not a hothouse; a race which owed its survival to the fact that the *tubercle bacillus* had ceased to exist would, on the whole, be a race hardly worth surviving. Personally, I am of opinion — and I think such opinion will be shared by most medical men who have been behind the scenes and have not allowed their sentiments to blind them — that if to-morrow the *tubercle bacillus* were non-existent, it would be nothing short of a national calamity. We are not yet ready for its disappearance."[28]

The third example was a columnist in the *Daily Mail* who confronted her readers with these questions:

"Are these puny-faced, gaunt, blotchy, ill-balanced, feeble, ungainly, withered children the young of an imperial race? Why has Mrs Jones had nine children six died, one defective? Nor is it for Mrs Jones to take the initiative. Isn't it for the leisured, the wise, to go to her and tell her what are the facts of life, the meaning of what she is doing, and what she ought to do? ... Mrs Jones is destroying the race!"[29]

Of the three, the writer in the *Daily Mail* was the first to act to address the differential birth rate. It was she who decided to tell Mrs Jones the facts of life and what she ought to do. Barr was so impressed by her actions that on 26th May 1921, he wrote to congratulate her:

"You and your husband have inaugurated a great movement which I hope will eventually get rid of our C3 population and exterminate poverty. The only way to raise an A1 population is to breed them."[30]

His letter was addressed to Dr Marie Stopes.

---

[1] For a brief history of Tuberculosis, see Chapter 6 of *In My Path* (1936) Sutherland, H. Pages 128-147.

2 Haycraft, J. B. (1895). *Darwinism and Race Progress*. London: Swan Sonnenschein & Co. Retrieved January 4, 2019, from https://archive.org/details/darwinismandrac01haycgoog/page/n6. Page 54.

3 *Ibid.*, page 55.

4 *Ibid.*, page 57.

5 Pearson, K. (1907). *A First Study of the Statistics of Pulmonary Tuberculosis*. London: Dulau and Co.

6 Drapers' Company Research Memoirs. (1908). *A Second Study of the Statistics of Pulmonary Tuberculosis: Marital Infection*. London: Dulau and Co. Retrieved January 4, 2019, from https://archive.org/details/b22419123/page/n1.

7 Pearson, E. (1938). *Karl Pearson: An Appreciation of Some Aspects of His Life and Work*. Cambridge: Cambridge University Press.

8 *Ibid.*, page 60.

9 Pearson, K. (1907). *A First Study of the Statistics of Pulmonary Tuberculosis*. London: Dulau and Co.

10 Newsholme, A. (1908). *The Prevention of Tuberculosis*. London: Methuen & Co. Page 167.

11 Eyler, J. M. (1997). *Sir Arthur Newsholme and State Medicine, 1885-1935*. Cambridge, U.K.: Cambridge University Press. Page 188.

12 Pearson, K. (1912). *Tuberculosis, Heredity and Environment: Being a Lecture Delivered at the Galton Laboratory for National Eugenics*. London: Dulau and Co., Ltd. Page 46.

13 Sutherland, H (Producer) (1911). *The Story of John M'Neil* [Motion Picture]. Retrieved January 4, 2019, from https://player.bfi.org.uk/free/film/watch-the-story-of-john-mneil-1911-online.

14 Barr, J. (1911). *The Aim and Scope of Eugenics*. Edinburgh: Neill & Co., Ltd. Retrieved January 6, 2019, from https://archive.org/details/b30617030. Page 21.

15 Eugenics Education Society (1912). *Programme and Time Table, First International Eugenics Congress*. Beverley: Minster Press. Page 20.

16 Barr, J. (1912, July 27). *President's Address Delivered at the Eightieth Annual Meeting of the British Medical Association*. British Medical Journal, 157-163. Page 157. Retrieved January 6, 2019, from https://www.ncbi.nlm.nih.gov/pmc/articles/PMC2334152/.

17 *Ibid.*

18 *Ibid.*

19 *Ibid.*, page 158.

20 *Ibid.*

21 *Ibid.*, page 159.

22 Sutherland, H. (1912, November 23). *The Soil and the Seed in Tuberculosis*. British Medical Journal, 2(2708), 1434-1437. Retrieved January 5, 2019, from https://www.ncbi.nlm.nih.gov/pmc/articles/PMC2334807/. Sutherland's article referenced Barr's views through the metaphor he used (the "soil and seed" of the title of Sutherland's article and was used in Barr's *The Aim and Scope of Eugenics*) and by the allusion to the doctrine of predestination.

23 *Ibid.*

24 *Ibid.*

25 Hunter, D. (1912, November 30). *Letter*. British Medical Journal, 1578-1579.

Retrieved January 7, 2019, from
https://www.ncbi.nlm.nih.gov/pmc/articles/PMC2334872/.
[26] Winter, J. (1980, April). *Military Fitness and Civilian Health in Britain during the First World War*. Journal of Contemporary History, 15(2), 211-244. Page 212.
[27] *Ibid*.
[28] Barr, J. (1918, September 21). *The Future of the Medical Profession*. British Medical Journal, 218-321. Retrieved July 16, 2018, from https://www.ncbi.nlm.nih.gov/pmc/articles/PMC2341835/.
[29] The article was *Mrs Jones Does Her Worst* by Dr Marie Stopes. Greer, G. (1985). *Sex and Destiny: The Politics of Human Fertility*. London: Picador (in association with Martin Secker & Warburg Limited). Page 309.
[30] Stopes, M. (1921). *Queen's Hall Meeting on Constructive Birth Control: Speeches and Impressions*. London: G.P. Putnam's Sons Ltd. Page 8. Given Barr's letter was read out at the 1921 Queen's Hall rally and printed in the published record of the event, it is reasonable to infer that Stopes endorsed his accolade.

Chapter 4
Cool Blue Paint.

Dr Marie Stopes and Mr Humphrey Roe, her second husband, opened "The Mothers' Clinic for Constructive Birth Control"[1] on 17th March 1921.[2] Situated at 61 Marlborough Road, Holloway, it was the British Empire's first birth-control clinic.

Its location on the corner of Marlborough and Kiver Roads meant that it was easy to find and, if a woman was too nervous to enter, she could walk past without drawing too much attention to herself. Any nervousness, however, would be dispelled on entry by the calm interior, described by Stopes as "Botticelli Blue, with reproductions of beautiful babies on the walls."[3] The *Star* newspaper gave a more fulsome description:

> "Fresh willow-blue curtains in the windows; on the walls clean white distemper and cool blue paint; a pedestal holds a little plaster model of a meditative baby angel looking just as though he had accomplished his flight 'from the everywhere into here'. And on the old Jacobean table a huge jar of pink-and-white roses with upclimbing branches of tender green. A place to disarm fear, to invite confidence in its callers."[4]

The female visitor would also have been relieved to find that all the nurses were female, thereby avoiding an awkward conversation with a man. In these quiet premises a woman could discuss her situation, receive information about conception or contraception, and contraceptives were provided free-of-charge or at cost.

The Mothers' Clinic offered one device, Stopes' own "Prorace" cervical cap which was akin to a rubber thimble placed over the cervix and covered the entrance to the uterus (womb).[5]

The mechanics of the cervical cap were briefly explained in the 6th edition of Stopes' book *Wise Parenthood*:

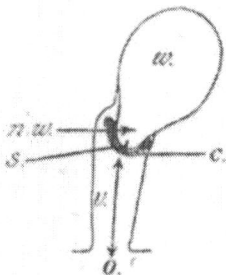

In the diagram, "o" is the vaginal orifice, "v" is the vaginal canal and "w" the womb. The rubber cervical cap "c" is placed over the neck of the womb "n.w.", meaning that it occludes the entrance to the womb (or *os*) "s". This barrier would ensure that during intercourse, sperms would be prevented from entering the womb, so fertilisation would not result. As Stopes herself explained: "It adheres by suction assisted by the spring of the firm rim against the circular muscles and remains firmly in place, whatever movement the woman may make."[6]

A second contraceptive method, such as a spermicidal quinine ointment would be applied to the cap as a backup.

The work of the Mothers' Clinic was performed by nurses, though a medical doctor, Jane Hawthorne was supposed to visit on a fortnightly basis for special cases.

According to Stopes' earliest biographers, the clinic was an instant success. In *The Authorized Life of Marie C Stopes*, Aylmer Maude[7] stated that the clinic "was very soon overtaxed to such an extent that it has hardly dared to advertise its existence."[8] Keith Bryant's biography said that "women poured in".[9]

In contrast, the actual numbers were disclosed in Ruth Hall's biography, *Passionate Crusader*. Hall's figures, based on the Clinic's books, showed that 518 women attended the clinic in 1921. Of these, 471 wanted contraceptive information and 47 sought help in becoming pregnant.[10] In other words, between two to three women would attend each weekday.

The founders of the clinic were an accomplished couple; as Stopes herself put it, they were "well off in an ordinary sense, intelligent, [and] socially rather powerful".[11] Roe was a flight pioneer whom, with his brother Alliott, had set up the British aircraft manufacturer AVRO (the company's name being a compression of Alliott Verdon Roe). He was wealthy, having invested £10,000 in AVRO before 1914 and sharing in the profits on the 10,000 aircraft produced during the War.[12] In 1917, he had joined the 100th Squadron of the Royal Flying Corps as an aerial observer and night-bomber.[13]

Stopes was a renowned paleobotanist who had travelled the world and was the first female lecturer at the University of Manchester. She was also the author of *Married Love* (1918), a best-selling book on human relationships that brought her fame and commercial success. Other books followed: *Wise Parenthood*, also in 1918 and *Radiant Motherhood* in 1920.

In addition, Stopes was appointed to the Cinema Commission, which classified films for release to the public,[14] and also to the National Birth Rate Commission.[15] Despite the official sounding name, the latter organisation was not a governmental body. It had been set up to investigate and make recommendations in relation to the falling birth rate. In the period of Stopes' involvement, the commission was headed by the Bishop of Birmingham and many eminent people of the day gave evidence, including Sidney Webb (part-founder of the Fabian Society), Mrs Bramwell Booth (of the Salvation Army) and Sir Arthur Conan-Doyle (creator of Sherlock Holmes).[16]

Dr Binnie Dunlop, the secretary of the Malthusian League, had introduced Stopes to Roe to help her raise the funds to publish *Married Love*. All three shared an interest in birth-control.

Dunlop's organisation propagated the ideas of the Rev. Thomas Malthus in the *Essay on the Principle of Population*. The Malthusian idea was that population tended to increase beyond the capacity to produce food and that, when over-population occurred, nature would redress the imbalance through war, famine and disease. Whereas Malthus had advocated limiting the population through abstinence from sex, contemporary Malthusians (the so-called "Neo-Malthusians") advocated the use of contraceptives (which were sometimes called "Malthusian devices").

Humphrey Roe's "strange preoccupation"[17] with birth-control had led him to propose the establishment of a clinic at St Mary's Hospital, Manchester in October 1917.[18] Despite Roe's offer to finance the clinic, the hospital had declined on the grounds that it might deter their other patrons.[19] Nonetheless, his preparations − including the equipment list and a logo − were useful in setting up the Mothers' Clinic.

The source of Stopes' knowledge of contraceptives depends on who you believe, because there are conflicting accounts.

The story promulgated by Stopes herself was that her knowledge of sex and contraceptives came from books in the British Museum. In 1911, she had married Reginald Ruggles-Gates and had, she said, paid "a terrible price for sex ignorance",[20] because it was only after she had read the museum's treatises on sex that she realised that Gates was impotent. Subsequently, their marriage was annulled on the grounds of non-consummation.

A different account was given by the American birth controller Margaret Sanger, who recalled that when she first met Stopes in 1915, Stopes "had never heard the words birth control and told me she had no knowledge of contraceptive technique".[21] The veracity of this story should be tempered, though, by Humphrey Roe's margin notes in his copy of Sanger's autobiography. He had written: "False. Damned Liar".[22]

Stopes' biographer June Rose debunked both of these stories when she found a 1911 letter, written within six months of Stopes' marriage to Ruggles-Gates, which revealed Stopes had an extensive knowledge of contraception[23] (and therefore sex) at that time.[24] The conflicting versions demonstrate the problem of separating fact from fiction when dealing with the life of Dr Marie Stopes. The situation was not improved by what one biographer, Clare Debenham, described as Stopes' "fluid relation to the truth."[25]

The Mothers' Clinic did not introduce contraceptives to Britain, nor did it make them widely available. People who wanted them − generally speaking middle and upper class women or prostitutes − knew where to get them, and, as historian John Peel pointed out there was "with the exception of the oral contraceptive... not a single birth control method in existence to-day which was not already available, and available in greater variety, in 1890."[26] What the clinic did do was to provide access to information about conception and contraception to the group which had the least access to it: poor and working-class women.

Birth control was not respectable in 1921, though Stopes argued that the Mothers' Clinic removed both "psychologically and socially the subject of Birth Control from the harmful atmosphere of... such persons who have tended to drag the subject into the gutter" and who had "coupled contraceptive information with other irritating, detrimental and harmful pursuits and attitudes."[27]

The logo of the Mothers' Clinic depicted a cylindrical lantern casting rays of light in all directions. The protective cover of the lamp appeared to be a mesh of fine wire, though on closer inspection it was the words "birth control" repeated many times over and, above and below, the slogan: "Joyous and deliberate Motherhood, A Sure Light in our Racial Darkness."[28]

This symbol and these words indicated that Stopes' aspirations were greater than merely providing contraceptives to the women of Holloway and it is these aspirations that we will examine in the next chapter.

---

[1] Wellcome Library. PP/MCS/E/10:Box62. PP/MCS/C.2. Letterhead of The Mothers' Clinic for Constructive Birth Control dated 8th December 1921.
[2] Hall, R. (1977). *Passionate Crusader: The Life of Marie Stopes*. New York: Harcourt Brace Jovanovich. Page 186.
[3] *Ibid.*, page 188.
[4] *Ibid.*
[5] Brand, P. (2007). *Birth Control Nursing in the Marie Stopes Mothers' Clinics 1921 to 1931*. De Montfort University. Page 216.

6 Stopes, M. C. (1920). *Wise Parenthood: A Practical Sequel to Married Love* (6th ed.). London: G.P. Putnam's Sons Ltd, London. Page 27. Retrieved January 3, 2019, from https://archive.org/details/cihm_990552/page/n7.

7 Maude, A. (1924). *The Authorized Life of Marie C. Stopes*. Covent Garden: Williams & Norgate. Page 140. Retrieved October 23, 2019, from https://archive.org/details/b29977587/page/140. Maude was a friend and biographer of the Russian novelist Tolstoy and, if not actually Stopes' lover, it was not for want of effort on his part. Indeed, June Rose included an excerpt of his letter to Stopes on the eve of her marriage to Humphrey Roe dated 17th June 1918 in which he wrote: "I have been bothering you with letters recently… Still I cannot let the eve of your third marriage pass without sending you my most cordial good wishes and fondest greetings" (Roe was Stopes' second husband). Maude's biography, *The Authorized Life of Marie C. Stopes* (1924) was, according to *The Spectator*, "a panegyric and not a biography," and it appears that much of the book had been written by Stopes herself. According to Ruth Hall (*Passionate Crusader: The Life of Marie Stopes*. New York: Harcourt Brace Jovanovich. Page 262.), when Stopes blamed Maude for poor sales, he responded: "You so impressed on me the importance of getting the Life out quickly, and I evidently rushed it to the point of scamping it and failed to correct some of the errors in your rough draft." While these aspects undermine the veracity of the book, it is nonetheless a useful source because it reveals what Maude and Stopes would have the reader believe.

8 Hall, R. (1977). *Passionate Crusader: The Life of Marie Stopes*. New York: Harcourt Brace Jovanovich. Page 190.

9 *Ibid.*

10 *Ibid.*

11 *Ibid.*, page 208.

12 *Ibid.*, page 138.

13 *Ibid.*, page 139.

14 Stopes, M. (1921). *Verbatim Report of the Town Hall Meeting under the Auspices of the Voluntary Parenthood League*. New York: Voluntary Parenthood League. Retrieved January 14, 2019, from https://archive.org/details/101553806.nlm.nih.gov. Page 18.

15 National Birth Rate Commission. (1920). *Problems of Population and Parenthood. Being the Second Report of and the chief evidence taken by the National Birth-rate Commission, 1918-1920*. London: Chapman and Hall, Ltd. Page viii. Retrieved January 28, 2019, from https://archive.org/details/problemsofpopula00natiuoft/page/n8.

16 *Ibid.*, page xiii.

17 Rose, J. (1992). *Marie Stopes and the Sexual Revolution*. London: Faber and Faber Limited. Page 142.

18 *Ibid.*, pages 142-3.

19 Hall, R. (1977). *Passionate Crusader: The Life of Marie Stopes*. New York: Harcourt Brace Jovanovich. Page 140.

20 Rose, J. (1992). *Marie Stopes and the Sexual Revolution*. London: Faber and Faber Limited. Page 78.

21 Soloway, R. (1997). *The Galton Lecture 1996: Marie Stopes, Eugenics and the Birth Control Movement*. In R. Peel (Ed.), Marie Stopes Eugenics and the English Birth Control Movement. London: The Galton Institute. Page 49.

[22] Hall, R. (1977). *Passionate Crusader: The Life of Marie Stopes*. New York: Harcourt Brace Jovanovich. Page 116.

[23] Rose, J. (1992). *Marie Stopes and the Sexual Revolution*. London: Faber and Faber Limited. Page 77.

[24] In her review of June Rose's book, Lesley Hall, Emeritus Wellcome Library Research Fellow and acknowledged expert on Stopes, wrote: "Even her most famous personal myth — that she married Ruggles Gates in complete sexual ignorance and took years, and a course of study in the 'Cupboard' in the British Museum, to realise that the marriage was unconsummated — subjected to scrutiny is seen to lie at some angle to the truth." Hall, L. Book Review, June Rose *Marie Stopes and the Sexual Revolution*. Retrieved 6th November 2019, from *Lesley Hall's Web Pages*: https://www.lesleyahall.net/jrose.htm.

[25] Debenham's comment followed her article on *theconversation.com* website: *Married Love: the 1918 book by Marie Stopes that helped launch the birth control movement.* Retrieved November 14, 2019, from theconversation.com https://theconversation.com/married-love-the-1918-book-by-marie-stopes-that-helped-launch-the-birth-control-movement-93108.

[26] Peel, J. (1963, November). *The Manufacture and Retailing of Contraceptives in England*. Population Studies, 17(2), 113-125. Retrieved April 22, 2018, from http://www.jstor.org/stable/2172841.

[27] *Brief on behalf of the plaintiff*. Wellcome Library. PP/MCS/H/4a:Box72.

[28] Stopes, Marie Carmichael. (1923). *Contraception (Birth Control), Its Theory, History and Practice: A Manual for the Medical and Legal Professions*. Page 397. Retrieved August 20, 2020, from https://archive.org/details/dli.bengal.10689.14738/page/n5/mode/2up.

Chapter 5
"Babies in the Right Place"

O n establishment in May 1921, the Mothers' Clinic was supported by patrons.[1] Three months later, Stopes founded the "Society for Constructive Birth Control and Racial Progress" (CBC). Stopes became the president, Humphrey Roe the secretary, and the patrons became vice-presidents.

As Stopes herself had remarked, the vice-presidents were "all names of world-wide significance".[2] They included: Sir James Barr (who was, as we have seen, a prominent physician and formerly president of the BMA), Sir William Bayliss (the distinguished Professor of Physiology at University College London), Dame Clara Butt (the concert singer), Edward Carpenter (the philosopher and poet), John Maynard Keynes (the economist), Sir William Arbuthnot Lane (the physician and surgeon), Lady Constance Lytton (the suffragette), Aylmer Maude (the biographer and translator of Tolstoy), Bertrand Russell[3] (the philosopher and mathematician), and H.G. Wells[4] (the writer).

At first sight, the support of these eminent people appeared to be far in excess of the needs of a small, poorly-attended clinic in a poor part of London. It is only when the aims of the CBC were taken into account that the need for their participation becomes clearer. In the short term, they bolstered Stopes' pre-eminence in the birth-control movement and affirmed the efficacy of the contraceptives used at the clinic.

The long term aims of the CBC were spelled out in the *Tenets of the CBC* which set out its goals (shown in full in

Appendix 1). The 17 tenets reveal that the CBC was intended as a national movement and that its ambitious goal was the transformation of Britons through the application of eugenic principles.

Tenet 12 expressed the hope that the Mothers' Clinic would be the catalyst for "the Ministry of Health to supply suitable help and contraceptive instruction to working-class women at the many Ante-natal Clinics, Welfare Centres, etc. already in existence all over the country."[5]

Tenet 16 stated the CBC's positive[6] aims, confirming that it was: "... profoundly and fundamentally a pro-baby organisation, in favour of producing the largest possible number of healthy, happy children without detriment to the mother" and "... to secure conception to those married people who are healthy, childless, and desire children." It also spelled out its negative intent to "furnish security from conception to those who are racially diseased, already overburdened with children, or in any specific way unfitted for parenthood." As the motto of the CBC put it, "Babies in the Right Place".

The positive aims would be achieved by undertaking a "serious and scientific study" of the hygiene of sex (Tenet 1) and obtaining "the best possible knowledge of scientific and technical details". These would be made available to those undertaking "the important social duty" of creating additional members of the community (Tenet 4).

The negative aims were specified in Tenets 9, 10 and 11:

"9. AS REGARDS THE POPULATION AT PRESENT. We say that there are unfortunately many men and women who should be prevented from procreating children at all, because of their individual ill-health, or the diseased and degenerate nature of the offspring that they may be expected to produce. These considerations would not apply to a better and healthier world.

"10. There are many women unfortunately so constructed — suffering from weakness of certain organs — that they would risk death if they were to attempt to bear children, and who, therefore, should not bear them.

"11. There are unfortunately many couples so ill-provided with this world's goods, or with means to acquire them, that they cannot support further children, and therefore should not bear them. Women, owing their own or their husband's incapacity to be self-supporting, may be permanently or temporarily in such a position owing to disaster or unemployment."[7]

Tenet 13 argued that knowledge of, and instruction in, contraceptive measures for normal and healthy people was "an hygienic and not a medical matter" (at this time, the policy of the BMA was that no one should have access to contraception except through a qualified medical doctor). On the other hand, "the problem of controlling conception on the part of those who are diseased, abnormal and unhealthy" was "a purely medical matter" and that might "involve measures which this Society would not advocate for general use."[8]

Stopes had specified the "problem" in her 1920 book, *Radiant Motherhood* as:

"... the vast and ever increasing stock of degenerate, feeble-minded and unbalanced who are now in our midst and who devastate social customs. These populate most rapidly, these tend proportionately to increase, and these are like the parasite upon the healthy tree sapping its vitality. These produce less than they consume and are only able to flourish and reproduce so long as the healthier produce food for them; but by ever weakening the human stock, in the end they will succumb with the fine structure which they have destroyed."[9]

The "measures which this Society would not advocate for general use" were also outlined in *Radiant Motherhood*. Stopes had written that she "would like to see the sterilization of those totally unfit for parenthood made an immediate possibility indeed made compulsory."[10] She added:

"... a very few quite simple Acts of Parliament could deal with it.
"Three short and concise Bills would be sufficient to afford the most urgent social service for the preservation of our race. They should be simply worded and based on possibilities well within the grasp of modern science.

"The idea of sterilization has not yet been very generally understood or accepted, although it is an idea which our civilization urgently needs to assimilate."[11]

Given that Stopes recommended X-Rays to sterilise men and women, it was appropriate that the chapter was entitled: *A New and Irradiated Race*.

Stopes lobbied politicians to further her aims. In September 1920, she sent a copy of *Radiant Motherhood* to Frances Stevenson, secretary (mistress, and later wife) to Prime Minister, Lloyd George.

According to Stopes' biographer June Rose, "she drew attention to the chapter on eugenics in which she commented on the tens of thousands of 'stunted, warped and inferior infants, who would invariably drain the resources of those with a sense of responsibility'". In the covering letter she urged Stevenson to get Mr George to read it because it would "help him in real fact more than a dozen Ministries will ever do."[12]

Stopes also wrote to parliamentary candidates in the 1922 general election asking them to sign a printed template that declared: "I agree that the present position of breeding chiefly from the C3 population and burdening and discouraging the A1 is nationally deplorable, and if I am elected to Parliament I will press the Ministry of Health to give such scientific information through the Ante-natal Clinics, Welfare Centres and other institutions in its control as will curtail the C3 and increase the A1."[13]

---

[1] Letterhead of The Mothers' Clinic for Constructive Birth Control dated 8th December 1921. Wellcome Library. PP/MCS/E/10:Box62.

[2] Rose, J. (1992). *Marie Stopes and the Sexual Revolution*. London: Faber and Faber Limited. Page 153.

[3] *Ibid.*, page 162.

[4] *Ibid.*, page 153.

[5] Maude, A. (1924). *The Authorized Life of Marie C. Stopes*. Covent Garden: Williams & Norgate. Page 222-6. Retrieved October 23, 2019, from https://archive.org/details/b29977587/page/222.

[6] The word "positive" is used here in the sense of "promoting". Eugenists referred to positive and negative measures, defined by Kevles in *In The Name Of Eugenics*: "'positive eugenics,'... aimed to foster more prolific breeding among the socially meritorious, and 'negative eugenics'... intended to encourage the socially disadvantaged to breed less — or, better yet, not at all." See: Kevles, D. J. (2004). *In The Name of Eugenics: Genetics and the Uses of Human*

Heredity (5th Printing ed.). Cambridge, Massachusetts: Harvard University Press. Page 85.

[7] Maude, A. (1924). *The Authorized Life of Marie C. Stopes*. Covent Garden: Williams & Norgate. Appendix C on pages 222-6. Retrieved October 23, 2019, from https://archive.org/details/b29977587/page/222.

[8] *Ibid*.

[9] Stopes, M. (1920). *Radiant Motherhood: A Book for Those who are Creating the Future*. London: G.P. Putnam's Sons Limited. Page 228-9. Retrieved August 24, 2019, from https://archive.org/details/radiantmotherhoo00stopiala/page/n5.

[10] *Ibid.*, page 231. Stopes had held such views since (at least) 1918, evidenced by her suggestion to the National Birth-Rate Commission on 28th October 1918: "May I suggest a very simple solution in regard to the hopelessly bad cases, bad through inherent disease, or drunkenness or character? A perfectly simple way would be sterilisation of the parent." (See: National Birth Rate Commission. (1920). *Problems of Population and Parenthood. Being the Second Report of and the chief evidence taken by the National Birth-Rate Commission, 1918-1920*. London: Chapman and Hall, Ltd. Page 133. Retrieved January 28, 2019, from https://archive.org/details/problemsofpopula00natiuoft/page/n8).

[11] *Ibid*.

[12] Rose, J. (1992). *Marie Stopes and the Sexual Revolution*. London: Faber and Faber Limited. Page 138.

[13] *Ibid.*, page 161.

Chapter 6

Battles with the Churches

The Christian churches had long-established views on the use of contraceptives, so it was inevitable that they would at some point express their opinion about Dr Stopes' activities. She seems to have anticipated this and the foreword of the first six editions of *Married Love* featured a letter from Father Stanislaus St John, a Jesuit priest. The mere inclusion of his letter would have scandalised Catholics and more so when he praised the book as a "piece of thoughtful scientific writing" which he had found "admirable throughout," adding:

> "… it seems to me that your theme could not have been treated in more beautiful or more delicate language, or with a truer ring of sympathy for those who, through ignorance or want of thought, make shipwreck of their married happiness."[1]

Father St John's praise acknowledged they were in "complete agreement" to that point, "but our ways part when you treat of birth control."[2] He then explained the Catholic position. Father St John's foreword did show that, while there might be disagreement about birth control, it could be expressed in a cordial manner. This was not to last because the positions of each side were irreconcilable.

On the one hand, you had Stopes claiming the moral authority of Almighty God and, on the other, you had Christians who thought that her behaviour was at best, outrageous, and at worst, blasphemous. Stopes' divine inspiration came about in

June 1920 when, she said, she had received a message from Almighty God. Given that the message was subsequently printed in *A New Gospel to All Peoples: A revelation of God uniting physiology and the religions of man*, it can still be read today:

> "The way in which the following words were written is exactly as follows:
> "During the last week of June 1920, I was, like most other members of the reading public, aware of the proposed Conference of the Anglican Bishops at Lambeth; I was not, however, intending to communicate with them.
> "That week it chanced that I spent an afternoon alone in the cool shades of the old yew woods on the hills behind my home: While penetrated by that calm beauty there came, suddenly and quite explicitly, exact instructions in the words which follow.
> "I was told: 'Say to my Bishops' — what is found in these pages. At the conclusion of the message I arose and went home instantly; sent for my secretary; and there and then, without going into the house, redictated to him what had been dictated to me.
> The message was then printed as quickly as could be arranged and a copy sent to each of the Bishops at the Conference."[3]

The *New Gospel* began: "My lords, I speak to you in the name of God. You are his priests. I am his prophet. I speak to you of the mysteries of the union of man and woman."[4]

It continued with what biographer June Rose described as "breathtaking certainty": "Paul spoke with Christ 1900 years ago. God spoke to me today."[5]

According to Rose:

> "Sexual union was not, Marie's *New Gospel* asserted, as the Christian Churches had mistakenly maintained, designed solely for the purpose of creating children. God commanded that couples should use the best means of birth control 'placed at man's service by Science'. Above all, the Bishops must teach their flocks that 'the pure and holy sacrament of marriage may no longer be

debased and befouled by the archaic ignorance of centuries...'"[6]

In every respect it was an extraordinary document, not least when it criticised the clerical error that:

"... led many of you Ministers of the [Anglican] Church into the false belief that you preserve your purity and your vigour only in celibacy... [which had]... led some of the Ministers of the Church to give instruction to youths committed to their charge that they shall exercise what they falsely call 'self-restraint' by means of wasting their own sacred secretions by their own hands... "[7]

A Catholic priest, Father F.M. de Zulueta wrote to Stopes describing her New Gospel as "a most profane compound of imaginary mysticism and pornography ... [that]... could only revolt anyone with a real sense of religion."[8]

The Lambeth Conference in 1920 was not swayed by *A New Gospel* and the Bishops uttered: "...an emphatic warning against the use of unnatural means for the avoidance of conception, together with the grave dangers — physical, moral and religious — thereby incurred, and against the evils with which the extension of such use threatens the race. In opposition to the teaching which, under the name of science and religion, encourages married people in the deliberate cultivation of sexual union as an end in itself, we steadfastly uphold what must always be regarded as the governing considerations of Christian marriage."[9]

Stopes claimed divine inspiration throughout her life. In her book *Radiant Motherhood*, she wrote of her vision of "the fine and splendid race" that she saw "as God's prophet."[10] Many years later (in November 1948) her recollection of a speech to the Voluntary Parenthood League in New York included embellishments that had religious overtones:[11] "... at the end of it, the audience surged forward and kissed my feet and the hem of my dress."[12]

The relationship between Stopes and the Christian churches was not helped by her "take no prisoners" approach when she criticised them. For example, a speech to the Women's

Freedom League on 21st March 1921 was reported in the *Daily News* as follows:

"Dr Marie Stopes said that the standard type of man and woman she would aim at would be 'a manly man and a woman who was strongly sexed and a truly feminine creature.' The present ideas of the Churches, she said, was a 'weak, under-sexed, over-neurotic, over-intellectual and ascetic person.' That was most dangerous and anti-racial, and was not Christian but Pauline. It was copied from the homosexual ideal of Diana, and was not only not of the highest form of humanity but was a slightly perverted form of humanity which must wither production. 'Whom did the [Anglican] bishops at the Lambeth Conference put in the chair to deal with the problems of married life? The unmarried, ascetic Bishop of London. What an impertinence to elect a man of that character to deal with the problem of the sexes!'"[13]

A similar report in the *Daily Mail* confirmed the account.[14]

On 12th November 1921, Stopes wrote to Cardinal Bourne, Britain's most senior Catholic:

"Right Reverend Sir, As you have expressed so unqualified disapproval to the application of scientific knowledge to the control of procreation of children and the Roman Catholic Church attacks birth control so consistently, it is the wish of our Society to meet and openly discuss these points of difference. I think a meeting and open discussion between the respective leaders of these two schools of thought would be most profitable, and as it is my wish only to know and ascertain the truth, I feel sure your time would not be wasted if you would meet me in debate."[15]

Bourne regarded the invitation warily. The incorrect salutation would not have assured him that he would have been treated with the dignity that his position demanded and, had he debated her, he would have advanced her cause. His reply declining the invitation said that the conference would be "useless" given that anyone competent to take part was already acquainted with the Catholic Church's position.

Stopes' reply protested that she was not acquainted with the Church's position, an unconvincing assertion, given it had been printed in the first six editions of *Married Love* .[16]

Subsequent events suggested that Bourne had been wise to decline the invitation. According to a report in the *Daily News* on 11th July 1922, "there were some animated passages during a conference on birth control held at Deptford Town Hall last night."

The representative of the Catholic Church, Father Mahoney, said "that the exponents of birth control would open the sluice gates to a great many evils, to the use of noxious and harmful drugs, to surgical operations, and would have dire results on the family life of England."

Stopes replied that "in its treatment of this subject the Roman Catholic Church seemed to be the incarnation of the devil."[17] When the protestant Bishop of Woolwich said he supposed that he was also "one of the accredited agents of his satanic majesty," she corrected him: "I said the Roman Catholic Church." The Bishop replied that he hoped that that kind of language would not be used because "it is not at all helpful".[18]

Perceiving that there was an increased amount of obscene literature on display, the Westminster Catholic Federation successfully lobbied for a question to be asked in the House of Commons in August 1921. What steps, "in the way of criminal proceedings" would the government take "to check the seriously increasing output of obscene literature having for its object the prevention of conception?"[19]

While Stopes was not responsible for these publications, her activities were seen as part of, as well as influencing, the zeitgeist.

In late 1921, Father Vincent McNabb, a respected Dominican preacher and Catholic intellectual, wrote about the CBC in the *Catholic Times*. He said that "its literature is almost incredibly obscene by its advocacy of unsocial and unnatural sin."[20]

The teachings of the Anglican and Catholic Churches on contraception were aligned at this time. This would have given Catholics a degree of comfort in that the Anglicans, the established church in Britain, were a bulwark against modern developments.

In October 1921 however, a conference of Anglican bishops was held in Birmingham. They were addressed by Lord Dawson of Penn who spoke on *Love – Marriage – Birth Control*. Dawson was King George V's doctor, president to the Royal College of Physicians,[21] and "the most admired and respected doctor of his generation".[22] In his speech, he:

> "… put forward with confidence the view that birth control is here to stay. It is an established fact, and for good or evil has to be accepted. Although the extent of its application can be and is being modified, no denunciations will abolish it."[23]

Dawson's support of contraception, and the impact of his speech, was to change the stated view of the Anglican Church. From that point on, the Catholic Church stood alone to defend the traditional Christian position.[24]

---

[1] Femina Books. (1967). *The Trial of Marie Stopes*. (M. Box, Ed.) London: Femina Books Ltd. Page 50.

[2] *Ibid*.

[3] Newspaper cutting from *The Star* dated 25th January 1922 *"Dr Marie Stopes as Prophet"*. Wellcome Library. PP/MCS/H/4a:Box72 PP/MCS/H.4a.

[4] Rose, J. (1992). *Marie Stopes and the Sexual Revolution*. London: Faber and Faber Limited. Page 136.

[5] *Ibid*.

[6] *Ibid*.

[7] Femina Books. (1967). *The Trial of Marie Stopes*. (M. Box, Ed.) London: Femina Books Ltd. Page 110.

[8] Rose, J. (1992). *Marie Stopes and the Sexual Revolution*. London: Faber and Faber Limited. Page 137.

[9] *Lambeth Conference Resolutions Archive 1920*. Page 21. Anglican Communion Office www.anglicancommunion.org/media. Retrieved August 28, 2019, from: https://www.anglicancommunion.org/media/127731/1920.pdf.

[10] Stopes, M. (1920). *Radiant Motherhood: A Book for Those who are Creating the Future*. London: G.P. Putnam's Sons Limited. Page 236. Retrieved August 24, 2019, from https://archive.org/details/radiantmotherhoo00stopiala/page/n5.

[11] For instance, see the Gospels: Luke 8:44, Luke 7:38 and Mark 5:28.

[12] *Married Love and Modern Life* by Dr Marie Stopes. *Woman's Magazine* November 1948. Page 88. Wellcome Library. PP/MCS/G/30:Box 70.

[13] Newspaper cutting from The Daily News dated 22nd March 1921 *Problem of the Sexes: Dr Marie Stopes and the 'Ascetic' Bishop of London*. Wellcome Library. PP/MCS/H/4a:Box72.

[14] *Ibid*.

[15] Letter from Marie Stopes to Cardinal Bourne dated 12th November 1921 Westminster Archdiocese Archive. BO5/59 Birth Control 1921-26.

[16] *Ibid*.

[17] Newspaper cutting from *The Daily News* dated 11th July 1922 *"Birth Control: Dr Marie Stopes' Reply to Priest"*. Wellcome Library. PP/MCS/H/4a:Box72.

[18] *Ibid*.

[19] Hall, R. (1977). *Passionate Crusader: The Life of Marie Stopes*. New York: Harcourt Brace Jovanovich. Page 206.

[20] *Ibid*., page 205.

[21] British Medical Journal. (1945, March 17). *Obituary Viscount Dawson of Penn*. British Medical Journal, pages 389-392.

[22] Lord Dawson's reputation was tarnished posthumously when it was discovered that he had administered a lethal cocktail of morphine and cocaine to the dying King George V in January 1936. It gives him the dubious honour of being Britain's sole regicide of the Twentieth Century. See *A king, a doctor, and a convenient death* by J.H.R. Ramsay, British Medical Journal 1994; 308: 1445 https://www.bmj.com/content/308/6941/1445.1.full.

[23] Penn, D. (1921). *Love-Marriage-Birth Control: Being a Speech delivered at the Church Congress at Birmingham, October 1921*. London: Nisbet & Co. Ltd. 22 Berners Street, W.1. Page 21. Retrieved March 25, 2019, from https://archive.org/details/lovemarriagebirt00dawsrich/page/n5.

[24] Vickers, M. (2013). *By the Thames Divided: Cardinal Bourne in Southwark and Westminster*. Gracewing Publishing. Pages 456-60.

Chapter 7

Competitors and detractors

The opening of the Mothers' Clinic gave Stopes "new authority as a social reformer"[1] and placed her in a pre-eminent position among the birth control pioneers,[2] for the moment anyway. Her position was, however, threatened by rivals who sought to reassert themselves, and by sleazy opportunists who used her name to promote their products.

In October 1921, the Malthusian League opened the Walworth Women's Welfare Centre in South London, which meant that the Mothers' Clinic was no longer the only birth control clinic in Britain.[3] The Centre was staffed by a qualified medical doctor, Dr Norman Haire, an Australian doctor from Sydney. It offered a contraceptive device known as the Mesinga pessary (what would today be called a diaphragm).[4]

The League launched a magazine, the *New Generation*, and they wrote to members of the CBC to garner support. Their approach annoyed Stopes,[5] for while they had discussed opening a birth control clinic for years, they had not acted. It perhaps seemed to her that, having been beaten to the punch by the Mothers' Clinic, they were trying to re-establish themselves to the detriment of the CBC.

Unscrupulous merchants were exploiting the Stopes name to turn a profit. A large board in Praed Street commanded "Every woman to read *Wise Parenthood*"[6] and in "the sleazy rubber shops in Charing Cross Road, in which medical appliances, pornographic novels and pills of dubious efficacy jostled for attention, an advertisement with a pointing finger signalling pessaries 'as recommended by Dr Stopes'."[7] Her books were placed in proximity to pornographic titles, and some booksellers would slip advertisements between the pages (such as *Dr Patterson's Famous Pills, the Great Remedy for Irregularities of Every Description* (most likely abortifacient pills)).[8]

Stopes was incensed by the publication of *Wise Wedlock* by the pseudonymous Dr Courtenay Beale which shamelessly plagiarised her work. She would have taken him to court if her solicitor had been able to find him.[9]

Despite these distractions, or perhaps because of them, Stopes was hard at work promoting her Clinic and her cause.[10] The highlight of her campaign was the Queens' Hall rally on 31st May 1921. On the night, in spite of a strike that restricted rail transport, "over 2,000 people packed the hall [and] some were standing at the back".[11]

Stopes' success, however, came at a cost: hubris. In November 1921, the *Literary Guide* described her as "a talented lady who has been advocating birth control so effectively that she is inclined to suppose that she is the inventor of it."[12] Stella Browne, also a birth control pioneer, commented: "she seems to be getting quite unbalanced in her egomania and conceit… she is making fresh enemies daily."[13]

Some of the enemies included those who should have been natural allies. For example, Stopes had alienated Margaret Sanger (the American birth-control pioneer whom Stopes had met in 1915)[14] when she addressed Mary Ware Dennett's Voluntary Parenthood League in New York in October 1921. While the speech was a success, Sanger had been angered that Stopes was speaking to a competitor of her own American Birth Control League and, when Stopes arrived in New York, Sanger was too busy to see her.[15]

Attacked from many quarters, Stopes sought to hit back through legal action. In late 1921, she wrote to Mr Cedric Braby, of Braby & Waller in The Strand, to seek legal redress against her critics and enemies. They included Stella Browne, the *New Generation* magazine,[16] Father McNabb, and the *Catholic Times*.[17]

Stopes was not, however, merely seeking legal redress. There were other factors at play, such as seeking to boost sales of her books[18] and to attack the Catholic Church. In a letter to Braby, Stopes told him of:

"… the aspect which I should like also brought out [in a court case], namely, the harm the Roman Catholics are doing to our nation as a whole, this would require some further material. I could give you a good deal of information: for instance in a return of Religious Creeds of prisoners for 1906, over one half of all the prisoners in Scotland were Roman Catholics, although they form a very small part of the total population. In similar ways one could bring out in Court that Roman Catholics on the whole are most immoral of the sections of our community, and for them to gain ascendancy is nationally very dangerous and harmful."[19]

While she acknowledged that "this would extend the case considerably," she suggested hiring "a Barrister clever enough to realise that, and clever enough to bring out such implications."[20]

On being advised not to proceed with legal action, she told Braby that she was not "entirely satisfied"[21] and that she found the time it took to obtain legal advice "most vexing".[22] By this time, she was seeking advice on whether she could sue *The Tablet*, a Catholic journal. She told Braby that she had been "speaking to an eminent lawyer the other day" and that he had "urged immediate action." She concluded with a warning: "Please tell your man to give an immediate opinion or I must go to someone else."[23]

In early 1922, Stopes found out that the *Fifth International Neo-Malthusian and Birth Control Conference* would take place at Kingsway Hall that July.[24] The president was Dr C.V. Drysdale (with whom Stopes had fallen out when she left the Malthusian League), and the conference prominently featured Margaret Sanger, John Maynard Keynes, and Dr Norman Haire whom would head the section on contraception.[25] The delegates would include several vice-presidents of the CBC, including Sir James Barr, Harold Cox and Sir William Arbuthnot Lane.

This major international conference would ensure that the Malthusian League dominated the birth control agenda in July and, if the event coincided with the announcement of government support, possibly beyond. In these circumstances, it was unsurprising that Stopes chose a course of action that would give her legal redress against her Catholic critics and obtain national publicity as the pre-eminent name in birth control.

During a lecture to members of the CBC in Essex Hall in the Spring of 1922, she announced:

> "It may interest the Society to know that I have issued a writ against a medical man in this country, and he will have to answer in the High Courts, and there will be a big case coming along."[26]

The trial of Dr Halliday Sutherland had begun.

---

[1] Rose, J. (1992). *Marie Stopes and the Sexual Revolution*. London: Faber and Faber Limited. Page 151.

[2] Hall, R. (1977). *Passionate Crusader: The Life of Marie Stopes*. New York: Harcourt Brace Jovanovich. Page 204.

[3] *Ibid.*, page 198.

[4] *Ibid.*

[5] Letter from Marie Stopes to all vice-presidents and members of committees dated 6th December 1921. Wellcome Library. PP/MCS/E/10:Box62. Stopes herself had been a member of the Malthusian League.

[6] Femina Books. (1967). *The Trial of Marie Stopes*. (M. Box, Ed.) London: Femina Books Ltd. Pages 235-6.

[7] Rose, J. (1992). *Marie Stopes and the Sexual Revolution*. London: Faber and Faber Limited. Page 163.

[8] Hall, R. (1977). *Passionate Crusader: The Life of Marie Stopes*. New York: Harcourt Brace Jovanovich. Page 204.

[9] *Ibid.*

[10] An affidavit during the Stopes *v.* Sutherland pre-trial litigation showed that the Mothers' Clinic was mentioned in newspapers at least 37 times between March 1921 and December 1922. The affidavit was drawn up under intense time pressure, so it is likely the actual number was higher. Wellcome Library. PP/MCS/H/4a:Box72.

[11] Rose, J. (1992). *Marie Stopes and the Sexual Revolution*. London: Faber and Faber Limited. Page 147.

[12] Hall, R. (1977). *Passionate Crusader: The Life of Marie Stopes*. New York: Harcourt Brace Jovanovich. Page 199.

[13] Hall, L. *Situating Stopes: or, putting Marie in her proper place*. Retrieved January 17, 2019, from https://www.lesleyahall.net/stopes.htm.

[14] Rose, J. (1992). *Marie Stopes and the Sexual Revolution*. London: Faber and Faber Limited. Pages 90-1.

[15] *Ibid.*, page 154.

[16] Hall, L. *Situating Stopes: or, putting Marie in her proper place*. Retrieved January 17, 2019, from https://www.lesleyahall.net/stopes.htm.

[17] Letter from Percy Braby to Marie Stopes dated 5th December 1921. Wellcome Library. PP/MCS/H/1:Box71.

[18] According to Lesley Hall: "A more cynical view was (reportedly) expressed by Lord Dawson, a leading light in the medical profession and himself sympathetic to birth control, who was alleged to have 'once told Dr Robert L. Dickinson that she told [him] that she guessed she would have to have a suit soon as her books were not selling sufficiently well. Shortly afterwards, she sued Sutherland." Lesley Hall (2013) *'The Subject is Obscene: No Lady Would Dream of Alluding to It': Marie Stopes and her courtroom dramas*, Women's History Review, 22:2, 253-266, DOI: 10.1080/09612025.2012.726114. Page 261.

[19] Letter dated 3rd December 1921 from Marie Stopes to Percy Braby. Wellcome Library. PP/MCS/H/1:Box71.

[20] *Ibid.*

[21] Letter from Marie Stopes to Percy Braby dated 21st December 1921. Wellcome Library. PP/MCS/H/1:Box71.

[22] Letter from Marie Stopes to Percy Braby dated 13th January 1922. Wellcome Library. PP/MCS/H/1:Box71.

[23] *Ibid.*

[24] The agenda for a meeting of the executive committee of the CBC in late April 1922 included the item: "Rumours of an International Congress for Birth Control arranged by [the] Malthusian League in London this Summer, of which we have not been informed." *Agenda of the Executive Committee of the CBC* dated 14th April 1922 Wellcome Library. PP/MCS/C/37:Box58.

[25] Malthusian League. (1922). *The Fifth International Neo-Malthusian and Birth Control Conference.* In R. Pierpoint (Ed.), Report of the Fifth International Neo-Malthusian and Birth Control Conference. London: William Heinemann (Medical Books) Ltd. Retrieved October 21, 2017, from https://archive.org/details/reportoffifthint00inteuoft.

[26] Femina Books. (1967). *The Trial of Marie Stopes.* (M. Box, Ed.) London: Femina Books Ltd. Page 83.

Chapter 8

"Birth Control"

The "medical man" was Dr Halliday Sutherland and the "big case" was to become the Stopes v Sutherland libel trial.

Sutherland was demobilised from war service in the Royal Navy and the Royal Air Force in March 1919.[1] Later that year, he was accepted into the Catholic Church at the Church of the Immaculate Conception, Farm Street, Mayfair.[2]

On 4th August 1920, he married Muriel Fitzpatrick.[3] They lived at Over, Gloucestershire, and he worked as the Deputy Commissioner of Medical Services for Tuberculosis at the Ministry of Pensions, based in Bristol.

On 7th July 1921, Sutherland attended a meeting of the Medico-Legal Society, a forum for doctors and lawyers to discuss issues of interest to both professions, in London. That evening, Professor Louise McIlroy presented a paper on *Some Factors in the Control of the Birth Rate*.[4] McIlroy was based at the Royal Free Hospital for Women and had recently been appointed the first woman professor of obstetrics and gynaecology at London University.[5] The audience of eminent doctors and lawyers included Earl Russell, Dr Armand Routh (Stopes' gynaecologist) and the playwright, George Bernard Shaw.

In the discussion that followed her paper, McIlroy remarked that she had to exclude many issues in the interests of time and that, had she covered these, they would have been there until after midnight. Commenting on the safety of contraceptives, she said:

"As to contraceptives being harmful, I did not go into that question. I have had no experience of the harmful result from the use of quinine. The most harmful method of which I have had experience is the use of the pessary. It does not remain in place. It can pass back natural discharges. In sexual intercourse there is no proof that the spermatorrhoea [sic] has some physiological beneficial effect on the woman and if you put a cap over the walls of the vagina the walls may be threatened. We are not decided whether it is so or not. In my opinion it is the cervix which is absorbed and flooded, not the vagina. The Church is out of date. The Church ought not only to show the way to heaven, but to show that we should live a proper and moral and clean life."[6]

The following week, Sutherland discussed the meeting at the Medico-Legal Society with Father Joseph Keating, a Jesuit priest and editor of *The Truth*, a monthly Catholic journal.[7] He then wrote a pamphlet for the Catholic Truth Society entitled *Do Babies Build Slums?*, in which he challenged the Malthusian claim that large families were the cause of poverty. The pamphlet contained an early form of the words that would eventually become central to the Stopes *v* Sutherland libel trial:

"In a London slum, a woman who studied philosophy (not medicine) at a German University has opened a birth control clinic, where women are taught a method of preventing pregnancy. This method is described by a distinguished doctor, Professor McIlroy, as 'the most dangerous of which I have had experience.'"[8]

Keating suggested that Sutherland expand his pamphlet into a book and, whilst on holiday in Inverness, he wrote *Birth Control: A Statement of Christian Doctrine Against the Neo-Malthusians*.[9] Keating revised the proofs.[10] The book was published on 27th March 1922 and it sold a modest 811 copies in Britain.[11]

In it, Sutherland attacked Malthusian theories root and branch: "… the path of the Malthusian League, although at first glance an easy way out of many human difficulties, is in reality the broad road along which a man or a nation travels to destruction; and as guides the Neo-Malthusians are utterly unsafe, since they argue from (a) false premises to (b) false deductions."[12]

Birth Control was set out like a long debating speech with headed sections containing assertions, arguments and supporting facts, and numbers and letters to guide the reader. The extract below gives a flavour of the book:

"2. Poverty in Britain due to other causes
"(a) Under-development
"Even if the theory of birth controllers, that a high birth-rate increases poverty, were as true as it is false, it could not possibly apply to Great Britain or to any other country open to commercial intercourse with the world because there is no evidence that the supply of food in the world either cannot or will not be increased to meet any actual or possible demand. Within the British Empire alone there was an increase of 75 per cent. in the production of wheat between 1901 and 1911. In Great Britain there has been not only an increase of population but also an increased consumption of various foods per head of the population. Moreover, if Britain were as well cultivated as is Flanders we could produce all or nearly all our own food.
"The truth is that in countries such as England, Belgium, and Bengal, usually cited by Malthusians as illustrating the misery that results from overpopulation, there is no evidence whatsoever to show that the population is pressing on the soil.
"On the contrary, we find ample physical resources sufficient to support the entire population, and we also find evidence of human injustice, incapacity, and corruption sufficient to account for the poverty and misery that exist in these countries. This was especially so in Ireland during the first half of the nineteenth century. Moreover, so far from high birth rates being the cause of poverty, we shall find that poverty is one of the causes of a high birth-rate."
"(b) Severance of the Inhabitants from the Soil.
"It was not a high birth-rate that established organised poverty in England. In the sixteenth century the greater

part of the land including common land belonging to the poor, was seized by the rich. They began by robbing the Catholic Church, and they ended by robbing the people. Once machinery was introduced in the eighteenth century, the total wealth of England was enormously increased; but the vast majority of the people had little share in this increase of wealth that accrued from machinery, because only a small portion of the people possessed capital. More children came, but they came to conditions of poverty and of child labour in the mills. In countries where more natural and stable social conditions exist, and where there are many small owners of land, large families, so far from being a cause of poverty are of the greatest assistance to their parents and to themselves. There are means by which poverty could be reduced, but artificial birth control would only increase the total poverty of the State, and therefore of the individual.

"From early down to Tudor times, the majority of the inhabitants of England lived on smallholdings. For example, in the fifteenth century there were twenty-one small holdings on a particular area measuring 160 acres. During the sixteenth century the number of holdings on this area had fallen to six, and in the seventeenth century the 160 acres became one farm. Occasionally an effort was made to check this process and by a statute of Elizabeth penalties were enacted against building any cottages "without laying four acres of land thereto." On the other hand, acres upon acres were given to the larger landowners by a series of Acts for the enclosure of common land, whereby many labourers were deprived of their land. From the reign of George I to that of George III nearly four thousand enclosure bills were passed. These wrongs have not been righted."[13]

The text of *Birth Control* was peppered with robust attacks on those with whom Sutherland disagreed. For instance, Dr C.V. Drysdale, president of the Malthusian League, had "… in order to bolster up an argument which is rotten from beginning to end…[not hesitated]…to launch without a particle of evidence a charge of gross hypocrisy against..." a religious sect that had not deserved it.[14]

Sutherland wrote that Lord Dawson's speech to the Congress of Anglican bishops in Birmingham in 1921 included "hoary fallacies" and said that Dawson had not spoken on behalf of a united medical profession.

"When a great leader announces the birth of a new epoch, it is meet that the rank and file remain silent; and at this Congress of the Church of England no jarring interruptions marred the solemnity of the moment. No old-fashioned doctor was there to utter a futile protest, and there was no simple-minded clergyman to rise in the name of Christ and give Lord Dawson the lie. Without dissent, on a public platform of the Established Church, presided over by a Bishop, and in full view of the nation, "the moth-eaten mantle of Malthus..." was donned. "It was a proud moment for the birth controllers, but for that national institution called *Ecclesia Anglicana* a moment full of shame."[15]

In Chapter VII, Sutherland listed *The Evils of Artificial Birth Control* which included the passage that was to be at the centre of the Stopes *v* Sutherland libel trial:

"6. SPECIALLY HURTFUL TO THE POOR".
"(b) Exposing the Poor to Experiment."
"Secondly, the ordinary decent practices of the poor are against these practices and indeed they have used them less than any other class. But, owing to their poverty, lack of learning, and helplessness, the poor are the natural victims of those who seek to make experiments on their fellows. In the midst of a London slum a woman, who is a doctor of German philosophy (Munich), has opened a Birth Control Clinic, where working women are instructed in a method of contraception described by Professor McIlroy as 'The most harmful method of which I have had experience'. When we remember that millions are being spent by the Ministry of Health and by Local Authorities — on pure milk for necessitous expectant and nursing mothers, on

Maternity Clinics to guard the health of mothers before and after childbirth, for the provision of skilled midwives, and on Infant Welfare Centres — it is truly amazing that this monstrous campaign of birth control should be tolerated by the Home Secretary. Charles Bradlaugh was condemned to jail for a less serious crime."

Charles Bradlaugh's "less serious crime" had taken place in 1877 when, with Annie Besant, he reprinted a Malthusian tract. They were prosecuted and imprisoned until the charges were later dismissed (see Appendix 3 for Dr Sutherland's summary of the case).

Stopes ordered a copy of *Birth Control* prior to its publication. According to Humphrey Roe:

"… when the book reached the house we glanced at it together and after reading some chapters of it I agreed with her that it was so badly written and so unconvincing an argument that the book was not worth the trouble of reading. We looked at the index to see if either of our names were mentioned in connection with the Clinic and not finding them there threw the book down and it was not until some time later that we discovered the libellous passages which form the basis of this action."[16]

On 12th April 1922, Roe wrote to Sutherland to invite him to debate birth control at a general meeting of the CBC,[17] but Sutherland did not reply.[18] Later that month, Stopes' reviewed *Birth Control* in the first edition of *Birth Control News* (the CBC's answer to the *New Generation*):[19]

"Dr Sutherland's book will impose only on those who are more ignorant than he is. It is nicely calculated to encourage those biased in their prejudice, for now when speaking against birth control they can say: A Doctor says so. They will probably forget that he is a Roman Catholic Doctor… The omissions from the book are quite as remarkable as its lies…"[20]

Since that review, the biographers of Stopes have followed her lead in suggesting that Sutherland's opposition was motivated solely by his Roman Catholic faith and have represented the dispute as "Catholics against contraceptives". This view not only ignores Dr Sutherland's background in tuberculosis which drew him to oppose eugenics, but it also misrepresents the dispute in two other ways as well.

Firstly, in *Birth Control* Sutherland attacked not only Stopes' clinic but also her eugenic program as well. The evidence for this is in the section that immediately follows "(b) Exposing the Poor to Experiment" which reads:

"(c) Tending towards the Servile State."

"Thirdly, the policy of birth control opens the way to an extension of the Servile State, because women as well as men could be placed under conditions of economic slavery. Hitherto, the rule has been that during child-bearing age a woman must be supported by her husband, and the general feeling of the community has been opposed to any conditions likely to force married women on to the industrial market. In her own home a woman works hard, but she is working for the benefit of her family and not directly for the benefit of a stranger. If, instead of bearing children, women practise birth control, and if children are to be denied to the poor as a privilege of the rich, then it would be very easy to exploit the women of the poorer classes. If women have no young children why should they be exempt of the economic pressure that is applied to men? And indeed, where birth control is practised women tend more and more to supplant men, especially in ill-paid grades of work. One of the birth controllers has suggested that young couples, who otherwise could not afford to marry, should marry but have no children, and thus continue to work at their respective employments during the day. As the girl would have little time for cooking and other domestic duties, this immoralist is practically subverting the very idea of a home! The English poor have already lost even the meaning of the word 'property,' and if the birth controllers had their way the meaning of the word 'home' would soon follow.

The aim of birth control is generally masked by falsehood, but the urging of this policy on the poor points unmistakenly to the Servile State."

The term "servile state" (borrowed from Hilaire Belloc's book of the same name) meant that "those who do not own the means of production shall be legally compelled to work for those who do, and shall receive in exchange a security of livelihood."[21] In other words, a slave state. And while the identity of "one of the birth controllers" is not specified, if it was not Stopes herself, then it was closely aligned to the views she promoted (for example, see article 11 of the *Tenets of the CBC* in Appendix 1).

The second reason is that Sutherland's opposition to eugenics began long before his conversion to Catholicism in 1919. Born in 1882, he had been "brought up a Scots Presbyterian" but was by 1904 "in theory an agnostic and in practice an atheist".[22] On the outbreak of World War I, he joined the Church of Scotland: "In August 1914 there came the hazards of war, and for me the time had come when it was expedient to make my peace with God. At a few hours' notice the Church of Scotland admitted me to her membership."[23] It was not until 1919, that he was accepted into the Catholic Church at the Church of the Immaculate Conception in Farm Street, London.[24]

As historian Ann Farmer has written,[25] Sutherland did not oppose eugenics and reproductive control because of the Catholic Church; he was drawn to the Catholic Church because of its consistent opposition to eugenics and reproductive control.[26]

---

[1] *The Air Ministry and Royal Air Force Service Records*. The National Archives. Retrieved January 17, 2019, from http://discovery.nationalarchives.gov.uk.

[2] Sutherland, H. (1934). *A Time to Keep*. Geoffrey Bles. Page 239. See also: Sutherland, H. (1956). *Irish Journey*. London: Geoffrey Bles. Page 11.

[3] *Souvenir of the Marriage of Mr Halliday Sutherland M.D. with Muriel Fitzpatrick*. (1920). London. Dr Halliday Sutherland archive in possession of the Sutherland family.

[4] *Proceedings of the Medical-Legal Society, 11 Chandos Street, W. July 7th 1922* [sic – the meeting took place in 1921, not 1922] Wellcome Library. PP/MCS/H/4a:Box72.

[5] British Medical Journal. (1968, February 17). *Obituary Notice Louise McIlroy D.B.E.* British Medical Journal, 451.

[6] *Proceedings of the Medical-Legal Society, 11 Chandos Street, W. July 7th 1922* [sic – the meeting took place in 1921, not 1922] Wellcome Library.

PP/MCS/H/4a:Box72 PP/MCS/H.4a. The passage is quoted from a transcript of the meeting. The reader will get a better understanding of what was said if the replace the word "spermatorrhoea" (a medical condition) with "sperm".

[7] Sutherland, H. (1934). *A Time to Keep*. Geoffrey Bles. Page 240.

[8] *Do Babies Build Slums?* Catholic Truth Society. Westminster Archdiocese Archive. BO5/59 Birth Control 1921-26.

[9] George Bernard Shaw may have helped Sutherland to write *Birth Control* by providing copies of the British Medical Journal. Source: Postcard from Shaw to Sutherland dated 4th August 1921 ("I will tell my people to send on the B.M.J."). Dr Halliday Sutherland archive in possession of the Sutherland family.

[10] Letter from Joseph Weld to Monsignor Jackman dated 23rd December 1922 Westminster Archdiocese Archive. BO5/59 Birth Control 1921-26.

[11] Sutherland, H. (1934). *A Time to Keep*. Geoffrey Bles. Page 240.

[12] Sutherland, H. (1922). *Birth Control: A Statement of Christian Doctrine Against the Neo-Malthusians*. London: Harding & More. Page 3.

[13] *Ibid.*, page 29.

[14] *Ibid.*, page 77.

[15] *Ibid.*, pages 146-7.

[16] *Witness Statement of Mr Humphrey Roe* Wellcome Library. PP/MCS/H/4a:Box72. Roe did not testify, so his evidence was not tested in the High Court. Had he done so, however, the cross-examining barrister might have undermined his testimony by pointing out that *Birth Control* did not have an index and that Stopes was mentioned by name ten times in the text.

[17] Letter from Humphrey Roe to Halliday Sutherland dated 12th April 1922 Wellcome Library. PP/MCS/H/4a:Box72.

[18] Sutherland, H. (1934). *A Time to Keep*. Geoffrey Bles. Pages 239-241.

[19] Hall, R. (1977). *Passionate Crusader: The Life of Marie Stopes*. New York: Harcourt Brace Jovanovich. Page 200.

[20] Rose, J. (1992). *Marie Stopes and the Sexual Revolution*. London: Faber and Faber Limited. Page 159.

[21] Belloc, H. (1912). *The Servile State*. T.N. Foulis Limited, London and Edinburgh. Page 6.

[22] Sutherland, H. (1956). *Irish Journey*. London: Geoffrey Bles. Page 11.

[23] Sutherland, H. (1934). *A Time to Keep*. Geoffrey Bles. Page 208.

[24] *Ibid.*, page 239.

[25] Farmer, A. (2008). *By Their Fruits: Eugenics, Population Control, and the Abortion Campaign*. Washington D.C.: The Catholic University of America Press. Page 139.

[26] In the conclusion to *Eugenics and Politics in Britain 1900-1914*. G.R. Searle wrote: "For those socialists prepared to base their case on the essential inequality of man, eugenics has proved to be extremely attractive, as can be seen from a study of the writings of socialist intellectuals from George Bernard Shaw to Professor J.B.S. Haldane, both of them 'reform eugenists' of a sort. True, trade union leaders have mostly ignored eugenics, and often seemed unaware of its very existence. It still remains a matter of some interest that the fiercest opposition to eugenics has come, not from the Labour/Socialist camp, but from Roman Catholics and from a certain kind of individualist liberal" Searle, G. (1976). *Eugenics and Politics in Britain 1900-1914*. Leyden: Noordhoff International Publishing. Page 113.

Chapter 9

Lies

Stopes wrote to Percy Braby of Braby & Waller about *Birth Control* on 4th May 1922. The letter shows that she recognised she now had the opportunity she had been waiting for.

She began: "I think we have given the Roman Catholics rope enough and now they have hung themselves," and she drew his attention to "the explicit libel [which] contains three important lies":[1]

"Page 101. Exposing the Poor to Experiment. (Lie No. 1).

"This implies that I am using the poor as experimental material, which is absolutely contrary to fact, and most injurious to my efforts to assist the poor in obtaining exactly the same reliable scientific information, which is available for the rich and educated.

"Further down in the paragraph, the following sentence occurs: "In the midst of a London slum a woman, who is a doctor of German philosophy (Munich)…"[2]

"It is evidence of malice that I should be described as a doctor of German philosophy with no mention of the fact that I am a doctor of English science of the London University and hold high positions in English Universities. This I can trace directly to Roman Catholic malice as exactly the same phrase has been used recently by a Roman Catholic priest.

"Lie No. 2. '… a Birth Control Clinic, where working women are instructed in a method of contraception described by Professor McIlroy as 'the most harmful method of which I have had experience'.

"This is a two-fold lie. In the first place the method of contraception given at the Clinic is the most wholesome known to medical science, has been authorised by the expert medical Committee of the CBC, and is used by the best doctors in this country and all over the world.

"The second aspect of this double lie is that Professor McIlroy did not say these words about me of anything done at the Clinic, and I hold in her own handwriting an explicit letter to that effect, of which I enclose a copy marked 'A'.

"Carrying on, page 102 contains the third lie, as follows:— Charles Bradlaugh was condemned to jail for a less serious crime.

"This is also a double lie. Bradlaugh in the first place was not condemned to jail. This however matters little, the worst part of it being that it here explicitly implied that I commit a crime by opening my Birth Control Clinic. This is an absolute lie: it is no crime but of great and beneficial assistance to the working-classes to come for exactly the same medical help which expensive Harley Street doctors give to the highest in the land.

"The advantages of taking action in this case are many… you will see at once we are dealing one blow here with the Roman Catholics, the recalcitrant medical profession as distinct from the good class medicals who are with me; also with the clerical element for I have private information that Sutherland is merely a tool of the Roman Catholic Church."[3]

Stopes had contacted Professor McIlroy to verify her remarks and, on 3rd May 1922, McIlroy replied that she had "not made the slightest reference" to her, nor mentioned her by name.[4]

Stopes was in a confident mood: "our case is impregnable, and it will do great damage to the Roman Catholics." Her instructions to Braby were clear:

"I want you to act immediately without further hesitation; to act effectively and to strike as hard a blow as the law will permit."[5]

The action permitted under the law would be on the basis of libel. To succeed, Stopes would need to prove that: "the words… written or printed or otherwise permanently recorded must be defamatory: that is, they must have injured the reputation of someone, [or] must have made people think worse of [her]."[6]

To be defamatory, the statement must have a "tendency to injure the reputation of the person to who it refers, which tends… to diminish the good opinion that other persons have of [her], and to cause [her] to be regarded with feelings of hatred, contempt, ridicule, fear, dislike, or dis-esteem".[7]

Braby arranged for writs to be served on Sutherland and on Vincent Waring of Harding & More, the publisher of *Birth Control*. Sutherland later recalled receipt of the writ in his memoir:

"I was at my Bristol office when a local firm of solicitors telephoned, on 13th May 1922, to say they were instructed to serve me with a writ for libel at the instance of Dr Marie Stopes. I told them to hold the writ until I found a London solicitor who would accept service, then wired two friends in London, a barrister and a journalist, to meet me in a quiet hotel in Dover Street at eight that evening.

"There at eight-o-clock I saw my two friends[8] and showed them the passage in the book on which I knew the writ had been issued. The barrister read it carefully, said that the words had been defamatory, that a plea of "fair comment" would fail, and that my only defence was "Justification," namely, that what I had written was true in substance and in fact. This is the hardest defence for any defendant in a libel action."[9]

In the eyes of the law, if the statement was true, then Stopes was not entitled "to recover damages in respect of an injury to a character which [she] either does not or ought not to possess."[10] Justification was a complete answer to the action, and would be the end to the matter.[11]

The law specified it was not necessary to prove that the statement was literally true, but that it was substantially true. So if, for example, a statement said that X had committed a crime and had been fined £1 and imprisoned for three weeks, but in reality X had been fined £1 and imprisoned for two weeks, the standard of substantial truth would have been met.[12]

The defence of "Justification" was risky, because an unsuccessful attempt to establish that the defamation was true might lead to "an aggravation of the original injury" and make things worse for the defendants.[13]

The first hearing on 26th May 1922 outlined a timetable which showed that the case would be ready for trial in July, just in time for the Neo-Malthusian World Congress… if all went to plan.

---

[1] Letter from Marie Stopes to Percy Braby dated 4th May 1922. Wellcome Library. PP/MCS/H/1:Box71.

[2] *Ibid.*

[3] *Ibid.*

[4] Letter from Louise McIlroy to Marie Stopes dated 3rd May 1922. Wellcome Library. PP/MCS/H/4a:Box72.

[5] Letter from Marie Stopes to Percy Braby dated 4th May 1922. Wellcome Library. PP/MCS/H/1:Box71.

[6] Odgers, W. (1897). *An Outline of the Law of Libel: Six lectures delivered in the Middle Temple Hall during Michaelmas Term 1896*. Macmillan and Co., Limited. Page 9.

[7] Salmond, J. W. (1916). *The Law of Torts: A Treatise on the English Law of Liability for Civil Injuries (Fourth ed.)*. Temple Bar: Stevens and Haynes. Retrieved January 18, 2019, from https://archive.org/details/cu31924022354173/page/n5. Page 450.

[8] Sutherland did not name his friends in *A Time to Keep* and, based on his letter to Cardinal Bourne dated 14th May 1922, they were Reginald Dingle and Victor Rabagliati. Westminster Archdiocese Archive. BO5/59 Birth Control 1921-26.

[9] Sutherland, H. (1934). *A Time to Keep*. Geoffrey Bles. Pages 239-241.

[10] Salmond, J. W. (1916). *The Law of Torts: A Treatise on the English Law of Liability for Civil Injuries (Fourth ed.)*. Temple Bar: Stevens and Haynes. Page 464. Retrieved January 18, 2019, from https://archive.org/details/cu31924022354173/page/n5.

[11] Odgers, W. (1897). *An Outline of the Law of Libel: Six lectures delivered in the Middle Temple Hall during Michaelmas Term 1896*. Macmillan and Co., Limited. Page 95.

[12] Salmond, J. W. (1916). *The Law of Torts: A Treatise on the English Law of Liability for Civil Injuries (Fourth ed.)*. Temple Bar: Stevens and Haynes. Page 465. Retrieved January 18, 2019, from https://archive.org/details/cu31924022354173/page/n5.

[13] *Ibid.*, page 464.

Chapter 10

"Sutherland undoubtedly wants rapping on the nose"

Before a case can come to trial, there are many painstaking hours given to establishing facts, citing the law, of claim and counter claim, documenting these and filing them with the Court. Given the amount of work, delays are almost inevitable.

Stopes' lawyers drew up a Statement of Claim, which set out the legal wrongs of which Sutherland was accused and which specified the remedies that they sought. The Statement cited the words that she alleged were defamatory.

"(b) Exposing the Poor to Experiment.
"Secondly, the ordinary decent instincts of the poor are against these practices and indeed they have used them less than any other class. But owing to their poverty, lack of learning and helplessness, the poor are the natural victims of those who seek to make experiments on their fellows. In the midst of a London slum, a woman who is a doctor of German philosophy (Munich), has opened a birth control clinic where working women are instructed in a method of contraception described by Professor McIlroy as 'The most harmful method of which I have had experience.'…"
"It is truly amazing that this monstrous campaign of birth control should be tolerated by the Home Secretary.

Charles Bradlaugh was condemned to jail for a less serious crime."[1]

Readers will have noticed that the following passage had been excluded: "When we remember that millions are being spent by the Ministry of Health and by Local Authorities — on pure milk for necessitous expectant and nursing mothers, on Maternity Clinics to guard the health of mothers before and after childbirth, for the provision of skilled midwives, and on Infant Welfare Centres —" The Statement of Claim enabled the Plaintiff to select words from the offending texts, even if it was to change its context.

Stopes asserted that by the words she had selected, the Defendants meant:

> "… that the plaintiff was taking advantage of the ignorance of the poor to subject them to experiments of a most harmful and dangerous nature; that she was guilty of disgraceful illegal and criminal practices for which she should be punished by a term of imprisonment; and that she was a person with whom no decent or respectable persons should associate."[2]

The upshot was that she had been "greatly injured in her credit character and reputation," and her position in relation to the Mothers' Clinic had "been brought into public scandal hatred and contempt."[3]

The Statement was the device by which Stopes applied to the Court to use its authority to prevent the continued publication of the defamatory words, and to claim damages (monetary compensation) from the defendants.

Sutherland's Defence, also filed with the Court, rebutted the assertions contained in the Statement of Claim.[4] It argued that "the said words in their natural meaning are true in substance and in fact."[5] Of course, the meaning of the words may become part of the dispute, so the law prescribes that the meaning is the one "reasonably given to it by the persons to whom it is published." In other words, determined in court.[6]

In addition to the main defence, alternatives were specified: "The said words in their natural meaning are fair and *bona fide* comment without malice on matters of public interest..." The Defence cited "the campaign of the Plaintiff and others in furtherance of such [birth] limitation" and listed "the publications of the Plaintiff in favour of such limitation and the unrestricted sale of the same."[7]

Another defence was that the parts of the libel that were factual were true and the parts of the libel that were statements of opinion were fair comment.

The law of defamation involves a conflict of rights (the right of the plaintiff to not be defamed against the defendant's right to speak freely), and the defence of "fair comment" seeks to balance these. As an expert on defamation, W. Blake Odgers, KC put it in 1895:

"The plaintiff's reputation must not be injured [and] the defendant's freedom of speech must not be restricted."[8]

The defendant had an "undoubted right to criticise and comment on the public acts of a public [wo]man", but not to "unnecessarily impute dishonourable motives, or maliciously pry into [her] private concerns".[9] The defence would work if it was "a fair comment on a matter which is of public interest or is submitted to public criticism".[10]

The use of alternative defences aimed to construct a safety net so that, if one of the defences failed, then an alternative might hold.

Sutherland's rebuttal concluded by stating that "if the Plaintiff's character and/or reputation have been injured such injury is due to the conduct and publications of the Plaintiff".[11]

As the reader will no doubt appreciate, the case had already become quite complex. For what was the plaintiff's reputation before *Birth Control* was published? What impact had Sutherland's words had? Further, how would the assertions of each side be proved in court?

Sutherland later observed: "Cases are won not so much by advocacy in the court as by hard work in the solicitor's office."[12] In addition to the application and interpretation of the law and assembling evidence, much of the solicitor's work deals with the minor details to ensure the case runs smoothly (for example, ensuring that sufficient copies of particular books are available for use in court).

Further information was sought, and answered, by both sides. Assertions were made and rebutted; facts were established and refuted. Evidence was assembled and witness statements were prepared, sworn and filed. And if the case did get to trial — for there was a chance that the parties might negotiate a settlement beforehand — the appearance of witnesses in court had to be arranged.

In addition to having a good grasp of the case at the strategic and tactical levels, the solicitor should anticipate the likely actions of the other side and prepare contingency plans. At the same time, the solicitor had to manage the passions and fears of their client, such as Stopes' belligerent letter to Braby in June 1922 which urged him to:

> "Please remember that in this case I want to strike the heaviest blows possible in all directions… Sutherland is inspiring other attacks, and undoubtedly wants rapping on the nose."[13]

All of this work takes place behind the scenes and makes litigation a time-consuming and expensive process.

While they act on behalf of their clients, solicitors (and barristers) are officers of the Court and have obligations to act in accordance with legal conventions and rules of conduct.

As mentioned, the documents in the case are lodged at the office of the Court, and the Court may become further involved through intermediate hearings held to make decisions in relation to the subsidiary issues in a case.

At these so called "directions hearings" each party to the litigation can seek direction from the Court on a particular issue. For example, part of Sutherland's defence relied on the laws in France and the United States, and Stopes successfully applied to the Court to have these struck out, on the grounds that it would unfairly delay the trial.[14] The Court's rulings on these issues are called "Orders".

Intermediate hearings in the Stopes *v* Sutherland case included an "Order for Particulars" (commands that information be provided) and an "Order for delivery of interrogatories and Discovery of Documents" (commands that questions be answered, and documents be provided). These interactions are a vital but largely unobserved part of the legal process.

In the legal battle between Stopes and Sutherland there were thirteen formal interactions of this kind between June 1922 and February 1923.[15] Stopes was steadily gaining the upper hand, because she received the Orders from the Court that she sought.

In November 1922, the plaintiff set the case down for hearing before a judge and a special jury,[16] a move intended to expedite the case. In December, the Court struck out further parts of Sutherland's defence, which included:

> "The exhibition at a shop at 64 Praed Street, Paddington, of the Plaintiff's books *Married Love* and *Wise Parenthood* together with books of a sensual description, such as *Five Nights*, *Thais*, or *The Monk's Temptation* and *The White Slaves of London* and *The Kinema Girl*."[17]

The Court ruled that these references "be struck out on the grounds that the same are irrelevant and tend to prejudice embarrass and delay the fair trial of the action and are an abuse of the process of the Court and are contrary to the Rules of Pleading."[18]

These interactions placed enormous pressure on the defence, not least because missing the deadline for a court order would risk losing the case. At one point, they were given 21 days to substantiate Sutherland's assertion that there was a campaign of birth control. While they did so, it placed a great strain on their resources. As Stopes remarked in a letter to Braby, she felt sorry for Sutherland because "no mortal man could give all of those details in twenty-one days or twenty-one years, in my opinion".[19]

Buoyed by these successes, Stopes began to focus on the anti-Catholic aspect of her case. The briefing to her the barrister included her earlier command that attention be drawn to:

> "... the harm the Roman Catholics are doing to our nation as a whole... on the whole [they] are the most immoral of the sections of our community, and for them to gain ascendancy is nationally very dangerous and harmful".[20]

In addition, Stopes wanted to use the trial to expose Catholic control of the press:

> "It is suggested that in cross-examination of defendants witnesses some might be made to admit that individual Roman Catholic Editors on papers otherwise supposed to be Protestant use their editorial position to suppress news about the Plaintiff and Constructive Birth Control which the public would otherwise get in their columns."[21]

These matters would not help her to win the case, but it would enable her to use the Court to expose those whom she described as "the ruling gang of Roman Catholics".[22]

These instructions revealed a fatal flaw in Stopes' approach to the case and showed that, for all her much-touted intellect, she fundamentally misunderstood the legal process. To win, the plaintiff should get the best legal advisers, trust them, and follow their directions. The side issues were, at best, distractions and, at worst, might undermine her case.

The side issues included Stopes asking Lord Dawson of Penn (whom, readers will remember was the King's physician who had spoken with such effect at the Birmingham Congress of the Anglican Church in October 1921) to attend the case. Dawson declined her invitation, giving the excuse that he was so busy he was "only allowing five minutes to each patient and eating his meals in his car".[23]

Another was Stopes' plan to compel Cardinal Bourne to testify in the trial by subpoena. Her counsel were "strongly opposed" to this idea,[24] no doubt, knowing that judges take a dim view of those who try to turn their court into a circus.

To achieve the win that Stopes desired, her legal team would have to address the issue at the heart of the dispute: that Sutherland had unjustifiably defamed her, that her reputation had been harmed and that, as a result, she was entitled to damages.

Importantly, the defence of Justification placed the burden of proof on the defendant, for "it is for him to prove that that statement is true, not for the plaintiff to prove that it is false."[25] In other words, once Stopes had proved that Sutherland had defamed her and that her reputation had suffered, the work of the plaintiff was largely done. It was for Sutherland and his lawyers to prove that the words in *Birth Control* were true. Given his remarks were wide-ranging and given the difficulty of the defence of Justification, the defence would likely lose.

On 13th January 1923, Stopes wrote to Sir James Barr and assured him that: "the best medicals are with us" and that she had: "... the very best lawyers... and I am sure they would not let me proceed unless I had a very good case."[26]

A "very good case", the "best medicals" and the "very best lawyers" might have caused her to feel confident but, of themselves, they do not win cases. Litigation is a risky activity and the outcomes are unpredictable. Even the best cases on paper fall apart in a courtroom when the human element comes into play.

There is a reason for the legal maxim: "witnesses ruin cases".

---

[1] Statement of Claim dated 15th June 1922. Wellcome Library. PP/MCS/H/4a:Box72.

[2] *Ibid.*

[3] *Ibid.*

[4] A similar defence was filed by the co-defendant, publisher Harding & More.

[5] *Defence of Defendant Halliday Gibson Sutherland* dated 31st July 1922 Wellcome Library. PP/MCS/H/4a:Box72.

[6] Salmond, J. W. (1916). *The Law of Torts: A Treatise on the English Law of Liability for Civil Injuries (Fourth ed.)*. Temple Bar: Stevens and Haynes. Retrieved January 18, 2019, from https://archive.org/details/cu31924022354173/page/n5. Page 454.

[7] *Defence of Defendant Halliday Gibson Sutherland* dated 31st July 1922. Wellcome Library. PP/MCS/H/4a:Box72.

[8] Odgers, W. (1897). *An Outline of the Law of Libel: Six lectures delivered in the Middle Temple Hall during Michaelmas Term 1896*. Macmillan and Co., Limited. Page 36.

[9] *Ibid.*, page 37.

[10] Salmond, J. W. (1916). *The Law of Torts: A Treatise on the English Law of Liability for Civil Injuries (Fourth ed.)*. Temple Bar: Stevens and Haynes. Retrieved January 18, 2019, from https://archive.org/details/cu31924022354173/page/n5. Page 480.

[11] *Defence of Defendant Halliday Gibson Sutherland* dated 31st July 1922. Wellcome Library. PP/MCS/H/4a:Box72.

[12] Sutherland, H. (1934). *A Time to Keep*. Geoffrey Bles. Page 250.

[13] Letter from Marie Stopes to Percy Braby dated 15th June 1922. Wellcome Library. PP/MCS/G/30:Box70.

[14] Court Order dated 24th October 1922. Wellcome Library. PP/MCS/H/4a:Box72.

[15] Various documents. Wellcome Library. PP/MCS/H/4a:Box72.

[16] Letter from Percy Braby to Marie Stopes dated 23rd November 1922. Wellcome Library. PP/MCS/H/1:Box71.

[17] Particulars of the Defendants, Harding & More Limited. Wellcome Library. PP/MCS/H/4a:Box72.

[18] Court Order 12th January 1923. Wellcome Library. PP/MCS/H/4a:Box72.

[19] Letter from Marie Stopes to Percy Braby dated 22nd October 1922. Wellcome Library. PP/MCS/H/1:Box71.

[20] Brief on behalf of the Plaintiff. Wellcome Library. PP/MCS/H/4a:Box72.

[21] *Ibid.*

[22] *Ibid.*

[23] Letter from Marie Stopes to Percy Braby dated 15th February 1923. British Library: Western Manuscripts MS58648 Vol.CCII(ff.124). Jan 1923-June 1923.

[24] Letter from Percy Braby to Marie Stopes dated 14th December 1922. Wellcome Library. PP/MCS/H/1:Box71.

[25] Salmond, J. W. (1916). *The Law of Torts: A Treatise on the English Law of Liability for Civil Injuries* (Fourth ed.). Temple Bar: Stevens and Haynes. Page 464. Retrieved January 18, 2019, from https://archive.org/details/cu31924022354173/page/n5.

[26] Letter from Marie Stopes to Sir William Arbuthnot Lane dated 13th January 1923. Wellcome Library. PP/MCS/B.12 (Gold Spring: letters to Dr Norman Haire and others).

Chapter 11

Money and Maintenance

In addition to his legal problems, Sutherland had a much more pressing need: he had no money with which to fight the case. At one point, he even planned to defend himself in court.[1]

Readers will recall that on receiving the writ, Sutherland had met two friends, one a journalist and the other a lawyer. As he wrote in a later memoir:

> "The journalist suggested that I should ask the [Catholic] Church to assist me. This I declined to do, although if the Church on hearing of the case decided to help me I would be only too glad to accept. In any case I knew nobody at Archbishop's House, and as a Catholic was unknown except for this book [*Birth Control*]. At that he left the room to telephone, and then returned. At ten o'clock he was called to the telephone by Monsignor Jackman [secretary to Cardinal Bourne], who sent this message: 'Tell Dr Sutherland that Cardinal Bourne will stand by him to the end.' Had it not been for that decision by His Eminence, I would have been ruined."[2]

Sutherland was told to write to Cardinal Bourne to inform him of the case, which he did on 14th May 1922.[3] The following day Bourne wrote to Mr Franey, the head of the Catholic Union:

"It seems to me that this is pre-eminently a case in which the Catholic Union ought to intervene by giving Dr Sutherland every assistance in its power."[4]

Franey, a barrister by profession, promised that he would "be delighted to advise him to the best of my ability"[5] and he promised to raise the issue at the Council of the Union. Subsequently, Franey told Bourne that the Council hoped to "secure for Dr Sutherland a substantial recognition of the work which he has done for the Catholic cause."

The "substantial recognition" was to allow Sutherland to address the Union's Annual General Meeting on 29th June 1922.[6] In his speech, Sutherland outlined his case. While he did not appeal for money at the meeting, the question of financial support was raised and people came forward to offer help.

At this point, Franey raised the spectre of "unlawful maintenance", the act of funding litigation that had nothing to do with you, and which the law prohibited.[7] A donor in these circumstances would face penalties, including the payment of damages and costs to the other party in the legal action.

The rules of maintenance were not clear cut. Ideally, an expert would have been consulted on the issue and would have determined whether contributing to Sutherland's legal expenses was maintenance. Without the funds to do so, however, the expert advice was neither sought nor given.

At the end of 1922, Joseph Weld of Witham, Roskam, Munster & Weld, solicitor to the Westminster Archdiocese, wrote to Monsignor Jackman:

"I have seen Mr Franey twice in reference to the case and he is obsessed with the idea that persons who give money to help the defendants in the Sutherland case, run a risk of an action for maintenance. It was, I feel sure, this attitude of his which prevented the appeal to the Catholic Union being successful in the Summer. You will remember Dr Sutherland addressed the Catholic Union with the object of interesting them in his case. He did not actually appeal for funds, but the question of raising funds was discussed and Mr Franey volunteered the opinion that the donors would run grave risks. Naturally, this opinion coming from a Barrister supplied

the excuse which is always ready in a man's mind when
he is asked for money."[8]

Weld was also critical of Franey's indecisiveness and
complained of the "great difficulties in the way of inducing Mr
Franey to act".[9]

When Weld learned that the plaintiff had applied to
have the case tried before a special jury (which meant that it
would come on for trial much sooner than he had expected) he
confided to Jackman: "We haven't near enough money to fight
the case at present," and that he was "getting very uneasy about
the case".[10]

It "would be monstrous were Dr Sutherland left in the
lurch by his fellow Catholics,"[11] he said, because "… one of the
worst libels" (in connection with Bradlaugh) had been inserted
by Father Keating when he was revising Sutherland's draft."[12]

Cardinal Bourne pledged £400 of his own savings to
Sutherland's legal fees, a sum which he later increased to £500.[13]
While it was a significant donation that provided an example for
others to follow, it was insufficient to fund the litigation to the
trial stage.

Weld's letters also revealed that Sutherland was not the
only one with money worries. When Sutherland received the
writ, he engaged a firm of solicitors and, while he had
subsequently moved to Charles Russell & Co, money was still
owing to the first firm:

> "Poor Mr Daly will be very upset. We don't seem to be
> able to get anything in. You probably know that he is a
> Catholic Clerk with a very large Protestant firm and he
> is afraid of his firm coming down upon him for not
> forcing Dr Sutherland to pay something on account."[14]

Edward Eyre of the Catholic Federation was more
supportive than Franey, though the Federation was smaller and
not as well-resourced as the larger Union.

A legal opinion on the issue of maintenance was not
received until mid-January 1923, a little over one month before
the case opened in the High Court. Mr Ernest Charles KC and
Harold Murphy of Charles Russell & Co opined:

"… if any individual or group of individuals belonging to that Church, moved thereto by the interest arising from a common religious faith, chooses to lend financial aid to Dr Sutherland in his Defence, he or they may do so without any apprehension that such assistance would constitute actionable maintenance. The question was expressly raised in Holden *v* Thompson (1907) 2 KB 489 and it was there held that where assistance, induced by a common religious belief, is given to a poor defendant the case falls within the specific exception to the law against maintenance founded on the interest arising out of charity."[15]

Further they advised that for maintenance to be proved, a plaintiff would have to show that had maintenance not been provided, the case would not have been defended. Given that Sutherland had at one stage contemplated defending himself, this did not apply. The plaintiff could not complain to the Court that, because of maintenance, the defence was better than it otherwise would have been.[16]

The settling of the maintenance issue meant that on the eve of the trial and after much uncertainty, Sutherland was able to raise funds to pay for his defence. Special collections were held for this purpose at Catholic Sunday masses.

At the end of January 1923, the parties learned that the High Court had fixed the trial for the third week in February.[17]

---

[1] Letter from Halliday Sutherland to Cardinal Bourne dated 14th May 1922. Westminster Archdiocese Archive. BO5/59 Birth Control 1921-26.

[2] Sutherland, H. (1934). *A Time to Keep*. Geoffrey Bles. Page 241.

[3] Letter from Halliday Sutherland to Cardinal Bourne dated 14th May 1922. Westminster Archdiocese Archive. BO5/59 Birth Control 1921-26.

[4] Letter from Cardinal Bourne to Mr Franey dated 15th May 1922. Westminster Archdiocese Archive. BO5/59 Birth Control 1921-26.

[5] Letter from Mr Franey to Monsignor Jackman dated 18th May 1922. Westminster Archdiocese Archive. BO5/59 Birth Control 1921-26.

[6] Letter from Mr Franey to Cardinal Bourne dated 31st May 1922. Westminster Archdiocese Archive. BO5/59 Birth Control 1921-26.

[7] Salmond, J. W. (1916). *The Law of Torts: A Treatise on the English Law of Liability for Civil Injuries (Fourth ed.)*. Temple Bar: Stevens and Haynes. Pages 547-9. Retrieved January 18, 2019, from
https://archive.org/details/cu31924022354173/page/n5.

[8] Letter from Joseph Weld to Monseigneur Jackman dated 23rd December 1922. Westminster Archdiocese Archive. BO5/59 Birth Control 1921-26.

[9] Letter from Mr Franey to Monsignor Jackman dated 23rd January 1923. Westminster Archdiocese Archive. BO5/59 Birth Control 1921-26.

[10] Letter from Joseph Weld to Monsignor Jackman dated 17th November 1922. Westminster Archdiocese Archive. BO5/59 Birth Control 1921-26.

[11] Letter from Edward Eyre to Monsignor Jackman dated 28th July 1922. Westminster Archdiocese Archive. BO5/59 Birth Control 1921-26.

[12] Letter to Monsignor Jackman dated 23rd December 1922. Westminster Archdiocese Archive. BO5/59 Birth Control 1921-26.

[13] Vickers, M. (2013). *By the Thames Divided: Cardinal Bourne in Southwark and Westminster*. Gracewing Publishing. Page 458.

[14] Letter from Joseph Weld to Monsignor Jackman dated 23rd November 1922. Westminster Archdiocese Archive. BO5/59 Birth Control 1921-26.

[15] Legal Opinion dated 16th January 1923. Westminster Archdiocese Archive. BO5/59 Birth Control 1921-26.

[16] *Ibid*.

[17] Letter from Braby to Stopes dated 26th January 1923. British Library: Western Manuscripts MS58648 (Jan 1923–Jun 1923) Vol.CCII(ff.124). Jan 1923-June 1923.

Chapter 12

The Gold Pin and Lambert

On the eve of the trial, Sutherland and the co-defendant, Harding & More, gave formal notice to the Court that they were including an additional defence, namely:

"The Plaintiff during the year 1921 at the said clinic advocated the use by certain women whose names are unknown to the Defendant of the said Gold Pin or wishbone pessary; and also invited one Norman Haire to fit such women with the said appliance."[1]

While the date of the formal notice was 16th February 1923, the defence would almost certainly have informally notified the plaintiff's solicitor at an earlier date.

How the defence came by the information is not known. One possible source was the letters page of *The Lancet*, in which a public spat between Haire and Stopes had taken place.

At the Neo-Malthusian World Conference in July 1922, Haire had addressed delegates on *Contraceptive Technique*. He criticised the cervical cap[2] and said the Mesinga pessary was the "the best contraceptive method available," basing his claim on 200 cases of its use in the previous year without a single failure.[3]

Stopes wrote to *The Lancet* on 12th August 1922 to contradict Haire and to boast that she had 1,000 successful cases. Haire's reply of 19th August referred to Stopes as a "non-medical woman" and said that "her ignorance of medical matters had led her to advocate, in her books, at her clinic, and elsewhere, the use of the Gold Pin pessary, which had been condemned by

British medical men as indisputably dangerous, giving rise to sepsis and abortions."[4] The bitter exchange of letters ceased only when the editor of *The Lancet* ordered that it be brought to a close.

The Gold Pin was also known as the "Gold Spring" or "Wishbone Pessary". A flyer published by the Mothers' Clinic said:

> "It requires either a physician or a nurse to put it in place as it has to be inserted by a carrier or introducer which holds the two little prongs together until they are in place within the uterus."[5]

Once the carrier or introducer was withdrawn, the prongs would separate and hold open the entrance to the womb. According to the flyer:

> "It is useful in avoiding pregnancy because it is the nature of the uterus to throw out any foreign body. This means that it will not retain the spermatozoa and therefore pregnancy cannot occur so long as the pessary remains in place."[6]

Medical opinions on the effect of the Gold Pin differed.[7] Some thought it would hinder conception, others thought it would promote conception (by facilitating the passage of sperm into the uterus) and yet others thought that, if conception did take place, the products would be expelled owing to the presence of the Gold Pin — in other words it was an abortifacient.[8] And therein lay the value of the Gold Pin to the defence: that on the one hand, its effects were uncertain and therefore experimental and, on the other, that it was an abortifacient.

Stopes was enthusiastic about the Gold Pin and had written about it in *Wise Parenthood*:

> "The advantages of [the Gold Pin] are that all consideration of the subject may be completed once and for all, and the spring should stay in place for years. No further anxiety or trouble on the part of the woman is required, but a visit twice a year to a nurse or doctor to

have the spring cleaned and examined. It is therefore, the one and only method (apart from actual sterilisation) which is applicable, and of real help to the lowest and most negligent strata of society. It is therefore a method of the greatest possible racial and social value, and should become widely known and practised."[9]

She added:

"Its chief value should be for the C3 mothers who are already sufferers from the over-production of children and have been rendered dull and careless through misery.
"All health workers, district nurses, and workers in schools for mothers know scores of such women, and many have appealed to me asking what they are to advise for women too careless to use any ordinary method. Welfare workers should see that C3 women have these springs inserted by qualified doctors or nurses."[10]

The cost of gold hindered the use of the Gold Pin on a large scale, so Stopes wrote to the Surgical Manufacturing Company, "to make to her own specifications 'a small simple pin of flexible vulcanite or celluloid medicated so as to be suitable for internal use'".[11]

In June 1921, one year before their spat in *The Lancet*, Stopes had discussed the Gold Pin with Haire at the Mothers' Clinic. She then wrote "to ask him if he would take on two or three cases which he would 'watch carefully'". He had refused on the grounds that since the Gold Pin "sometimes, at least, acts as an abortifacient, I cannot try it without risking my professional reputation and rendering myself liable to a criminal prosecution".[12]

Any concern that Stopes had about the involvement of the Gold Pin in the trial would have intensified when, on 15th January 1923, her solicitor, Mr Percy Braby, wrote to her to provide an update on the evidence of her witnesses. He remarked: "None of them seem to like the Gold Pin."[13]

Stopes met one of her supporters, Dr Harold Chapple, a gynaecologist at Guy's Hospital, who told her the less said about the Gold Pin, the better.[14] On 19th January, she wrote to her medical witnesses and, referring to her "useful talk" with Dr Chapple, relayed his recommendation: "our doctors [should] not to be lured into saying anything about the Gold Spring". A template of what they should say was enclosed with the letter.[15]

The result was that the statements of Stopes' medical witnesses in relation to the Gold Pin became uniform. Readers have already read the names of Sir James Barr, Sir William Bayliss, Dr Jane Hawthorne, Sir William Arbuthnot Lane and Dr Harold Chapple earlier in this book. For the purposes of explaining how the witness statements were altered, two other witnesses are now introduced: Dr George Jones (a venereologist and member of the CBC) and Dr Meredith Young (the Medical Officer for Health for Cheshire).

In relation to the Gold Pin, the Witness Statement of Bayliss[16] exactly matched Barr's,[17] and Lane's was an abbreviated version of both.[18] The Witness Statements of Hawthorne[19] and Chapple[20] were almost identical, and Jones's closely matched these.[21] Young was the only medical witness to differ, merely stating: "I have no experience of the Gold Pin though I am acquainted with other appliances of precisely the same nature (intrauterine stems)."[22]

Unfortunately, none of the witness statements prior to Stopes' interference have survived (or if they have, this author has not seen them), so a "before" and "after" comparison is not possible. On the other hand, it is possible to reconstruct a glimpse of the changes to Dr Jane Hawthorne's statement. In Braby's letter to Stopes of 15th January 1923, he stated that Hawthorne did not like the Gold Pin, basing his remark on the "settled" (in other words, completed) witness statement.[23] Stopes' letter to Hawthorne of 19th January sought permission to excise "the fibre being caught in the spring" from the settled statement.[24] This detail is telling in that it indicates Hawthorne's practical knowledge of the device.

It was extraordinary that Stopes had written to her medical witnesses, not least because the collation of evidence was the job of the solicitor. If Braby did not know of Stopes' interference on 19th January, he would have found out when he received Hawthorne's amended witness statement for inclusion in the brief. As a result, it is difficult to conclude that Braby did not know about Stopes' interference, and one wonders if he knew about it in advance, or acceded to it after the fact. Either way, Stopes' conduct was unconscionable.

Stopes' letter to Hawthorne is also of interest because of her remark that she did "not want Lambert gratuitously dragged into the case".[25] The allusion to Lambert suggests that they were involved in relation to the Gold Pin and that Hawthorne was aware of it. It also raises the question why Lambert might be dragged into the case and why Stopes did not want this to happen.

"Lambert" was E. Lambert & Sons & Watkins, manufacturers of surgical appliances in Dalston and correspondence between Lambert and Stopes provides part of the answer. H.W. Lambert met Stopes to discuss pessaries at the end of February or at the beginning of March 1920.[26] From time to time, Stopes received requests for contraceptives and she referred these to Lambert for fulfillment.

In October 1920, E.W. Lambert wrote to Stopes about a request he had received "for the 'Gold Spring' or 'Wishbone' Pessary, as described in the new edition of your book *Wise Parenthood*."[27] Being "rather in the dark as to which pessary to send this customer" Lambert asked (or as he obsequiously put it: "we shall esteem it a favour if you will enlighten us... ") if it was one of their products. Her reply explained that it was an American device, and that she had sent money to America for it "to have samples to see if you can manufacture it".[28]

In January 1921 Lambert wrote again: "We have been given to understand you are recommending a Gold Pin or Wishbone Pessary & as we are having some enquiries for it, should be pleased if you could let me have a pattern or give us some idea of its description."[29]

Stopes provided the name and address of the American manufacturer, the cost of the device, and specified that it must be put in place by a fully-trained doctor. In relation to women making enquiries about the Gold Pin, Stopes added: "If they wish to know of a doctor who would handle it, I should recommend Dr. Jane L. Hawthorne of 150, Harley Street, London W."

The letter revealed that Stopes had facilitated the use of the Gold Pin, and that Dr Haire, Dr Hawthorne, and possibly other doctors, were involved as well.

On the eve of the opening of the Mothers' Clinic, E.W. Lambert wrote to Stopes to request that she send "those people who can afford to pay" direct to their premises in Dalston which, he pointed out, was only a short tram ride away. He also donated 144 cervical caps free of charge for use at the Mothers' Clinic.[30]

In her reply, Stopes promised that the nurse would send people "who live in your neighbourhood to you direct in suitable cases."[31] She thanked him for the caps saying that it would be "very acceptable assistance for the poor members".

Stopes did not want Lambert "dragged into the case" because, Gold Pin aside, it might reveal their business dealings,[32] and show that her operations were not confined to the Mothers' Clinic (see Appendix 2 for an outline of the business dealings between Lambert and Stopes).

Stopes' letter to Lambert concluded she could not forsee what demand there might be for the services of the Mothers' Clinic and, with no sense of how ironical her words would later become, added:

"It will be an interesting experiment."[33]

---

[1] Further Particulars of Justification Under Paragraph 4 of Defendant Sutherland's Defence dated 16th February 1923. Wellcome Library. PP/MCS/H/4a:Box72.

[2] Malthusian League. (1922). *The Fifth International Neo-Malthusian and Birth Control Conference*. In R. Pierpoint (Ed.), *Report of the Fifth International Neo-Malthusian and Birth Control Conference*. London: William Heinemann (Medical Books) Ltd. Pages 272-3. Retrieved December 1, 2019, from https://archive.org/details/reportoffifthint00inteuoft/page/272.

[3] *Ibid.*

[4] Wyndham, D. (2012). *Norman Haire and the Study of Sex*. Sydney: Sydney University Press. Page 99.

[5] *"Notes re 'Gold Pin' or 'Wishbone' Pessary"* Page 60a of the Brief on Behalf of the Plaintiff. Wellcome Library. PP/MCS/H/4a:Box72. PP/MCS/H.4a.

[6] While the flyer said that pregnancy could not occur, it skipped over the issue of whether conception could take place. The page number "60a" suggests that the flyer was included in the brief after it had been completed. *"Notes re 'Gold Pin' or 'Wishbone' Pessary"* Page 60a of the Brief on Behalf of the Plaintiff. Wellcome Library. PP/MCS/H/4a:Box72.

[7] Dr Norman Haire spoke about the Gold Pin at the Neo-Malthusian Conference in July 1922. He said: "There are a number of different types of Interuterine Pessaries. The first known as the Gold Pin, Wishbone, Butterfly or Brooch Pin. It is usually made of gold and silver or gold and platinum. The button remains in the vagina outside the cervix, while the hollow stem occupies the canal of the cervix and the uterine cavity. It must be inserted by a doctor. As it is hollow it

can be left in during the menstrual period. It is left in for six or twelve months. It was originally introduced for facilitating impregnation in cases of stenosis [constriction] of the cervix, and is not a preventative of conception. Conception often takes place in spite of it, or perhaps because of it, and if the pessary is not soon removed, abortion follows. The cervix is kept patent [open, unobstructed] by it, and the way is thus left open for the entry of septic organisms from the exterior which may reach the uterus and give rise to pathological conditions. The use of this instrument has been followed by abortion and by inflammatory conditions. It is not a reliable contraceptive; it often acts as an abortifacient, and in my opinion is a dangerous instrument." Malthusian League. (1922). *The Fifth International Neo-Malthusian and Birth Control Conference*. In R. Pierpoint (Ed.), *Report of the Fifth International Neo-Malthusian and Birth Control Conference*. London: William Heinemann (Medical Books) Ltd. Pages 275-6. Retrieved December 1, 2019, from https://archive.org/details/reportoffifthint00inteuoft/page/274.

[8] According to Stopes' biographer Ruth Hall: "Even Marie's own witnesses found it impossible to deny that its action might be that of an abortifacient." Hall, R. (1977). *Passionate Crusader: The Life of Marie Stopes*. New York: Harcourt Brace Jovanovich. Page 233.

[9] Stopes, M. C. (1920). *Wise Parenthood: A Practical Sequel to Married Love* (6th ed.). London: G.P. Putnam's Sons Ltd, London. Pages 36-7. Retrieved January 3, 2019, from https://archive.org/details/cihm_990552/page/n7.

[10] *Ibid.*, pages 37-8.

[11] Hall, R. (1977). *Passionate Crusader: The Life of Marie Stopes*. New York: Harcourt Brace Jovanovich. Page 233.

[12] Rose, J. (1992). *Marie Stopes and the Sexual Revolution*. London: Faber and Faber Limited. Page 168.

[13] Letter from Braby to Stopes dated 15th January 1923. Wellcome Library. PP/MCS/H/1:Box71.

[14] Letter from Stopes to Arbuthnot Lane dated 19th January 1923. Wellcome Library. PP/MCS/B.12.

[15] Letter from Stopes to Barr dated 19th January 1923. Wellcome Library. PP/MCS/B.12.

[16] Witness Statement Sir William Maddock Bayliss. Wellcome Library. PP/MCS/H/4a:Box72.

[17] Witness Statement of Sir James Barr. Wellcome Library. PP/MCS/H/4a:Box72.

[18] Witness Statement of Sir William Arbuthnot Lane. Wellcome Library. PP/MCS/H/4a:Box72.

[19] Witness Statement of Jane Lorimer Hawthorne. Wellcome Library. PP/MCS/H/4a:Box72.

[20] Witness Statement of Harold Chapple. Wellcome Library. PP/MCS/H/4a:Box72.

[21] Witness Statement of George Jones. Wellcome Library. PP/MCS/H/4a:Box72.

[22] Witness Statement of Dr Meredith Young. Wellcome Library. PP/MCS/H/4a:Box72.

[23] Letter from Braby to Stopes dated 15th January 1923. Wellcome Library. PP/MCS/H/1:Box71.

24 Letter from Stopes to Hawthorne dated 19th January 1923. Wellcome Library. PP/MCS/H/1:Box71.
25 Letter from Stopes to Hawthorne dated 19th January 1923. Wellcome Library. PP/MCS/B.12.
26 Letter from H.W. Lambert to Stopes dated 3rd March 1920. British Library: Western Manuscripts MS58638 Vol.CXCII. 1920-1929.
27 Letter from E.W. Lambert to Stopes dated 4th October 1920. British Library: Western Manuscripts MS58638 Vol.CXCII. 1920-1929.
28 Letter from Stopes to E.W. Lambert dated 5th October 1920. British Library: Western Manuscripts MS58638 Vol.CXCII. 1920-1929.
29 Letter from E.W. Lambert to Stopes dated 4th January 1921. British Library: Western Manuscripts MS58638 Vol.CXCII. 1920-1929.
30 Letter from Lambert to Stopes dated 15th March 1921. British Library: Western Manuscripts MS58638 Vol.CXCII. 1920-1929.
31 *Ibid*.
32 Stopes had extensive commercial dealings with Lamberts and aspects of the business relationship are discussed in Appendix 2.
33 Letter from Stopes to Lambert dated 13th March 1921. British Library: Western Manuscripts MS58638 Vol.CXCII. 1920-1929.

Chapter 13

The Bombshell in the Enemy's Camp

On 16th February 1923, five days before the trial and the day on which the Gold Pin was formally introduced into the case, Sutherland wrote to Cardinal Bourne. He was in a jubilant mood. "One of the leading birth controllers had turned King's evidence!" he said, referring to Dr Norman Haire's inclusion in the trial.[1] He also wrote: "The Great News tonight is that Leslie Scott, KC, Plaintiffs' leader, has thrown up his brief."[2]

The previous year, Percy Braby had consulted Sir Hugh Fraser for help in choosing a barrister. Fraser's first two picks were declined: one had acted for the Catholic Church and Stopes thought he might be "got at",[3] while the other did not have a good record (Braby had briefed him in several cases, but he had lost each one through his own fault).[4] This left Sir Leslie Scott KC and Mr Patrick Hastings KC, both of whom were described by Braby as "favourites at the Bar".[5]

Neither choice entirely satisfied Stopes, because Scott was a High Church Anglican and Hastings was a Labour MP. Of the two, Scott was chosen to represent Stopes in the High Court.

At the beginning of 1923, Braby was told that Sir Leslie Scott would be so busy at the end of the month and at the beginning of February that "it may be impossible for him to do full justice to this case." Scott recommended Hastings as an able replacement. Braby counselled Stopes against making a change, most likely because they were close to trial.[6]

Understandably, Stopes wanted "every consideration and attention possible" to be given to her case[7] and she suggested increasing Scott's fee "to induce him to take a greater interest".[8]

A conference was planned, and postponed several times because of Sir Leslie's workload.

Stopes' letters to Braby reveal that there may have been a clash between Stopes and Scott. She described him as "a bit of a nuisance" and asked Braby to "please try to drum into [his] head which I fear is very incapable of receiving impression…" in relation to certain aspects of the case.[9] She suggested that it would be wiser to devote their attention to Patrick Hastings, because "it seemed to me that in ten minutes he had got the hang of the position more usefully than Sir Leslie in all these weeks."[10]

Sir Leslie returned the brief on 13th February 1923, ostensibly because of the very large number of cases he had in hand, and he was replaced by Mr Patrick Hastings KC.[11]

Any change was not ideal and, a mere eight days before the trial, less so. While Hastings had already been involved in the case to some extent, it was as a junior barrister. It may have been at this point, on the eve of the trial, that Stopes made an offer to settle out of court.[12] If Sutherland would apologise, she would stop the proceedings and pay his costs. The offer was declined.

While the case had shifted in Sutherland's direction, it had not moved sufficiently for him to expect a win. The solicitor for the Westminster Archdiocese, Mr Weld, gave Monsignor Jackman his view on 17th January 1923:

"I have just read through the Proofs of Dr Sutherland's witnesses. The evidence he has got together is very strong, but I am a bit doubtful whether it is sufficient to prove his plea of Justification."[13]

The case was for Stopes to win. If all went to plan she would, at last, win a very public victory. The tangible signs of victory would be great, including the payment of damages, a published apology, and the award of costs against Sutherland. The intangible benefits, however, would be far greater. Publicity, pre-eminence in the birth control movement and, best of all, the silencing of all her critics.

[1] Letter from Halliday Sutherland to Cardinal Bourne dated 16th February 1922. Westminster Archdiocese Archive. BO5/59 Birth Control 1921-26.

[2] *Ibid.*

[3] Letter from Stopes to Braby dated 27th November 1922. British Library: Western Manuscripts MS58647 (1913-1922) Vol.CCI(ff.170). 1913-1922.

[4] Letter from Braby to Stopes dated 22nd November 1922. British Library: Western Manuscripts MS58647 (1913-1922) Vol.CCI(ff.170). 1913-1922.

[5] Letter from Stopes to Braby dated 27th November 1922. British Library: Western Manuscripts MS58647 (1913-1922) Vol.CCI(ff.170). 1913-1922.

[6] Letter from Braby to Stopes dated 13th January 1923. British Library: Western Manuscripts MS58648 (Jan 1923–Jun 1923) Vol.CCII(ff.124). Jan 1923-June 1923.

[7] Letter from Stopes to Braby dated 15th January 1923. British Library: Western Manuscripts MS58648 (Jan 1923–Jun 1923) Vol.CCII(ff.124). Jan 1923-June 1923.

[8] Letter from Stopes to Braby dated 16th January 1923. British Library: Western Manuscripts MS58648 (Jan 1923–Jun 1923) Vol.CCII(ff.124). Jan 1923-June 1923.

[9] Letter from Stopes to Braby dated 2nd February 1923. British Library: Western Manuscripts MS58648 (Jan 1923–Jun 1923) Vol.CCII(ff.124). Jan 1923-June 1923.

[10] Letter from Stopes to Braby dated 6th February 1923. British Library: Western Manuscripts MS58648 (Jan 1923–Jun 1923) Vol.CCII(ff.124). Jan 1923-June 1923.

[11] Letter from Stopes to Braby dated 13th February 1923. British Library: Western Manuscripts MS58648 (Jan 1923–Jun 1923) Vol.CCII(ff.124). Jan 1923-June 1923.

[12] The source for this information was the *Southern Cross* newspaper which reported a speech that Sutherland made during his Australian tour of 1939-40: "In reference to the Birth Control Libel Case…[Dr Sutherland] said that he had regarded it as an honour to represent the Catholic point of view. He could have achieved but little had it not been for the support accorded him, especially by the late Cardinal Bourne. He went on to mention a circumstance in connection with the case which had not been made public. The [defendant's] legal adviser, Sir Charles Russell, informed him before the trial that the plaintiff was prepared to stop the proceedings and to pay his (Dr. Sutherland's) costs if the slightest apology were made. In discussing this development with Cardinal Bourne, the Cardinal asked him whether it had changed his mind about proceeding with the case. He replied that he was still determined to fight the case in the courts, and the Cardinal said to him that he could not advise any other procedure in view of such a determination." *Southern Cross.* (1939, October 20). *Echoes Of Famous Law Case, A.R.P. At Sea.* Southern Cross, page 9. Retrieved January 20, 2019, from https://trove.nla.gov.au/newspaper/article/167762630

[13] Letter from Joseph Weld to Monsignor Jackman dated 17th January 1923. Westminster Archdiocese Archive. BO5/59 Birth Control 1921-26.

Dr Halliday Sutherland in Spain in around 1903.

The Sutherland family in 1910. Standing (from Left to right): Joan (holding Wasp, Daddles lies at her feet), Halliday, Francis. Seated (from left to right): Dr John Francis Sutherland, Jane Henrietta Sutherland (nee McKay).

Dr Halliday Sutherland in 1910.

Number of Deaths in the United Kingdom from—	England and Wales.	Scotland.	Ireland.	Total.
1. Smallpox	10	1	1	12
2. Typhus Fever	24	14	56	94
3. Puerperal Fever	214	87	41	342
4. Erysipelas	1,033	191	92	1,316
5. Rheumatic Fever[1]	2,024	112	159	2,295
6. Enteric Fever	2,344	367	362	3,073
7. Scarlet Fever	3,220	233	99	3,552
8. Diphtheria	5,732	674	283	6,689
9. Influenza	9,297	425	1,720	11,402
10. Whooping-Cough	10,255	2,480	809	13,549
11. Measles and German Measles	12,672	1,154	587	14,413
12. Diarrhoea and Dysentery[2]	10,658	2,177	1,747	14,582
13. Cancer[3]	31,745	4,551	3,338	39,634
*14. Bronchitis	42,204	5,167	7,845	55,216
*15. Pneumonia[4]	46,967	10,452	4,102	61,521
16. Phthisis[5]	39,839	6,415	8,828	55,082
{ Other forms of Tuberculosis	16,262	3,655	2,851	23,768
All Causes of Death	524,221	77,296	77,334	678,851

* These headings unquestionably include many deaths from Pulmonary Tuberculosis.

[1] Excludes Rheumatism of Heart, but includes Acute Rheumatism of Heart.
[2] Includes Epidemic Diarrhoea or Infective Enteritis, Diarrhoea (undefined), Dysentery, Enteritis, and Gastro-Enteritis.
[3] Includes Carcinoma and Sarcoma.
[4] Includes Lobar and Broncho-Pneumonia.
[5] Pulmonary Tuberculosis and Phthisis not otherwise defined.

A table showing the deaths from various diseases in 1907. From *The Control and Eradication of Tuberculosis* edited by Dr Halliday Sutherland.

A scene from *The Story of John M'Neil* Britain's first public health cinema film produced by Dr Sutherland in 1911.

The Regent's Park "Open-Air" Bandstand School in 1913.

The "Open-Air" Class in Regent's Park in June, 1911.

A class in the "Open-Air" Bandstand School, 1911.

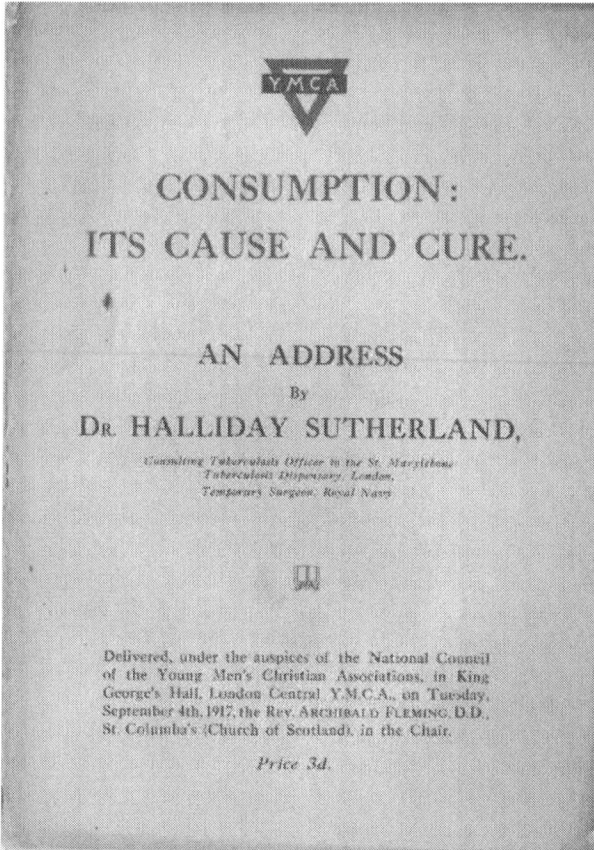

Dr Sutherland described eugenists as "race breeders with the souls of cattle-breeders" in his 1917 speech, *Consumption: Its Cause and Cure.*

PART 2

THE TRIAL

DAY 1

Wednesday, 21st February 1923

Chapter 14

Opening Speech of Mr Patrick Hastings[P]

T he Royal Courts of Justice resemble a cathedral that rises high above the pavement in London's Fleet Street. The case listed as Stopes *v* Sutherland took place in Court 4, the Lord Chief Justice's Court.

In a 1934 memoir, Sutherland wrote:

> "The trial, which lasted for six days, commenced on 21st February 1923, before the Lord Chief Justice of England, Lord Hewart, and a special jury. That morning four large tin boxes stuffed with evidence were carried across the Strand into the Law Courts. The case was opened by the plaintiff's leading counsel, Sir Patrick Hastings,[1] with whom were Sir Hugh Fraser and Mr. Metcalfe. I was defended by Mr. Charles, KC, now Lord Justice Charles, Mr. Rabagliati, and Mr. Harold Murphy. For the publishers, Messrs. Harding & More, were Serjeant Sullivan, KC,[2] and Mr. Theobald Mathew. The public benches and gallery were crowded."[3]

The tension between each side was no doubt intensified as the parties were brought into proximity; Stopes and Sutherland had never met and this was the first time that they had occupied the same room. At 10 am the Judge entered the Court and the jury were sworn in.

In civil matters the order of proceedings is that the plaintiff leads the case, is followed by the defence, followed by the jury's decision, followed by judgement. The pleadings — an outline of the plaintiff's allegations — were read by Sir Hugh

Fraser. This was followed by Mr Patrick Hastings KC's opening speech for the plaintiff.

"If your Lordship pleases, Members of the jury…"

Of all of those present in the courtroom, the twelve most important men were anonymous, passive and, in terms of the court transcript, barely visible.

Hastings said that Sutherland had attacked both the character of the plaintiff and her life's work: "What is said of Dr Stopes in effect in this case is that her writings amount to a criminal offense."[4]

The powerful opening was followed by a melodramatic and false assertion that: "… if the verdict is against her in this case there would be no reason at law why she should not be committed at once to take her trial at the Central Criminal Court."

Hastings read the words that were at the centre of the libel and explained: "I have called your particular attention to the words 'a woman who is a Doctor of German Philosophy.' That of course was intended by this gentleman to suggest that Dr Stopes was a person probably of German origin with some German degree, who was foisting herself on the poor as a person who was English and with English qualifications. I can only hope that before this case is over, whatever else may happen, that Dr Sutherland may feel utterly ashamed of himself for having said that."[5]

Hastings listed Stopes' extensive qualifications and contrasted these with the single qualification that Sutherland had mentioned in the defamatory passage in *Birth Control*. He touched on her remarkable career travelling the world and studying paleobotany. He mentioned her failed first marriage, describing Ruggles-Gates (albeit not by name) as "obviously a man of peculiar habits", and explained that it had led her to abandon all of this (including a salary of £600 per annum) to satisfy a "divine call"[6] to advocate constructive birth control.[7] While this was something that people might laugh at, it was "her duty which she is compelled to, to carry on this work".[8] It was, he said, "a very courageous thing for a woman to undertake"[9] not least because of the shadow that Charles Bradlaugh had cast over birth control.

He described Stopes' marriage to Humphrey Roe as "a stroke of good fortune in antithesis to her bad fortune... and their married life is one of complete happiness as compared to what had happened before."[10] He pointed out that Roe was "a gentleman of means" which he mentioned, he said, because it had been suggested in some quarters that Stopes' involvement in contraceptives was motivated by money.[11]

Hastings said that Stopes' beliefs were entirely different to Bradlaugh or any Malthusian:

> "What she believes in, and what she is seeking to teach is this; that the only possible chance of happiness for married people is to realise that marriage, and all that it conveys, is intended to be a joy to both and not a curse to either. She is in the course of her researches, has heard not one, not hundreds, probably not thousands, more like tens of thousands of cases, which must be known to everyone of us, of women whose life is made a misery by the fear of being forced to have children when their health is bad — poor people with 8 or 10 children and no income, whose lives are made a curse to them."[12]

Sutherland was entitled to say that she was wrong, but he was not entitled to say "that she is a criminal for expressing her views, that she is experimenting on poor people who are too poor and ignorant to defend themselves."[13]

Hastings read out the preface written by Father Stanislaus St John which had been printed in the first six editions of *Married Love*. He said the priest had praised the book and that he had outlined the points of difference between Stopes' own position and that of the Catholic Church in language that was polite and respectful. In contrast, Sutherland had described the book "as a criminal and obscene publication".[14]

Mr Charles objected: "I do not know where in the libel this is described as a criminal and obscene publication."

"Really you must allow me to open my case in my own way," replied Hastings.

"I am sorry, I do not want to interrupt unreasonably," said Charles, perhaps implying that it had been a reasonable interruption, his point being that the alleged libel was phrased more subtly than presented in Hastings' simplistic summary.

The peculiar banter between advocates was formal, impeccably polite and even, at times, obsequious. Yet the legal battle was no less vicious for it.

Following the interruption, Hastings gave a copy of *Married Love* to each member of the jury. He read Stopes' preface aloud:

"More than ever today, happy homes are needed. It is my hope that this book may serve the state by adding to their numbers. Its object is to increase the joys of marriage, and to show how much sorrow may be avoided. The only secure basis for a present-day State is the welding of its units in marriage, but there is a rottenness and danger at the foundation of the state if many of the marriages are unhappy. Today, particularly in the middle classes in this country, marriage is far less really happy than its surface appears. Too many who marry expecting joy are bitterly disappointed, and the demand for 'freedom' grows; while those who cry aloud are generally unaware that it is more likely to have been their own ignorance than the 'marriage-bond' which was the origin of their own unhappiness. It is never easy to make marriage a lovely thing; and it is an achievement beyond the powers of the selfish, or the mentally cowardly. Knowledge is needed and, as things are at present, knowledge is almost unobtainable by those who are most in want of it."[15]

He then took the jury through the various sections of the book.

"Now out of this book, as I told you, some of the passages no doubt, taken and read in a cold-blooded court, would horrify people who lived 30, 40 or 50 years ago and they will no doubt be used to try and horrify you. I venture to think there is only one thing you can think of in this case when you see this lady in the box: was she doing this for a motive of good or was she not? Because, if you read that book from the point of view of a person who wants prurient writing, you can see many things in it which are prurient. If you do not want such a book, you may see in it many things which are very very beautiful."[16]

It was a point well made, especially because the standards of obscenity had changed from the times of Bradlaugh.

Hastings then said that "this book is only part of a whole" and told the Court that Stopes was also a "President of a Society" the name of which was garbled, possibly by the shorthand writer, as the Society for "Constructional [sic] Birth Control and Racial Progress". He said that the Society was "entirely intended for exactly the same purpose as this book".

He mentioned the names of some of the vice-presidents of her Society who came from all walks of life and whom, he said, he was going to call to give evidence. They included "some of the greatest doctors in the civilised world," and said their appearance would enable the Court to "see the sort of people who are associated with this criminal, carrying out the criminal class of work, publishing obscene indecent literature."[17] Hastings said Stopes had not received financial gain from the venture and "practically every penny that has come in, has gone straight out in the Constructive Birth Control and Racial Progress and the Clinics and the other things in which she is concerned."

He said that the plaintiff issued her writ because Stopes was:

> "...doing something which ran contrary to the views of those — I am not saying who they are — who accept the tenets of the Roman Catholic Church, and no doubt they thought the best way of bringing her to book was to say she was a criminal, and, if possible, make people think she was a German, and to suggest she was dishonest. I think you will agree that if somebody is doing that sort of thing, there is a moment when you have got to stop them."[18]

Hastings was carrying out the instructions in his brief to attack the Catholic Church,[19] and he referred to Catholicism no less than ten times in his opening speech.

"Dr Sutherland is entitled to say that and he is entitled to write it: he is entitled to say the Roman Catholic Church does not like it, but you must play fair."[20]

According to Hastings, if Britain were to go back to the old days of obscenity, Sutherland himself might get six months for something he wrote in *Birth Control* and, for similar reasons, newspapers could not publish warnings about venereal disease without risking the imprisonment of the editor.

Hastings knew the defence would be aiming to prove their assertion that "Bradlaugh was condemned to jail for a less serious crime" was true. The two criteria for Bradlaugh's crime — the publication of "obscene libels" — were that the publication included details that would lead to "desires of lust, and excite libidinous thoughts" and that it was "inconsistent with the morals of society".[21]

Hastings sought the Lord Chief Justice's permission to get the jury to read four sentences from *Married Love* quietly to themselves.[22] He said he did not propose to read it out aloud unless Mr Charles desired it.

Charles replied that he did not want to read any of these things aloud, but that he would have to insist that they were. The likely reason was because one test for obscenity was whether the words would scandalise an audience when read aloud.[23]

Hastings asked Charles twice whether he objected, and he answered that he could not.

The passages from *Married Love* read by the jury were: "Assuming now that the two are in the closest mental and spiritual, as well as sensory harmony: in what position should the act be consummated? Men and women, looking into each other's eyes, kissing tenderly on the mouth, with their arms round each other, meet face to face. And that position is symbolic of the coming together of the two who meet together gladly."[24] And "It should be realised that a man does not woo and win a woman once and for all when he marries her: he must woo her before every act of coitus, for each act corresponds to a marriage as other creatures know it."[25]

These words were not of a scandalous nature, said Hastings, but were: "… perfectly frank, perfectly outspoken, written as a father might say to his son, or a mother to her daughter."

Hastings told the Court that Dr Stopes would be appearing in the witness box the next day and said: "I am going to be very short indeed in examining her, because the view I personally take of a case such as this is that the plaintiff comes and gives you just an outline of her or his work."[26]

He pointed out that the burden of proof was on the defendant and that, as plaintiff, Stopes was entitled to say: "You libelled me; you have got to prove it; I am not going into the witness box at all; you cannot cross-examine me."[27] This of course begged the question why Stopes was appearing in the witness box at all. That she did suggests that she sought personal publicity, because it gave her an opportunity to speak in the case.

Hastings presented her appearance as brave and, given she would undergo cross-examination, perhaps it was. He told the jury:

> "If they [the defence] succeed in satisfying that this lady is a person who has sunk so low as to write obscene libels — if you think that this is the case, then, of course, there will be an end of this case. But if you think she is a lady who has devoted her life to what she believes is an honest, desirable duty, and a duty which she is bound to perform, which she is performing honestly, truly and well, then you may take into your consideration at the conclusion of this case what you may think of a person who disagrees with her views, puts forward a libel of this sort, and then comes into a Court of law and seeks to justify it…"[28]

He concluded:

> "The case cannot be won by me; I can have nothing to do with this. This lady herself is the person who will satisfy you, and it must be, almost in a minute, whether she is right or whether she is wrong… I should think you would not have much difficulty in coming to a conclusion as to the verdict you ought to give."[29]

Having completed his powerful opening speech, Hastings sat down and the first witness was introduced.

---

[1] Hastings received a knighthood in 1924 meaning that on the day of the trial he was "Mister" not "Sir". Sutherland's account was written in 1934.

[2] The salutation "Serjeant" designated that Sullivan was a Serjeant-at-Law of the Irish Bar, an office that dated back to 1261. The title lapsed when he retired, so he was the last one. The title pertained to the Irish Bar, but Sullivan was still known as "Serjeant Sullivan" when he practiced in England.

[3] Sutherland, H. (1934). *A Time to Keep*. Geoffrey Bles. Dr Sutherland's description of the jury as "special" most likely means that the trial would take place in front of a jury, and that jurors were chosen specifically for the trial.

[4] Femina Books. (1967). *The Trial of Marie Stopes*. (M. Box, Ed.) London: Femina Books Ltd. Page 43.

[5] *Ibid.*, page 44.

[6] *Ibid.*, page 47.

[7] *Ibid.*, page 46.

[8] *Ibid.*, page 47.

[9] *Ibid.*

[10] *Ibid.*

[11] *Ibid.*

[12] *Ibid.*, page 48.

[13] *Ibid.*, page 49.

[14] *Ibid.*, page 51.

[15] *Ibid.*, page 52.

[16] *Ibid.*, page 53.

[17] *Ibid.*, page 54.

[18] *Ibid.*, page 56.

[19] Brief on Behalf of the Plaintiff. Page 8. Wellcome Library. PP/MCS/H/4a:Box72.

[20] Femina Books. (1967). *The Trial of Marie Stopes*. (M. Box, Ed.) London: Femina Books Ltd. Page 56.

[21] Sutherland, H. (1936). *Laws of Life*. New York: Sheed & Ward. Pages 21-27.

[22] Femina Books. (1967). *The Trial of Marie Stopes*. (M. Box, Ed.) London: Femina Books Ltd. Page 59.

[23] Sullivan, S. A. (1952). *The Last Serjeant: The Memoirs of Serjeant A.M. Sullivan*. London: Macdonald. Page 303.

[24] Stopes, M. C. (1918). *Married Love* (6th *ed.*). London: A.C. Fifield. Page 48-9. Retrieved August 28, 2019, from https://archive.org/details/married_love/page/n1.

[25] Femina Books. (1967). *The Trial of Marie Stopes*. (M. Box, Ed.) London: Femina Books Ltd. Page 48.

[26] *Ibid.*, page 61.

[27] *Ibid.*

[28] *Ibid.*

[29] *Ibid.*, page 62.

Chapter 15

Testimony of Sir James Barr[P]

Sir James Barr was called to the witness box for examination by Sir Hugh Fraser.

On entering the box, witnesses were sworn to tell the truth. They were then questioned by the barrister for the party they were supporting, known as the "examination-in-chief". This was followed by the cross-examination, in which barristers for the other parties questioned the witness. The witness might then be re-examined by their advocate, for instance, to address any matters that arose during the cross-examination. The witness was then dismissed and leaves the witness box.

In big trials, senior barristers lead the case assisted by their juniors. Hence, following Hastings' opening speech, his junior, Sir Hugh Fraser, examined Sir James Barr.

Sir James' bald head and distinguished grey beard gave him an august appearance, but in case anyone was in doubt, his many achievements were recited: a doctor of medicine for 47 years, Order of the British Empire, Fellow of the Royal College of Physicians, sometime President of the BMA and vice-president of the CBC. A substantial background for a substantial witness.

In the examination, Sir James said he thought the Mothers' Clinic was doing "an enormous amount of good".[1] Two further questions established that Barr had made "a special study of the question of birth control" and that he had "written a good deal on the subject".[2]

Of the method of contraception used at the Mothers' Clinic, Barr said: "So far as I understand it, and I know it perfectly well, it is a simple method and perfectly harmless."[3]

Fraser's next question concerned the efficacy of the cervical cap when used in conjunction with a quinine pessary. According to Barr, it was "effective and safe" and there was "not the slightest" danger.

Fraser concluded with questions on the Gold Pin. It was established that Barr's concerns with this device were on the minor ground that it required: "… a medical man to insert the Gold Pin, and I think that any method should be so simple that a woman can carry it out herself; that is the only objection I have to a Gold Pin."

On this point Barr differed from Stopes, who thought it was a good method for women "too careless or too stupid" to be relied on to use contraceptives.[4]

Barr did not believe that the Gold Pin was used at the clinic and, asked if he had any objection to its use if a doctor were involved, he answered:

> "Not in the slightest; the check pessary has been one which has been in use for many years, not simply for this purpose but for afflictions of the uterus, the same thing with this Gold Pin."

Fraser's examination was brief — no more than 19 questions.

◆   ◆   ◆

Mr Ernst Charles KC, barrister for the defence, rose for the cross-examination and he was to ask six times as many questions. The aim of cross-examination is to undermine the credibility of the witness and to challenge their evidence. In vernacular and grossly over-simplified terms, the aim is to show that the witness is lying, or stupid, or both.

Sir James had written a great deal about birth control and he was one of the leading physicians in Britain, if not the world. Given an attack at these strongpoints would be futile, Mr Charles aimed his questions at places that were less well defended: the uncertain effect of the Gold Pin, and Sir James' practical knowledge of the cervical cap. He began where Fraser had left off, on the topic of the Gold Pin.

Charles: "It was invented to encourage conception, was it not?"
Barr: "I do not know what the origin of the Gold Pin is."
Charles: "You wouldn't be surprised to know that is was called a wishbone pessary?"
Barr: "Yes."
Charles: "Which keeps the womb open?"
Barr: "Yes."
Charles: "And the result would be to allow conception to take place, would it not?"
Barr: "I think anything in the uterus at all would prevent conception, it does not matter what it is."[5]
Charles: "I can leave it if you do not know, because I can prove the history of the Gold Pin quite easily. You do not know, at any rate, with your medical knowledge that it was originally intended to encourage and make conception possible, in cases where for some physical reason it was impossible?"[6]
Barr: "Well, I do not know anything about that part of it, but so long as it was in the uterus, I do not see how conception could take place."[7]

Charles was, most likely, intending to undermine Barr's evidence when, later in the trial, he would introduce witnesses whom, while they were not as distinguished as Barr, had greater expertise in this area of medicine.

Charles: "Would you consider that it would be a proper thing to leave a spring or a Gold Pin in a woman's body for years?"
Barr: "It ought to be taken out occasionally, but I do not see that it would do any harm even if left [in] for a long time."
Charles: "Have you never heard — of course I will tell you quite frankly I am going to call some distinguished gynaecologists who have experienced the harm they do — have you never heard of these Gold Pins doing infinite harm to women who have had them in?"

Barr: "Never."

Charles then asked the question that was to trouble the Plaintiff's case throughout the trial: "In truth and in fact is this Gold Pin an abortifacient, not a contraceptive?"

The problem they faced was that at the time abortion was illegal, though according to one historian there was "a tacit although unofficial understanding that doctors could perform therapeutic abortion if the life of the mother was in danger."[8]

If Stopes' witnesses admitted that the Gold Pin was an abortifacient, it would jeopardise her case. The alternative answers, that it promoted or prevented fertilisation were inconsistent outcomes that lent weight to the assertion that it was an experimental device.

> Barr: "Of course inserting anything into the uterus, if the woman was pregnant, would be an abortifacient, but that is inserted before she is pregnant to prevent her getting pregnant."
> Charles: "You mean to say it prevents conception starting or taking place at all; it may prevent birth, but also conception?"
> Barr: "I think so."
> Charles: "How?"
> Barr: "Any irritant or anything in the uterus, that would create a certain amount of stimulus; there must be a certain amount of stimulus; if there is contraction, it would prevent conception."
> Charles: "Have you tried it upon any patient?"
> Barr: "No."
> Charles: "Have you known any cases where it has been tried?"
> Barr: "Not that particular form."
> Charles: "I am only asking about this particular form?"
> Barr: "No not the Gold Pin"
> Charles: "You have no experience?"
> Barr: "I have no experience."

Having got what he wanted, Charles changed the subject: "Now I want to ask you about the check pessary. That is what is called an occlusive pessary. That is supposed to make a complete seal. It is a rubber cap, is it not?"

"Rubber cap, yes," Barr replied.

Charles' question was imprecise in that "check pessary" might have referred to the cervical cap, used at Stopes' clinic, though it might just as easily be applied to what would today be called a diaphragm.

The cervical cap fitted over the cervix and, (as mentioned earlier) was akin to a rubber thimble.[9] Fertilisation was prevented by the rubber barrier that stopped the entry of sperm into the uterus. The rim of the device provided a seal by pressing in on the cervix and held the device in place by suction. The Mesinga cap was used at Dr Haire's Walworth Clinic. It also prevented fertilisation with a rubber barrier. The key difference was that the seal provided by the rim pressed out against the vagina to hold it in place.

The fact that both devices were made of rubber and were of similar appearance added to the confusion. While answering Charles' questions, Barr appears to have confused the two.

Charles: "If it is going to be effective, the rim round the cap had to fit hard up against the walls of the vagina?"
Barr: "Not necessarily."
Charles: "It must fit very firmly?"
Barr: "Not necessarily."
Charles: "Do you say it would do to have it loose?"
Barr: "Perfectly loose."[10]
Charles: "So a woman if she had it in, within her body, for, I will say two or three weeks, with the ordinary movements, what would happen then?"
Barr: "It would remain in position"
Charles: "Even if it was loose?"
Barr: "Even if it was loose, and it is a very simple matter to take it out and put it in again. It is a simple matter to take it out and wash it and put it in again."[11]

Charles next referred to the opinions of other doctors in relation to contraceptives and of the opinions expressed by Professor McIlroy. Hastings objected to Charles' questions (described in the transcript as "an altercation")[12] on the grounds that citing the opinions of other physicians and asking Barr whether he agreed with them was, in effect, allowing their views to be submitted as evidence.

Barr confirmed that he was a vice-president of the Society for Constructive Birth Control. Charles then referred to *Married Love*, describing it as a book that had "been much praised by my friend." In the formal, polite language of the Court, "my friend" referred to Hastings. He read a passage concerning "scientific motherhood" (what we would today call artificial insemination) for Australian women who were deprived of mates by the War.

> "What do you say, Sir James Barr, as a doctor, to obtaining..." At this point, he broke off: "... it is almost too horrible to talk about —"

Again Hastings objected. Asking a question was one thing, but Charles should not, he said, tell the Court that it was too horrid to contemplate.

Charles asked Barr if it was something of which he approved. Would he, as a medical man, carry it out? Barr replied that he would not. When asked why, Barr replied that he did not know, and that it was a matter of scientific experiment.[13]

Would he leave *Married Love* or *Wise Parenthood* lying about the house for his children or young servants to look at? After disclosing that his children were all grown up, Barr conceded that he probably would not, "if they were under age".[14]

◆   ◆   ◆

Serjeant Sullivan KC, barrister for the co-defendant, Harding & More, rose to cross-examine Sir James, his southern Irish accent in contrast with Barr's Ulster brogue.[15]

Sullivan's questions related to the words: "Charles Bradlaugh was condemned to jail for a less serious crime." In Bradlaugh's trial, the prosecution sought to prove two things: "First, that the book was obscene in itself; and secondly, that it tended to corrupt public morals because not only the married, but also the unmarried, and any boy or girl, could buy it for sixpence, and thereby learn how they might give way to passion without fear of results."[16]

Sullivan said to Barr: "Is there any relation between cause and effect in some physical excitements and some moral results?"[17]

Barr was baffled. "Between physical excitements and moral results?"

"Yes," Sullivan replied. "Is there sometimes connections in the nature of cause and effect?"

"What do you mean by 'moral results'?" said Barr, still puzzled.

"I want to know, do some physical practices become demoralising — do they break down the character of the young who indulge in them?" said Sullivan. Barr replied: "I do not think so. I have never heard of such a case."

Sullivan asked if Barr had read *Married Love* and was told that he had looked it over, but had not read it from cover to cover. "Have you not taken the trouble to ascertain its contents?"

"I approve of the principle of the book, therefore I do not think it necessary to read it," replied Barr.

Sullivan said: "May I suggest Sir James, that a good principle might be so phrased as to be lost in a most objectionable phrase? Do you suggest that to advocate the principle of birth control, there need be no limit to the language or the ideas that are used for propagation; do you suggest that?"

Sullivan's ornate phrasing had again hidden the question from Barr.

"That there need be no limit?" asked Barr.[18]

Sullivan confirmed the question and Barr responded that "all language should be expressed in decent phraseology".[19] As we have seen, Barr had already admitted that he had not read *Married Love* and Sullivan ensured that this point was not lost on a juror, perhaps weary at the end of a long day.

Sullivan: "Precisely. Then you have never examined this book, which is so highly recommended by your Clinic, to ascertain by what ideas and by what language your principle has been advocated?"
Barr: "No, I have not."
Sullivan: "Have you ever sought to ascertain what restrictions are put on the distribution of the book?"

Barr: "I am told it is not distributed very widely, though in fact it is married women that come to the clinic."

Sullivan: "Do they bring their marriage certificates with them?"

Barr: "I do not know; I should think not."

Sullivan: "Have you read the book yourself to show that it appeals to persons outside of married life, that although the idea is to confine it to wise married women, that is only an idea; have you read the book?"

Barr: "Yes I have read it, but I mean to say, I have not read it from cover to cover."

In his "quiet and beautifully modulated voice",[20] the Lord Chief Justice clarified whether *Married Love* could be bought "in ordinary booksellers' shops".

In his next few questions, Sullivan interwove questions about the clinic and the "check pessary" with references to the seamier side of London.

Sullivan: "You know that your Clinic is a place where women can learn at any rate how to indulge in sexual intercourse without fear of bearing children; is that not true?"

Barr: "Yes, quite true."

Sullivan: "Though they have not been called Clinics, are there not establishments well known in this City for many years?"

Barr: "I do not know of anyone except another; there are only two that I know of."

Sullivan: "Your check pessary is a new invention, is it?"

Barr: "No."

Sullivan: "That is so widely advertised by this book. The essence of the Clinic is teaching the use of the check pessary, is not it?"

Barr: "Yes."

Sullivan: "Is this the first establishment in the City of London, do you think, where young people have, or any person has, learned the use of check pessaries?"

Barr: "I do not know anything about that."[21]

Sullivan questioned Barr if he had also noticed that "in shops, rubber goods stores, and largely advertised, these three books [*Married Love, Wise Parenthood* and *Radiant Motherhood*] displayed in juxta-position to these check pessaries?" No doubt, Sullivan asked the question to justify the statement about a "monstrous campaign of birth control", but Barr replied that he had not.

The next questions related to the books coming into the hands of the young. Sullivan asked if it were desirable that a book which alluded to "the tricks of prostitution for the purpose of giving pleasure to their patrons" would come into the hands of adolescents. Barr replied that he was "strongly in favour of teaching sexual matters to children" so that they would acquire the knowledge "gradually" rather than "all at once" when they were grown up. Pressed to answer though, Barr said that it was not desirable.

Sullivan asked Barr to "take the book now and glance through it" and, after a pause, directed him to descriptions of the sex organs and "a description of the act of copulation". Having looked at the passages, Barr said that the passages were purely a matter of physiological knowledge.

Sullivan: "Assume it is perfectly accurate?"
Barr: "Yes, it is a pure matter of physiological knowledge. Every student should be taught the like of this."
Sullivan: "My question is, is it desirable that it should be broadcasted amongst the young?"
Barr: "I think that every young person ought to know it."
Sullivan: "That is not my question; is it desirable that it be broadcasted, to be picked up at the pleasure of the young buying this book?"

From this moment on, Sullivan continued to assert that it was detrimental, but Barr refused to concede the point. Following discussion between the Lord Chief Justice and the barristers about it constituting a crime, and whether Bradlaugh had been imprisoned for a lesser crime, Sir James left the witness box.

The case was adjourned until 10.15 am the following day.[22]

Summary of Day 1.

So ended the first day of the Stopes *v* Sutherland libel trial. Hastings' opening speech had skilfully portrayed a charitable scientist who, motivated by the public good, enabled poor women to have access to knowledge about contraception. She had established a society whose officials were men and women of great eminence. Despite this, she had been attacked by a Roman Catholic doctor and, while he was entitled to criticise her work, his criticisms were vicious and unfair.

Sir James Barr had been a prestigious witness. It was preposterous to suggest that this eminent man would support a disreputable cause, let alone something that was more than the crime for which Charles Bradlaugh had been imprisoned.

In the cross-examination, the defence showed that Barr was not familiar with the check pessary nor the Gold Pin. Barr said that there was nothing offensive or prurient about the plaintiff's books, while the defence portrayed the uncontrolled distribution of Stopes' books as being more extensive than the one which had led Bradlaugh to prison.

The impact on the anonymous twelve men of the jury was not recorded.

---

[1] Femina Books. (1967). *The Trial of Marie Stopes*. (M. Box, Ed.) London: Femina Books Ltd. Page 62.

[2] *Ibid.*

[3] *Ibid.*, page 63.

[4] Stopes, M. C. (1920). *Wise Parenthood: A Practical Sequel to Married Love* (6th ed.). London: G.P. Putnam's Sons Ltd, London. Page 37. Retrieved January 3, 2019, from https://archive.org/details/cihm_990552/page/n7.

[5] Femina Books. (1967). *The Trial of Marie Stopes*. (M. Box, Ed.) London: Femina Books Ltd. Page 63.

[6] *Ibid.*

[7] *Ibid.*, page 64.

[8] Brand, P. (2007). *Birth Control Nursing in the Marie Stopes Mothers' Clinics 1921 to 1931*. De Montfort University. Page 237.

[9] *Ibid.*, page 216.

[10] Femina Books. (1967). *The Trial of Marie Stopes*. (M. Box, Ed.) London: Femina Books Ltd. Page 64.

[11] *Ibid.*

[12] *Ibid.*, page 65.

13 *Ibid.*, page 67.

14 *Ibid.*, page 68.

15 British Medical Journal. (1938, November 26). *Obituary Sir James Barr, M.D., F.R.C.P.* British Medical Journal. Pages 1117-8.

16 Sutherland, H. (1936). *Laws of Life.* New York: Sheed & Ward. Page 24.

17 Femina Books. (1967). *The Trial of Marie Stopes.* (M. Box, Ed.) London: Femina Books Ltd. Page 68.

18 *Ibid.*

19 *Ibid.*, page 69.

20 Sutherland, H. (1934). *A Time to Keep.* Geoffrey Bles. Page 252.

21 Femina Books. (1967). *The Trial of Marie Stopes.* (M. Box, Ed.) London: Femina Books Ltd. Page 69.

22 *Ibid.*, page 73.

DAY 2

Thursday, 22nd February 1923

Chapter 16

Examination of Dr Marie Stopes

D r Marie Stopes took the oath on the commencement of the second day of the trial. *The Daily Graphic* reported (somewhat breathlessly): "You might have imagined that Joan of Arc had come to life again. With clasped hands and upturned eyes, the woman in the box declared she was the transmission of a message sent by Almighty God."[1]

According to biographer Ruth Hall, her:

> "… appearance created a favourable impression… [and she] gave no hint of nervousness. Neither did she look at all like the sex-mad, money-seeking Jezebel portrayed by extremist magazines like *Plain English* and *John Bull*. Under the voluminous fur coat that Humphrey had given her, she wore a plain dark dress, with an innocent white Quaker collar and cuffs. Her hats were furred and feathered somewhat extravagantly, but at that period she wore no make-up, and her hair was its natural chestnut colour."

In his examination, Hastings began with her qualifications and achievements. To the remarkable life that had been outlined the previous day were added the study of botany, palaeontology and zoology at London University where, in her first year, she had won a scholarship and twice gained a Gold Medal. To this was added the fellowship of her college and of the Geological Society, membership of the Royal Society of Literature and the Linnaean Society (the world's oldest biological society);[2] her qualification as a Doctor of Science at

London University and her doctorate from Munich University. Her travels had taken her to many countries on behalf of research societies, to Belgium and France, around the world once, to America five times and to Japan on behalf of the Royal Society.

The previous day Hastings had said that the time Stopes was in the witness box would "be very short indeed," and his questions reiterated the requirement for brevity:

"I do not want to go into any great detail about it…"
"I want you to tell me quite shortly, in a sentence or two, about…"[3]

Hastings appears to have been apprehensive that Stopes would make long speeches. Certainly she did not appear to be intimidated by the witness box and seemed to relish the attention it provided. But while her utterances might provide good copy for the press, in order to win the case the less said, the better.

Hastings' question about her first marriage to Ruggles-Gates drew a 70-word answer, so he reminded her: "… if you could keep your answers as short as you can, because this is only the fringe of the case that I am dealing with at the moment. May I take it your experience during that period ended in extreme unhappiness?"[4]

"Yes," she replied. One word. Good.

"Was it after that that you started upon this campaign which we are discussing here, of what has been popularly been called 'birth control'?"

"Yes," but then she added "… and the wider campaign involved in that, the wider part of my work."

Hastings ignored her hint. "I am only asking about the one."[5] He asked her about her books and her position as a "Commissioner on the Royal Commission on 'Birth Control'". He must have been referring to the National Birth Rate Commission which, as mentioned above, despite the official-sounding name, was not a governmental body.

Hastings asked four brief questions about the Commission that enabled her to confirm that she had served on it for two years, that the Bishop of Birmingham was the

President and that there were "all classes of witnesses, such as medical and other witnesses called before the commission".

He then turned to "… a few general questions about the objects of your campaign. First of all, I want to ask you this general question: Is the reduction of the birth rate any part at all of your campaign?"

It was a deliberate closed question and Hastings would have expected the answer to be "no".

"No" would have differentiated her views from those of the Neo-Malthusians at whom Sutherland's book had been aimed. "No" would have made his reference to Bradlaugh, who had published a Malthusian tract, wholly off the mark. "No" would have removed her from the controversy of aiming to reduce or alter the composition of the birth rate. Stopes, on the other hand, had not spent her time and money to give one-word answers and replied:

"Not a reduction in the total birth rate, but reduction of the birth rate at the wrong end of the social scale and increase of the birth rate at the right end of the social scale."

This reference to her wider campaign was at odds with the charitable scientist that Hastings had portrayed in his opening speech. If Stopes' birth control campaign did aim to alter the social makeup of Britain, the defence could then argue that Sutherland's criticism was fair comment on a public matter and, given that the outcome of her activities would not be known for some time, point to the experimental nature of the venture.

Perhaps for this reason, Hastings glossed over her answer: "I may summarise that by saying the birth of children at the best period of their mother's life for children and for the mother."[6]

"That is so," Stopes replied.

The discrepancy between Stopes' answer and Hastings' summary was noticed and the Lord Chief Justice said: "That previous answer seemed to indicate something a little different from that."

Mr Charles, perhaps revealing too much eagerness at his opponent's discomfiture, added: "I thought so."

109

Hastings backtracked: "I am sorry: it may be my fault because I am trying to keep your answers as short as possible. Would you, in your own words, describe to us in a few sentences what are the objects and purposes of your Society?"

Having got her way, Stopes explained the wider part of her work:

> "The object of the Society is, if possible, to counteract the steady evil which has been growing for a good many years of the reduction of the birth rate just on the part of the thrifty, wise, well-contented, and the generally sound members of our community, and the reckless breeding from the C3 end, and the semi-feebleminded, the careless, who are proportionately increasing in our community because of the slowing of the birth rate at the other end of the social scale. Statistics show that every year the birth rate from the worst end of our community is increasing in proportion to the birth rate at the better end, and it was in order to try to right that grave social danger that I embarked upon this work."[7]

Stopes explained why she had written her books ("there was nothing that gave guidance to the normally healthy pair who started with love and who desired to maintain a loving happy home").[8] Asked if she had "at any time ever the intention or desire to pander to improper feelings of anybody?" she replied confidently: "Oh, of course not."

Discussion of the clinic made it clear that Stopes and Roe were financing the operation, including paying secretaries to handle the enormous private correspondence that Stopes was receiving.

Hastings said: "So far as you know has any one of your nurses, or anyone with whom you are associated, practiced any experiment of any kind upon any person, rich or poor?"

Stopes replied: "Absolutely not; that is the cruel libel."

Confirming that Humphrey Roe was a man of means and that she could live in ease and comfort in the country if she so desired, Hastings sat down, and Mr Charles stood for the cross-examination.

[1] Hall, R. (1977). *Passionate Crusader: The Life of Marie Stopes*. New York: Harcourt Brace Jovanovich. Page 224.

[2] *The Linnean Society*. (2019, September 17). Retrieved from The Linnean Society of London: https://www.linnean.org/the-society.

[3] Femina Books. (1967). *The Trial of Marie Stopes*. (M. Box, Ed.) London: Femina Books Ltd. Page 75.

[4] *Ibid.*

[5] *Ibid.*, page 76.

[6] *Ibid.*

[7] *Ibid.*, page 76-7.

[8] *Ibid.*, page 77.

Chapter 17

Cross-examination of Dr Marie Stopes by Mr Ernst Charles

Mr Charles began by asking: "I do not know whether you would like me to call you Dr Stopes, or Mrs. Stopes, or Mrs. Roe, I will do which you please."

"I am Dr Stopes if you please," she replied.

"Dr Stopes if you please," said Charles, making a weak joke in a case already devoid of humour.

Charles knew that Stopes was confident and highly intelligent. Perhaps sensing that she did not intend merely to be a passive witness, but to go on the attack, he focused his questions on tedious minutiae. He remarked that she was not a doctor in the ordinary sense of the term. She replied she was a doctor in the legal sense of the term, a Doctor of Science.[1]

> Charles: "As you would be if you were a Doctor of Music?"[2]
> Stopes: "Quite so."
> Charles: "Or a Doctor of Laws?".
> Stopes: "Quite so, and I would be entitled to the courtesy title 'Doctor'."

Charles supposed that "if I were a Doctor of Laws I might write a book on strictly sex questions and call myself 'Dr Charles'." Stopes pointed out that on the title page of her book she had styled herself as a Doctor of Science. Telling the Court that he did not want to underrate her greatly distinguished career, he pointed out that she had no medical degree.

The next few questions dealt with how she had obtained Sutherland's book, to which she replied that she purchased it. Charles stuck with the minutiae: "Purchased it, yes. I dare say that if you had asked, you would have got one free."

"I did not think of asking," said Stopes.

Charles' next questions sought to undermine the very basis for the case before the court by implying that she had started the court action to promote her cause rather than because of genuine feelings of hurt. He pointed out that once she had received the book, it had been three weeks before her husband had written to Sutherland to challenge him to a debate. Stopes agreed that the debate would have given publicity to the content of the book and that she had called attention to it by reviewing it in her Society's newspaper, *Birth Control News*.

Stopes seized the initiative and asked Charles to read the review.[3] The exchange between Charles and Stopes illustrates the tension in the courtroom.

Charles: "I know you would like me to read the review and I will. It is a very pleasant and well considered one for an opponent."[4]

Hastings: "Let us have the questions, please."

Charles: "Very well. However you did at any rate. I will read it; do not be afraid?"

Stopes: "I am not afraid."

Charles: "It will amuse us I think."

The Lord Chief Justice: "The witness says in not a very loud voice that she is not afraid."

Charles: "No she is not afraid; I shall read it; I am sure she is not afraid of me."

Stopes: "No."

Charles: "The book was not sent to you for review was it?"

Stopes: "Oh, I do not think so, no."

Charles: "Quite so. Now here is the review. It is not too long and rather snappy: 'Dr Sutherland's book will impose only on those who are more ignorant than he is.' — that is the beginning, he is a Doctor of Medicine?"

Stopes: "Yes, undoubtedly."

Charles: "'It is nicely calculated to encourage the biased in their prejudice, for now, when speaking against birth control they can say: 'A doctor says so.' They will probably forget that he is a Roman Catholic doctor. The omissions from the book are quite as remarkable as its lies. We could fill columns in illustration of this, but space is too valuable.'"

Charles moved to the next point so seamlessly that he made it look like he had anticipated Stopes' reaction. He asked her if many doctors had spoken against birth control prior to Dr Sutherland's book. She replied that they had, but in a scattered way (such as in the pages of the *British Medical Journal*) but not in a book called *Birth Control* that could be read by the public.

He quoted Stopes' announcement to the CBC in which she had said that, following all of the libels and slanders made about her but which she had not addressed, "… I therefore would like all members of the Society to know that in the interests of the Society, I have served a writ on a medical man in this country… "

"And in truth, and in fact, this action is launched for that purpose, is it not?" said Charles.

"Not only," Stopes replied.

"Let me read it again and see what else you say," said Charles and he read it again.

Stopes replied that it did not sound quite like the language she would have used, but accepted that it was approximately what she had said. When Charles said that he was reading from the shorthand note of the meeting, she replied: "they very often garble what one says." She argued that she was acting as the both the President of a Society and as a private individual. As President, she "had been attacked in such a slanderous manner, it matters to the Society that the President should be cleared. All the members of the Society are implicated if their President is made out to be a criminal and to have performed experiments on the poor."

She had also been injured as a private individual and "was forced to bring the action."

Charles said that worse things had been said about her. He quoted from a 1919 report in the *New Witness* and asked her if she had read it. It had described the "peculiar horror" of *Wise*

Parenthood and had commented: "Our readers may remember that for writing a similar but not quite so pernicious book, Bradlaugh and Mrs Besant were hounded out of decent society."[5]

Stopes said she had not read it given she had between 20 to 50 press cuttings per day. Charles continued: "But vile as the *Handmaiden of Death* is, the number of readers it may debauch is probably small. From that point of view, Dr Marie Stopes' *Wise Parenthood* is infinitely more dangerous."

Hastings objected suggesting that it was an odd way to read the article and then ask Stopes if she had read it. The Lord Chief Justice suggested: "would it not be better to let her look at the criticism and tell you if she read it."[6] Stopes said the article had been written in 1919 and that since then thousands of articles had been written.

Charles then put it to her that there was the strongest feelings both for and against contraceptives.

"It is a much discussed question, yes," replied Stopes.

He then said that the Birth Rate Commission, an august body on which she had been questioned by Hastings earlier, were among those who disapproved of artificial birth control: "And on the Birth Rate Commission, not Birth Control Commission, but Birth Rate Commission, that your Counsel has referred to, is it not a fact that out of all the people on the Birth Rate Commission the only people who directly approved of contraceptive methods was yourself and three others."

Stopes contradicted him: "No, that is not so."

"I am going to read the resolution," Charles assured her, holding a copy of *Problems of Population and Parenthood*, the 423-page report of the National Birth Rate Commission.

Stopes told him that she would find the resolution if he gave her the book. Charles, however, did not hand over his book. He put it to her that of the 40 or so distinguished members of the Commission, no one else approved of birth control other than one or two others, advocating voluntary control and self-restraint.

Again, Stopes contradicted him: "That is control of birth; the distinction you draw is not a real one."

"Dr Stopes, I am afraid I do not accept that in the least; I suggest that it is a very real one. What we are objecting to here is the artificial birth control, check pessaries, Gold Pins and things. Self-restraint, I think they all approve of in this book. Read at the beginning of the Roman figures, an argument on the use of contraceptives, that is by the whole of the Commission," said Charles.

He was referring to the "Notes of Reservation" section on page clxiii of the report.[7] These "reservations" were statements by which some members of the Commission would record their dissent from the views of the Commission as a whole.

He quoted from one reservation (Paragraph I) that 12 members (not including Stopes) had signed: "Further although we recognise that a reckless increase of the population is not to be desired, we hold the opinion that every effort should be made to arrest the decline in the birth rate." He called attention to the names including the President of the Mothers' Union who represented 250,000 women, "largely of the working-class."[8]

Charles read from another (Paragraph III), signed by 11 members (but not Stopes) which said that "all artificial contraceptive methods by mechanical or chemical contrivances, if habitually employed by normally constituted individuals, are harmful." He contrasted it with the reservation that followed (Paragraph IV), signed by Stopes and three others which said: "most artificial contraceptive methods at present employed are harmful, but that the use of the best contraceptive methods is much less detrimental than any other course open to millions of people."

Stopes said: "I do not understand your question; you have been reading this out; what question do you want to ask me about it?"[9]

"I want to ask you whether at this Birth Rate Commission, the majority who signed Reservations were dead against any artificial contraceptives?" said Charles.

"No that is not true," replied Stopes.[10]

"We have it here, you know?" said Charles.

"I say that this is very unfair under the circumstances; I think I should be warned of this," Stopes protested.[11]

While she might have thought it unfair, it was in fact fair and in accordance with legal procedure. Hastings had raised the National Birth Rate Commission in the examination, which meant that Charles was entitled to cross-examine Stopes on it. Once again, Charles had been prepared, and Stopes was learning the perils of unnecessarily putting herself in the witness box.

Charles moved to Stopes' books. Having previously confined her to minutiae, he would now draw upon what she had written. This had several advantages. Firstly, by quoting passages from her written works, the defence of Justification could be advanced without aggravating the libel. Secondly, the articulate woman in the witness box would be limited to answering questions about what she had written, not giving speeches for the newspapers.

Charles explained that he would ask some questions in relation to her book *Wise Parenthood* and he re-read the passage from *Birth Control* at the centre of the trial. While the defamatory passage in *Birth Control* had not mentioned her books, the defence had brought them into the trial under the ambit of the "monstrous campaign."

He turned to *A Letter to Working Mothers*, aiming to show that there was more to Stopes' work than improving relations between husbands and wives. He quoted a passage which stated that the Gold Pin was for: "The most difficult cases of all and at the same time, those most urgently needing to exert reliable control over conception and the women who are dissolute, harried, overworked and worried."[12]

He then read from the 7th edition of *Wise Parenthood*:

"The advantage of this method is that all consideration of the subject may be completed once and for all, and the spring should stay in place for years. No further anxiety or trouble on the part of the woman is required, but a visit twice a year to a nurse or doctor, to have the spring cleaned or examined. It is therefore the one and only method (apart from actual sterilisation) which is applicable and of real help to the lowest and most negligent strata of society. It is, therefore, a method of the greatest possible racial and social value if its further use proves to be satisfactory. If not, such cases should be sterilised."[13]

It differed from the 9th edition, in which she had written that women using the Gold Pin should visit the doctor "every second or third month" to have it cleaned and examined.

Charles asked her why she had made this "complete modification".

Stopes replied that in the 9th edition she was "only making a little more explicit what I have already said," carefully avoiding the implication that in the 7th edition she had been wrong, and that she had corrected the error in the 9th edition.

But Charles contradicted her: "I am afraid we cannot have that. I am going to suggest when you wrote the 7th edition you thought that the sort of period that you suggested for cleaning this pin was expressed sufficiently, whereas when you came to the 9th, you had learned by experience that it had to be examined and cleaned more often."

His point was that she had not reinforced what had been written previously, but had said something new, based on what she had learned, from experience of the use of the Gold Pin. Stopes protested: "I had no experience on that whatever —"[14]

Hastings intervened to say that Charles had interrupted her answer. She was, he said, about to explain why the change was made. Following discussion about the rules of evidence, the question was re-read to Stopes and she asserted:

"I had no experience of the medical practice of this pin at all; I have only drawn attention to the fact that medical practitioners in various parts of the world use it; I recommend to persons requiring it, that they should go to the necessary medical practitioner to get it; my source of information is the medical profession."[15]
Charles: "In truth and in fact, have you sent up women from this Clinic to a doctor to be fitted with the Gold Pin."
Stopes: "No."
Charles: "You never have?"
Stopes: "Never."[16]
Charles: "Never to Dr Haire?"[17]
Stopes: "I never sent anyone from the Clinic. I know what you are asking. I have received from unknown correspondents letters asking me to give them the addresses of medical persons and have given, on two or three occasions, the address of a gynaecologist and obstetrician."
Charles: "Was that Dr Haire?"

Stopes: "Yes, he is a gynaecologist and obstetrician."

Charles: "Did Dr Haire tell you that he would not use this Gold Pin because it simply produced an earlier abortion?"

Stopes: "On the contrary, Dr Haire came to my clinic and asked me to send him subjects for the Gold Pin."

Charles: "There will be a conflict of evidence about that."

Stopes' sensitivity on the matter of the Gold Pin had led her to lie to the Court.[18]

Charles cited her words in the 9th edition which spoke of a "drawback so serious" that the use of the Gold Pin "was believed to jeopardise the bearing of future children". "You had found that out, had you?" he asked, again implying an experiment.[19]

"I had found out nothing; I had my sources of information," replied Stopes. It was a nice distinction.

Charles was about to move on, but Hastings interrupted to ask him to read the next three lines in the 9th edition, which he did: "Sufficient observation has not yet been made on this point, so I should only advise its use by women who have already have had all the children they ought to have."[20]

And, having met the request, Charles took the opportunity to read the paragraph that followed:

"Its chief value should be for the C3 mothers who are already sufferers from the over production of children and have been rendered adult [sic] and careless through misery. All health workers, district nurses and workers in schools for mothers, know scores of such women, and they have appealed to me asking what they are to advise for women too careless to use any ordinary method and yet who continue to give birth to unaesthetic infants who are only an expense and drag upon the community. Although the cost of the gold spring pessary is immensely less than the cost of upbringing an enfeebled child, yet the outlay may seem heavy. The gold spring there [sic] may be unobtainable by just those people who most need it. Steps are being made that a similar and less expensive article of a similar kind may be available, but the difficulties to be overcome are very great. I confess I am less hopeful than I was a year ago that a really satisfactory fool-proof method may be found speedily. Innumerable fresh devices have been brought to my notice since I wrote this book, but serious drawbacks attach to them."

"Is that a question?" said Stopes, and the Lord Chief Justice explained: "No, I think the origin of that was this, that your learned Counsel requested Mr Charles to continue reading a little further."[21]

Hastings said: "The request I made was that Mr Charles should read the next three lines."

"I dare say. My friend desired me to read the part he wanted and not the part that he did not," countered Charles.[22]

Hastings' assertion that Stopes' work was merely the charitable promulgation of contraceptives was unwinding, exposed at first by her statements during the examination, and now by her books in the cross-examination. The uncertain nature of her project was being exposed and, if one had to wait to see how things would turn out, then surely it could be called an experiment.

Charles asked: "Are you making inquiries still?"[23]

"I do not know what you mean by inquiries."

"Inquiries in order to find, or try to find, what you call a foolproof method?"

"I am always inquiring for further knowledge of truth, yes always."

In the next few questions, Stopes repeated that she had always recommended the fitting of the Gold Pin and "all medical devices" by a doctor. "Nobody but a doctor can insert it; there is no risk. If you give a woman that Pin, she does not know what to do with it; nobody but a doctor can possibly insert it; you have to go to a doctor, nobody but a doctor knows how."

It was a good answer that portrayed her as the inquiring scientist in search of the truth, who insisted on the appropriate medical care for women who used the devices she wrote about.

Charles asked her if she had known of cases where the use of the Gold Pin had produced disastrous results. She replied that she had read medical papers, and had first-hand knowledge of over 1,060 cases that had gone well and "second-hand" cases where it had gone wrong: "because the woman neglected it and did not go to her doctor."

Charles warned: "I am afraid that there is more than one actual pin going to be produced in Court here."

"Those pins are the responsibility of the doctor who inserted them," said Stopes.[24]

Charles then moved to the next subject for cross-examination. "Now then, let me pass from that and go to this check pessary. That is what you recommend very much, is it not?"[25]

"I do not know which one you are referring to," she said.

"I am referring to the small occlusive pessary," replied Charles.

"To the small occlusive pessary for the cervix — the cervical cap, yes," said Stopes.

Charles asked her if she agreed with Sir James Barr that it could be put in loosely. Stopes said she didn't think that Charles' question to Barr made it clear what was being asked. Sir James was correct: the cervical cap was loose in relation to the vagina if it were attached to the cervix, the vagina and the cervix being different parts of the body.

> Charles: "I am sure Sir James Barr was anxious to let us know quite accurately what he thought."
> Stopes: "I think to him it would appear quite clear, but I did not think it was quite clear from your question just now."

Stopes was right; the term "check pessary" was ambiguous. Charles asked: "In your opinion ought it to fit tight or close?" and Stopes decided to test Charles' knowledge in the area of her expertise. "What to?" she asked.

> Charles: "Ought that occlusive pessary to be fitted so as it is a complete occlusion?"
> Stopes: "Occlusion of what?"
> Charles: "That it lets nothing out or nothing in, let me put it in plain terminology?"
> Stopes: "It adheres."
> Charles: "Nothing into the womb and nothing out of the womb?"

Stopes: "While it is attached to the cervix it would fit quite tightly to cervix, it does not adhere tightly to the vagina."

Charles: "I only want to see that we are in agreement. In your view in order for it to be effective, it must adhere closely to the cervix?"

Stopes: "To the cervix, yes."

He asked how long it could be left in for. In the course of her work, Stopes had specified different times and he went through the different editions of her books.[26]

Stopes pointed out that she had warned that, if the woman had even "trifling ill health," it should be removed.[27]

Charles asked who would be the judge of what constituted "trifling ill health". "What harm do you suggest it could do her?" said Stopes, perhaps expecting that Charles did not know.[28]

But Charles had been briefed: "The harm is that there might be secretions which, stemmed back in the womb by this occlusive pessary, would give rise to sepsis and trouble," he replied.

Stopes was reluctantly drawn into an explicit explanation that the cap would be gently squeezed off by the secretions.

Charles: "Then you do say that it is unsafe to leave it in for three weeks, except in perfect health?"

Stopes: "I am not sure whether it is advisable or not; some people tell me that it is advisable and some people say that it is not advisable."[29]

Charles: "You are not sure whether it is advisable or not, but you advise people to use them; is that pretty nearly experiment?"

Stopes: "Is that a question 'is it experiment' — which is the question?"

It would appear that Charles had made the point he had wanted to make, had shut down her speechifying from the witness box, and had piqued her temper in the process.

It was Hastings who spoke: "Never mind."

Stopes addressed the Lord Chief Justice: "You see, my Lord, these caps were invented in 1881 by a medical man and they have been used under medical supervision since 1881; that is over 40 years they have been used and used successfully; and to ask me now if it is an experiment to suggest using what has been in general use for over 40 years, I can only answer it is a ridiculous question."

Charles asked if *Married Love* had anything to do with birth control, to which Stopes replied: "very little… just indicating there are methods, but not being very explicit". Charles said that if it was a book designed to encourage happy marriages, then why was the artificial insemination of women mentioned in it.

Stopes said she had learned of this from Marion Piddington, an Australian woman who was campaigning for "scientific motherhood" by artificial insemination of women from a eugenically desirable donor.[30] She asked if she could give "rather a long answer". Hastings said she could as long she stopped when directed. Charles said: "So long as it is an answer I do not mind, but if it is a speech I object."[31]

It was a long answer that mentioned the Piddington system (for adjusting workers' wages) in South Australia, that Mr Piddington was a "very, very important man in Australia", that Mrs Piddington had sent reports of scientific motherhood to Stopes, that she had a "serious system… to deal seriously with an important social problem" and that Stopes had been asked to include it in the book. Two-hundred and forty words later, presumably when Stopes drew breath, Charles interrupted.

"Is that the answer?" he asked.[32]

"That is the beginning of my answer," she replied.

"Do not let me for a moment interrupt you, I would not interrupt you for the world," said Charles. "I was only venturing to ask you, even if you had heard of it possible in other countries, why you thought it necessary to introduce this matter of insemination of a woman with the seed of other men into a book sold [and] broadcast to old and young, called *Married Love*?"

One-hundred and seventy-five words later, during which Stopes explained that it enabled men who had been rendered sterile by syphilis or gonorrhoea in youth which made it impossible to have children, Charles asked: "Is that the end of it or the second chapter?"

"I do not know how much I have to say in order to answer you," replied Stopes.

"I am afraid I have been waiting for an answer of any sort. May I put the question again?" and he did.

A summary of her answer was: "Because I think it is a matter of great scientific and racial interest..." and later, "Because I think all scientific knowledge relating to such a subject should be in the possession of all rational people".[33]

Charles turned to her role as God's messenger: "Dr Stopes are you a Prophet of God?"[34] He referred to her pamphlet *A New Gospel to all Peoples* in which she had claimed that she had received a message from God and which He commanded her to transmit to the Bishops of the Anglican Church.

> Charles: "Do you not say it is the transmission of a message saying direct from the Almighty God through you?"[35]
> Stopes: "I say that."

Charles read from the pamphlet after which he asked if the art of contraception was included in the *New Gospel*. Stopes confirmed that it "undoubtedly" was. Charles read a passage and, noting the uncanny similarities between God's speaking style and Stopes' writing style, asked: "Does not that sound especially like an extract from one of the published works of one Marie Stopes?"[36]

> "All my works are not of my own knowledge, but of the instructions I receive of what I am to do," she replied.

Charles quoted from the *New Gospel*: "This error has led some of the Ministers of the Church to give instruction to the youths committed to their charge that they shall exercise what they falsely call "self-restraint" by means of wasting their own sacred secretions by their own hands. Thus keeping themselves altogether from the love of wedlock."

> Charles: "Did the Almighty God send that to you?"
> Stopes: "Yes."

Charles: "That the priests of the Church recommend boys in their charge to masturbate?"[37]

Charles no doubt hoped that this example would justify the comparison with the blasphemous libels of Bradlaugh. Having completed his questions, he sat down.

---

[1] Femina Books. (1967). *The Trial of Marie Stopes*. (M. Box, Ed.) London: Femina Books Ltd. Page 80.

[2] *Ibid.*, page 81.

[3] *Ibid.*

[4] *Ibid.*, page 82.

[5] *Ibid.*, page 84.

[6] *Ibid.*

[7] National Birth Rate Commission. (1920). *Problems of Population and Parenthood. Being the Second Report of and the chief evidence taken by the National Birth-rate Commission, 1918-1920.* London: Chapman and Hall, Ltd. Page clxii. Retrieved January 28, 2019, from https://archive.org/details/problemsofpopula00natiuoft/page/n8.

[8] Femina Books. (1967). *The Trial of Marie Stopes*. (M. Box, Ed.) London: Femina Books Ltd. Pages 86-7.

[9] *Ibid.*, page 87.

[10] *Ibid.*, page 88.

[11] *Ibid.*

[12] *Ibid.*, page 91.

[13] *Ibid.*

[14] *Ibid.*, page 93.

[15] *Ibid.*, page 94.

[16] *Ibid.*

[17] *Ibid.* Page 95.

[18] Rose, J. (1992). *Marie Stopes and the Sexual Revolution*. London: Faber and Faber Limited. Page 168.

[19] Femina Books. (1967). *The Trial of Marie Stopes*. (M. Box, Ed.) London: Femina Books Ltd. Page 95.

[20] *Ibid.*

[21] *Ibid.*, page 96.

[22] *Ibid.*

[23] *Ibid.*, page 97.

[24] *Ibid.*, page 98.

[25] *Ibid.*, page 99.

[26] *Ibid.*, page 100.

[27] *Ibid.*, page 101.

[28] Some writers suggest that the dangers of the contraceptive devices were exaggerated by the defence, so it is worth stating that (1) devices were not manufactured to the high standards that a modern consumer would expect; (2) the legal protection of consumers was not as developed as it is today (Stopes *v* Sutherland took place nine years before the landmark Donoghue *v* Stevenson decision of 1932); and (3) if sepsis (the presence of germs and their harmful

toxins in human tissue) did occur, antibiotics were not available. Penicillin was not discovered until 1929. Even today, boxes of sanitary napkins carry warnings for toxic shock syndrome.

[29] Femina Books. (1967). *The Trial of Marie Stopes*. (M. Box, Ed.) London: Femina Books Ltd. Page 102.

[30] Wyndham, D. (1996). *Striving For National Fitness: Eugenics In Australia 1910 To 1930s*. Sydney: Department of History, University of Sydney. Page 72. Retrieved November 6, 2019, from http://www.kooriweb.org/foley/resources/AEK1201/eugenics/eugenics1.pdf.

[31] Femina Books. (1967). *The Trial of Marie Stopes*. (M. Box, Ed.) London: Femina Books Ltd. Page 105.

[32] *Ibid.*, page 106.

[33] *Ibid.*, page 107.

[34] *Ibid.*

[35] *Ibid.*, page 109.

[36] *Ibid.*, page 110.

[37] *Ibid.*

Chapter 18

Cross-examination of Dr Marie Stopes by Serjeant Sullivan

Serjeant Sullivan, barrister for Harding & More (publisher) stood for his cross-examination of Stopes. As he was later to write in his memoirs: "The lady made things rather difficult for herself at the outset of her cross-examination, when I asked her to take her own book in her hand and asked her would she prefer that I read them aloud before I cross-examined. I am bound to say to her credit that she blushed and protested, "It would be an outrage for anyone to read this book aloud in this atmosphere." I observed that the atmosphere was of a court of justice and asked her if she could suggest any atmosphere in which this publication might be read aloud. She could not do so, coming perilously near to adopting the settled criteria of what in law is called an obscene libel."[1]

It was an unpleasant affair, not least because Sullivan's questions were at times unclear and Stopes, not unreasonably, had difficulty understanding them. For example: "Have you, in the course of your investigations considered whether the apprehension of the responsibility of parenthood might be a deterrent to acts of impropriety?"[2] Stopes replied that she considered it "insulting to womanhood".

For her part, Stopes gave long-winded answers and, when these did not answer the question, Sullivan became frustrated. She made a short speech and was mid-way through another when he interrupted: "I have no objection to an answer."

"I really rather object to this at the most vital part of the case," said Hastings. "This lady has given, I should have thought, quite a reasoned and not an unduly long answer. To interrupt in the middle of a most important answer seems a little hard."

The Lord Chief Justice insisted that Stopes be given the opportunity to complete her answer. She did and, when she had finished, Sullivan asked his next question: "Have you finished your answer?"

It was Hastings who spoke, again asking Stopes: "After that, would you keep your answers a little shorter."

"I will try, but it is very difficult sometimes," she said.

"Have you finished your answer?" repeated Sullivan.

The building tension between Sullivan and Stopes continued until she lost her temper. That she did so was understandable, given she had been in the witness box for several hours. She was provoked by an indecipherable question: "And do you permit that other people, at all events, might hold the opinion that the doctrine that any child is a curse if it is demoralising to the race?"[3]

Stopes asked for the question to be repeated and Sullivan repeated a version of it: "Do you deny the right of other people to hold the opinion that teaching any woman that any child, or any married couple that any child is a curse, is demoralising the whole institution of matrimony? Do you permit that opinion to other people?"

"I try not to be stupid, but it is difficult to understand the meaning of that question," said Stopes.

"If you do not succeed, I will sit down," Sullivan replied, and for once there was no mistaking his meaning.

The Lord Chief Justice intervened, saying: "There is a little ambiguity about the word 'any.' I do not think that you mean any whatsoever; you mean a child in ordinary circumstances."

Sullivan: "I mean a child born in wedlock."
The Lord Chief Justice: "Say the 12th after the 11th?"
Sullivan: "Yes."

At this point, Stopes asked: "Do you mean feeble-minded imbeciles?"

Sullivan said: "I put that to you. Do you admit the right of any persons to hold the opinion that teaching married people that any child to be born of them is a curse is itself a debasement of marriage? Do you deny the right of people to hold that opinion?"

Stopes replied: "I deny the right of anyone to maintain that an imbecile or monster or degenerate or diseased child — if you include this in your question — I am not clear do you include those in your question?"

He did not answer, but proceeded to the next question: "And, furthermore, do you claim the right to publish anything that to you seems fit, because you in your opinion think it is beneficial?"

"Yes," she replied.

"Very well then, we understand."

Sullivan sat down, abruptly ending the cross-examination.

◆　　◆　　◆

Hastings stood to re-examine the witness. He was entitled to do this to address points that had arisen during the cross-examination, and he presumably did not want her last moment in the witness box to be characterised by the intemperate language she had used. He sought clarification in relation to some of the names of the people involved in the National Birth Rate Commission and said: "that is all I have to ask".

At this point, Stopes was supposed to leave the witness box, but she was reluctant to relinquish her place at the centre of the Court's attention. "There is one more thing that I ought to be asked," she said.

The Lord Chief Justice observed: "She wishes to make another point," which was a cue for Stopes to make a speech to the Court: "There is one more important point, my Lord and jury, which I have not been asked about, and that is the subject of this libel — an enormous mass of irrelevant matter has been dragged in."

Hastings said: "Do you think you might safely leave that to me?"

"I have not been asked about it," replied Stopes.

"If you want to make the speech that otherwise I should make, I shall be glad. I think you may leave it to me. I know how much irrelevant matter has been introduced," said Hastings.

"I have not been asked the question and I want to answer," replied Stopes.

It was not the first time that she had insisted on getting her way and had overridden Hastings to get it. Hastings said:

"I do not want in the least that you and I should part. Tell me the question you want me to ask and I will ask you."

"Always supposing that it arises out of the cross-examination," said the Lord Chief Justice, reminding them of the Court's rules.

Hastings said: "May I guess that the question that you want to be asked is whether you have ever performed an experiment on the poor."

Given Hastings had asked Stopes that question during his examination, her complaint must have been that the barristers for the defence had not asked her. Stopes' misunderstanding of the legal process — that she (and not the Court) would determine what "experiment" meant, and that she could not specify the questions the defence should ask — meant that the witness box in Court 4 of the High Court became an expensive classroom.

Hastings was right, and Stopes replied: "That is the subject of the libel."

He said, "I thought it was," and then said the reason the defence had "not dared" to ask that question was because they knew that she had not performed any experiments on the poor. His inference was no doubt directed to the jury as much as to his client, and Charles angrily interjected: "I do not think my friend ought to say that. Your Lordship begged us, as I understood, to confine ourselves to instances. If your Lordship thinks otherwise now, I can refer to a dozen cases of experiments."

Stopes did not want to be a bystander in this fight: "I wish you would, sir."

"It is not fair for my friend to say that and he must know it is not under the circumstances," said Charles, implying that Hastings had used underhand tactics.

"No one shall say that to me in Court," said Hastings, but Charles continued: "My Lord stopped both of us and, quite naturally, we understood it as meaning: do not put every single case; get instances; that is enough. Now I could put a very, very great many."

The Lord Chief Justice intervened and, following discussion, said: "Dr Stopes wishes to reiterate her evidence that she has never made or caused to be made, an experiment upon anybody."

Hastings: "That is so, is not it?"[4]
Stopes: "Yes, the method used at the Clinic was indicated by a medical man in 1881, and had been used for over 40 years by the middle class and the best people in England under the advice of Harley Street, and to describe them as experiments is a gross misuse of the English language."

It was a point well made, but to what effect? The case was not confined to the clinic nor to cervical caps; it now included the Gold Pin, her books and the "monstrous campaign" of birth control as well. Further, the altercation had enabled Charles to assert three times and unchallenged, that there had been experiments.

Hastings' eloquent opening speech had indicated the plaintiff's path to victory — a charitable scientist trying to help her poorer sisters and a social project that was aligned to *Married Love*. Over the course of the testimony, however, an alternative view had been presented: a woman who claimed to be the messenger of the Almighty God, who promoted a far-reaching "racial and social" agenda for Britain and for Britons, and who advocated devices whose effects were not precisely known and possibly dangerous. The reaction of individual jury members is not recorded, but certainly the testimony of Dr Marie Stopes, sourced from her statements and her writings, were enormously useful to the defence.

Stopes resumed her seat, having been in the witness box for over three hours.[5]

---

[1] Sullivan, S. A. (1952). *The Last Serjeant: The Memoirs of Serjeant A.M. Sullivan*. London: Macdonald. Page 302.

[2] Femina Books. (1967). *The Trial of Marie Stopes*. (M. Box, Ed.) London: Femina Books Ltd. Page 126.

[3] *Ibid.*, page 128.

[4] *Ibid.*, page 131.

[5] Hall, R. (1977). *Passionate Crusader: The Life of Marie Stopes*. New York: Harcourt Brace Jovanovich. Page 216.

Chapter 19

Testimony of Nurse Maud Hebbes[P]

S ir William Arbuthnot Lane was supposed to have followed Stopes, however, he was not in Court and Nurse Maud Hebbes was put in the witness box instead. Hebbes, a fully qualified midwife and maternity nurse of over fifteen years' experience, had worked at the Mothers' Clinic from the beginning. Early in the examination she confirmed that around 1,700 women had attended the Clinic for advice about birth control.

Hastings asked if Hebbes had ever seen a woman named Beatrice Parkinson. She said she didn't remember.

Beatrice Parkinson had been mentioned in "The Defence", the pre-trial legal document produced to respond to the Plaintiff's Statement of Claim. It said: "In or about the month of May 1921, a working woman to wit one Beatrice Parkinson was so instructed by a certain person dressed as a nurse whose name is unknown to this Defendant."[1] At this stage of the trial, it appeared likely that Parkinson would appear as a witness for the Defendants to testify about her visit to the Mothers' Clinic.

Hastings asked Hebbes if she had: "… ever at any time performed any experiment upon any poor person… or at any person at your Clinic."

"Never," she replied.

Hebbes' duties were to interview the women and find out why they were there. Sometimes it was because they wanted a child, sometimes because they were having babies too frequently, in which case Hebbes was able to show them a device that would enable them to control conception by placing a "little rubber cap over the cervix".[2]

She told the Court that the method had been known for 30 years. If there was any difficulty, Dr Hawthorne would attend the clinic, whenever required.

Hastings' examination concluded with questions about the Gold Pin: "Have you yourself at this Clinic, had anything to do with the method of the golden pin?"

Hebbes: "Never."
Hastings: "Have you ever practised it or advocated it?"
Hebbes: "I know no one who has ever used it."

Her answer was a non-sequitur, but Hastings chose not to press the issue.

◆　　◆　　◆

Mr Ernst Charles began his cross-examination by asking for the books of the Clinic. Hastings objected on the basis that these records were equivalent to the medical records of patients held by a doctor, and Charles did not receive the books.

Hebbes said that in the majority of cases, the check pessaries were given away. Charles then turned to Hebbes' examination of women prior to fitting the check pessary and questioned her about her ability to identify disease or any abnormality that would make the use of the pessary inadvisable. The "simple examination" would detect an abnormal condition but perhaps not a diseased condition.

The cross-examination turned to the secretions from a diseased condition, and how long the cervical cap should be left in. Hebbes replied it should not be left in for longer than two days. Then Charles asked about the "doubtful" impact of quinine on the vagina (a quinine pessary was used as a spermicide in conjunction with the cervical cap), but Hebbes did not answer the question.

Charles wanted to know whether the women who attended the clinic were married — did Hebbes ask them? Hebbes believed that they were, and pointed out that that the cap could not be placed in a virgin.

About the Gold Pin, Hebbes admitted that she had read about it but that she had never known of one that was fitted. The cross-examination touched on the frequency of Hawthorne's attendance at the clinic (in theory, on fortnightly Fridays, but in practice not regularly), and Charles questioned Hebbes' ability to detect disease in a patient.

At this point, Stopes interrupted the trial, though what she said was not recorded in the transcript. Charles observed: "Dr Stopes is speaking rather louder than she intends."

"It was an excessive enthusiasm," said Hastings.

"I say rather louder than she intends. Please do not think that I am attributing anything wrong. I heard her, so possibly the jury might hear it."

Towards the end of the cross-examination, Charles asked Hebbes about the attendance of Beatrice Parkinson. She replied that she did not recall a person by that name visiting the clinic.

◆   ◆   ◆

Charles sat down, and Mr Theo Mathew began the cross-examination for the co-defendant, Harding & More. He focussed his questions on the use of an "air rim" pessary which had been mentioned in *Wise Parenthood*. Hebbes said that this device had not been used at the clinic, though some women attending the clinic had used it unsuccessfully.

◆   ◆   ◆

Following Mathew's brief cross-examination, Hastings re-examined Hebbes, obtaining confirmation that air-rim pessaries had not been provided at the clinic, that a statement that the check pessary could be left in all of the time had been made by the manufacturer and had nothing to do with the clinic, and established the form of questions asked for each person attending the clinic. At that point they turned to the next witness, Sir William Arbuthnot Lane.

---

[1] Defence of the Defendant Halliday Gibson Sutherland dated 31st July 1922. Wellcome Library. PP/MCS/H/4a:Box72.
[2] Femina Books. (1967). *The Trial of Marie Stopes*. (M. Box, Ed.) London: Femina Books Ltd. Page 133.

Chapter 20

Testimony of Sir William Arbuthnot Lane[P]

S ir William Arbuthnot Lane was, like other witnesses in the case, a leading physician and, in his case, a brilliant surgeon. His contribution to medicine was as a pioneer of new surgical instruments and techniques. To his brilliance as a surgeon, he added innovative techniques such as the so-called "no touch" technique which reduced the risk of infection, the use of steel pins and plates and the development of new surgical tools.[1]

Lane was a "tall and rather thin man with a clever and uncommon face" who looked younger than his 66 years.[2] Photographs show a distinguished face, framed by neatly cut grey hair and eyes that gave a steady, confident gaze.

Sir William was the last witness of the day and the examination and cross-examination were more sedate than those of the previous witnesses. He confirmed that he was, amongst other things, a Fellow of the Royal College of Surgeons, a Consulting Surgeon at Guy's Hospital, London and a vice-president of the CBC.[3]

Lane was not unacquainted with the social problems of the age because as "… surgeon to the Hospital for Sick Children for very many years… [he] saw intense misery and distress, and also home trouble and drink and drunkenness, entirely due to multiple pregnancy."

Lane belonged "to a great many of these Societies [because] I am intensely interested in humanity". The work of Dr Stopes had come to him as "a matter of intense interest" because: "… I felt that we had come across a real philanthropist at last, and an intelligent one, I may say."[4]

Hastings asked Lane if he had any experience of the occlusive pessary, and he confirmed that he had advised a number of women to use them.[5]

In his next few questions, Hastings sought to ask Lane about the views of other doctors. Before doing so, he consulted the Lord Chief Justice so that he could avoid breaking the rules of evidence in relation to "hearsay".

Hastings asked Lane if he was "well acquainted with the views of many other medical men on this subject," and quickly added that Lane should not say what they were. He then asked if he knew the view of "such a well-known name in the medical profession as Lord Dawson's?" Lane replied that Hastings knew Lord Dawson's views as well as he did.

Cryptically, Hastings then said: "Sir William, if I only could tell the Jury what I knew, I should be delighted; unfortunately I am not allowed to."

He then abruptly changed the subject, which no doubt left everyone in suspense… what was it that he wanted to announce? Did it relate to Lord Dawson? The next questions concerned the alleged dangers from the pessary. Lane confirmed that there was no danger from these. The pessary had been known for many "years and years".

Asked if there was "anything… that she has done at the Clinic which would properly be described as an experiment upon poor people?" Arbuthnot Lane replied:

"No. We are experiments ourselves; I take it we exist as experiments in this world. I cannot regard anything that she has done, in the nature of an experiment."[6]

◆　　◆　　◆

In Charles' cross-examination, he asked Lane whether the pessary should be fitted by a midwife or a doctor. Was it a medical device which should be applied by a doctor? Would it not be best for a doctor to examine the woman in case there was the presence of disease? What if the woman was "following out the directions given by Dr Stopes in her books, she may keep it in a week or possibly three weeks?"

Arbuthnot Lane answered these questions in a plain, matter-of-fact manner: if there was a problem, the woman would remove the cap "dust it with a little powder and put it in the drawer; if the children or the cat have not played with it she could use it the next morning."[7]

Charles asked if a cap left in place would cause "grave trouble." No it would not, said Lane, though he added that it would be "very dirty" and "very smelly".

Charles asked if the dirt would be dangerous given its position, to which Lane relied:[8] "These women are not very clean as a rule, if they leave them in there long, they are very dirty in their habits and are otherwise dirty, then their vaginas would be dirty; I do not think it would make any material difference. As a rule these people do not leave them in so long."

Likely intrigued by the earlier mention of Lord Dawson, Charles asked if Dawson would be giving evidence in the case. Lane replied that he did not know.

◆   ◆   ◆

Charles was followed by Sullivan, who asked: "Sir William, you were enthusiastically in favour of these books. To how many of your young lady acquaintances have you presented *Married Love*?"

To which Lane replied: "I do not quite understand you. Did you say to whom did I present it?"

The question was repeated, and Lane answered: "I am not a bookseller,"[9] adding that he "circulated the views for nothing, very widely too."[10]

On further questions, Lane said that the information contained in Stopes' books would do no harm and might do a "great deal of good".

Later in the cross-examination, with Sullivan and Lane talking at cross purposes, Sullivan pressed for an answer. Arbuthnot Lane replied: "Well I do not always understand you. I have a difficulty in understanding what you mean."

Sullivan asked about the impact on morality and its consequences, artificial insemination and, with that, the second day of the trial had ended.

The case was adjourned until 10.15 am the following day.[11]

Summary of Day 2

So ended the second day of the Stopes *v* Sutherland libel trial. The highlight had been Stopes' appearance in the witness box. Her testimony exposed the wider racial and social program behind her clinic, putting her at odds with the selfless charitable woman depicted in Hastings' opening speech. It also revealed that her work was of public significance, so it was not unreasonable for someone to criticise it.

Stopes' appearance in the witness box had not only damaged her case, but it was also unnecessary. The burden of proof was on the defence to prove that Sutherland's words were true in substance and in fact, not on Stopes to refute what had been written about her. Her answers in the examination and in cross-examination, greatly assisted the defence.

Hebbes and Lane had been competent witnesses, but it was Stopes who had dominated the day.

Overnight, the Plaintiff's barristers may have prepared for the appearance of Beatrice Parkinson and the Defence may have prepared for Lord Dawson.

What the members of the jury made of all of this is not recorded.

---

[1] Brand, R. A. (2009). *Sir William Arbuthnot Lane, 1856–1943*. Clinical Orthopaedics and Related Research, 467(8). Retrieved September 23, 2019, from https://www.ncbi.nlm.nih.gov/pmc/articles/PMC2706364/.

[2] Kingston University. *Sir William Arbuthnot Lane (1856-1943)*. Retrieved September 23, 2019, from HHARP: Historic Hospital Admissions Records Project: http://www.hharp.org/library/gosh/doctors/william-arbuthnot-lane.html.

[3] Femina Books. (1967). *The Trial of Marie Stopes*. (M. Box, Ed.) London: Femina Books Ltd. Page 144.

[4] *Ibid*.

[5] *Ibid*., page 145.

[6] *Ibid*., page 146.

[7] *Ibid*., page 147.

[8] *Ibid*., page 148.

[9] *Ibid*., page 149.

[10] *Ibid*., page 150.

[11] *Ibid*., page 152.

DAY 3

Friday, 23rd February 1923

Chapter 21

Testimony of Dr Harold Chapple[P]

The third day of the trial saw the remainder of the plaintiff's witnesses give testimony: Dr Harold Chapple (gynaecologist at Guy's hospital and the son-in-law of Sir William Arbuthnot Lane), Sir William Maddock Bayliss (Professor of General Physiology at University College London), Dr Meredith Young (Medical Officer for Health for Cheshire), Dr Jane Hawthorne (a Harley Street doctor who attended the Mothers' Clinic), and Dr George Jones (a medical doctor).

They were followed by Mr Ernst Charles KC's opening speech. The sole witness for the defence that day was Professor Ann Louise McIlroy (professor of Gynaecology at London University and consultant at the Royal Free Hospital for Women).

Dr Harold Chapple was the first witness of the day. He confirmed he was a qualified medical doctor and a gynaecologist at Guy's Hospital.

In the examination, Mr Patrick Hastings KC asked him about his experience, both among the wealthy and the poor, about his familiarity with the varying views of medical men about birth control, the work at the Mothers' Clinic, and about Stopes' books. He was supportive of Stopes in all of his answers, as one would expect from a witness from the Plaintiff.

◆　　◆　　◆

For the defence, Mr Ernst Charles KC commenced his cross-examination with a question about the differences of opinion among doctors, and the propriety of giving knowledge of contraceptives "gratuitously to poor people" when previously "these matters have among decent people been not much talked about."

Chapple did not answer the question, and asked: "Why should the poor be deprived on knowledge which the rich can enjoy?"

Charles asked him about the book in the hands of young people under 16, necessitated by the criterion for Bradlaugh's crime of criminal obscenity, and Chapple replied that if people had arrived at the stage at which they were interested in sex problems, then they should "most certainly read *Married Love*".

By now Charles could see that he had a confident witness who was going to use the court as a platform to propagandise Stopes' work. He changed tack: "You are the son-in-law of Sir William Arbuthnot [sic], are you not?"

> Chapple: "Incidentally, I am. I hope you do not think any the worse of me for that."
> Charles: "No, but I was only wondering why we were getting the same opinion?"
> Chapple: "But you can only have one opinion on that, you know."
> Charles: "I am afraid you are wrong there"
> Chapple: "That means that you are imputing to me that I am giving this opinion because I am the son-in-law of Sir Arbuthnot Lane?"
> Charles: "Do not think that, Dr Chapple. Please believe that I believe at any rate, that you give your evidence honestly and truly."

If the plaintiff's witnesses were going to be unanimous in their evidence, then Charles wanted to ensure that their unanimity was a weakness, not a strength. He drew attention to the similarity within the group to undermine the veracity of each individual.

He asked about the effect of Stopes' writings on young people and Chapple replied that it would be better that they get their "opinions from a beautifully expressed book rather than obtain them from more sordid sources."

Charles asked if he included "the passage about artificial insemination" in his opinion. Again, Chapple didn't answer the question: "You know, if you take —"

Charles: "Do you agree with that? Do you agree — I want your answer if you please?"
Chapple: "If you take a book —"
Charles: "Do you agree — I want your answer, if you please?"

Chapple compared *Married Love* to Chapter 20 of Leviticus, which dealt with adultery, incest and bestiality. Charles challenged him, asking if he was seriously comparing *Married Love* to the Bible. Chapple said the book addressed "really serious problems, which we as a serious body should try to face."

The Lord Chief Justice asked for further information about these serious problems. Charles resumed his cross-examination and again met Chapple's refusal to answer questions, and his tendency to answer questions with further questions. "You must not ask me questions," Charles told him, "I am here to ask you to answer the questions I put to you."

Charles was determined to ensure that if he was not going to get the answers he wanted or, for that matter, any answers at all, then the jury would notice that Chapple was evading his questions.

Charles asked about the Gold Pin and, by now predictably, Chapple replied: "As far as the Gold Pin is concerned, I have no knowledge of it from practical experience."[1]

What Charles did not know was that Chapple knew enough to have told Stopes on the eve of the trial: "we ought not to be lured into details about it whatever," and that he "wanted all of the doctors to agree" on this point.[2]

Asked if doctors had ever heard of the Gold Pin, Chapple said "they would not be in the slightest bit interested in it; of course, they would not."[3] In that case, said Charles, "Why bring it to the notice of fully sexed girls under 16?"

"She need not read the book; there is no compulsion in the question of birth control," replied Chapple.

Discussion followed on the desirability of bringing such knowledge to the attention of young people, and Chapple pointed out: "These books are frankly written for married people."

Charles said: "… they are written for married people, but sold to anyone."

At one point, Chapple complained: "The questions that I am being asked are based on selected passages from this book without the sense of the book. When you go into anatomical details, perfectly obviously there are certain things that to the mind that is not familiar with them, are possibly unattractive, but we are dealing with a very serious problem, and we are a serious body of people."

Charles: "What do you say that serious problem is?"

Chapple: "I say that serious problem is the question of birth control. I fancy that if you did my work for five minutes at Guy's hospital and you did not believe in birth control, you would not be able to look at it."

Charles: "Nobody has indicated any view adverse to birth control."

Chapple: "The whole of the questions I am being asked are based on selected passages of the book instead of dealing with the problem as a whole."

Charles: "Forgive me for saying so, but this is not a State trial of birth control; we are dealing here with observations that have been made about a Clinic and the books recommending artificial forms of contraception; that is what we are dealing with."

The exchange revealed the differences in the way the two sides approached the trial. One sought a platform on which it could promote its racial and social program, while the other dealt with the legal issues on which the case would be decided.

Charles turned to the specific problems of the cervical cap. "Would not every movement of the woman tend to dislodge it?"

Chapple: "No."

Charles: "You have not had any experience of complaints that they do dislodge this occlusive pessary?"

Chapple: "These, used with the ordinary amount of intelligence, are perfectly satisfactory."

Charles: "That is rather a vague phrase. What do you say is the average normal amount of intelligence of what I describe as the very poor and helpless people in, say, Holloway? Do they know much about it?"

Charles stuck to the point to ensure that Chapple's testimony was not about vague abstractions, but concerned with the gritty particulars. In response to a question on the possible constriction of the blood vessels of the uterus[4] and the possibility of producing congestion, Chapple replied: "I should doubt that. I do not think that the grip would be anything tight enough."

Charles: "You would doubt it, but it would be very possible, would it not?

Chapple: "What point are you driving at?"

Charles: "The point I am driving at is this; is it not a fact that a check pessary, if it is going to act at all, risks the constriction of the neck of the womb bringing about congestion by the engorgement of the blood vessels?"

Again, Chapple answered the question with a question: "Yes; and if it did?"

Charles: "Would that be good?"

Chapple: "It would not do any harm"

Charles: "It would not?"

Chapple: "It does not do harm, that is the point."

Charles turned to the period of time a cervical cap should be left in place. Three weeks was "commonly advised" by doctors, according to Chapple.

At the end of the cross-examination, the differences between the cervical cap and the Dutch (or Mesinga) pessary (what would today be called a diaphragm) were discussed. While similar in appearance, they differed in the mechanics of how they were held in place. As mentioned, the cervical cap used by Stopes had a ring which had to fit tightly around the cervix in order to keep its position.[5] In contrast (and as mentioned earlier), the Dutch pessary was held in place by pressing out against the walls of the vagina.[6]

The Lord Chief Justice clarified matters: "One fills up the end of the vagina and the other closes the mouth of the cervix."

"Occludes the mouth of the cervix," Chapple corrected him,[7] saying that the differences between the two were a matter of "trivial importance".

"You think it a matter of trivial importance?" asked Charles, who then pointed out that Dr Stopes had devoted a whole page of the book to the difference.[8]

Charles thanked Chapple, ending his cross-examination. While Chapple had frustrated Charles' attempts to get him to answer questions, Charles was not a feisty brawler who had to win every exchange. From his viewpoint, if the witness cooperated, good, but if they did not, that would be in his favour as well, because the jury would observe the obfuscation.

◆   ◆   ◆

Mathew cross-examined Chapple for the co-defendant. Seeking to place Stopes' books in proximity to the one published by Charles Bradlaugh, his questions related to whether Chapple thought it was desirable that young people should read a "dirty book". Chapple thought that it was not objectionable in the least.

---

[1] Femina Books. (1967). *The Trial of Marie Stopes*. (M. Box, Ed.) London: Femina Books Ltd. Page 161.
[2] Letter from Stopes to Hawthorne dated 19th January 1923. Wellcome Library. PP/MCS/B.12.
[3] Femina Books. (1967). *The Trial of Marie Stopes*. (M. Box, Ed.) London: Femina Books Ltd. Page 162.
[4] *Ibid.*, page 167.
[5] *Ibid.*
[6] *Ibid.*, page 169.
[7] *Ibid.*
[8] *Ibid.*

Chapter 22

Testimony of Sir William Bayliss[P]

Sir William Bayliss had received a knighthood for his services to medicine only the previous year. He was Professor of General Physiology at University College London.[1] While he was not a medical doctor — he abandoned medicine to focus on physiology — his work and the discoveries he made were of great importance to medicine. These included the discovery of hormones as a means by which the organs of the body could be controlled, and in relation to the physical state of cells in the body.[2]

Hastings' examination was brief — no more than eight questions. Bayliss had read all of Stopes' books and publications, and thought that they served: "… a most excellent purpose of instruction, in what I may call a noble and elevated way, in matters of sexual relations".

◆   ◆   ◆

Charles' cross-examination asked him whether it was desirable that people be taught as to the possibilities of their sex.[3]

Bayliss replied: "Yes, certainly," and he continued to praise Stopes' books.

Charles asked about the suitability of teaching contraception, the Gold Pin, and artificial insemination and the impact that this knowledge would have on the young.

"It does no harm whatever to clean minds," Bayliss replied.

In his brief appearance in the trial, Bayliss was a prestigious advocate for the works of Dr Stopes and had no doubt made a good impression for the jury.

The barrister for the co-defendant did not cross-examine Bayliss.

---

[1] Femina Books. (1967). *The Trial of Marie Stopes*. (M. Box, Ed.) London: Femina Books Ltd. Page 172.

[2] British Medical Journal. (1924, September 13). *Obituary: Sir William Bayliss*. British Medical Journal, 489-90.

[3] Femina Books. (1967). *The Trial of Marie Stopes*. (M. Box, Ed.) London: Femina Books Ltd. Page 173.

Chapter 23

Testimony of Dr Meredith Young[P]

The next witness, Dr Meredith Young, was the Medical Officer for Health in Cheshire and was responsible for 17 maternity and child welfare centres, which were chiefly attended by working-class mothers and their babies.[1]

Hastings' examination revealed that she had read "everything" Stopes had ever written, she said, "they are clean, well and beautifully written books, with a high ideal." Of the Mothers' Clinic she said: "I consider it extremely well and ably run, that the nurses are capable and well qualified, and I think it is all good."[2]

♦   ♦   ♦

Charles began his cross-examination by asking Young if she approved: "... of the methods of this sort being broadcasted to everybody, young and old?"

He specified that the methods included the check pessary, the Gold Pin and artificial insemination?[3] If Charles' questions were similar to those asked of earlier witnesses, so too were the answers he received: "If they do not learn it in a cleanly and proper manner, they will learn it in a dirty and sordid manner," said Young.

When Charles asked about the inclusion of artificial insemination, Young answered that it "was a necessary corollary to the rest of that book". On being pressed, however, she modified her answer to "Obviously it is unnecessary… " and in the course of questions revealed it had been "… practised for the last 30 years".[4]

Charles turned to the Gold Pin: "Do you have any views about the Gold Pin yourself?"

Young: "No, nothing worth mentioning really."[5]
Charles: "You know, do you not, it was first introduced to induce conception?"
Young: "Yes."
Charles: "You agree?"
Young: "Yes, I know that."
Charles: "It only brings conception if it is left in and taken out when the conception takes place."
Young: "I do not follow."
Charles: "It was first introduced to encourage and allow conception?"
Young: "To make conditions possible for conception to take place."
Charles: "And having made conception possible, conception took place and the woman became pregnant, but no birth could take place if the pin remained in position; it had to be withdrawn?"
Young: "The Gold Pin would, naturally, later on tend to induce abortion."

This revelation was very damaging. Only the day before, Charles had drawn attention to the differences between the 7th and the 9th editions of *Wise Parenthood* as to how frequently the Gold Pin should be examined and cleaned. No warning had been given that the Gold Pin tended to induce abortion, nor the detrimental impact that this might have on the poor women in whom the device had been placed.

Charles was followed by Mr Theo Mathew who cross-examined Young for the co-defendant. Following that, Hastings rose to re-examine Young on matters arising from the cross-examination.

♦   ♦   ♦

Hastings' aim was likely to counter the damage done by Young's revelations about the Gold Pin. In the course of this re-examination, the Lord Chief Justice asked about inter-uterine stems. Young stated that conception was "just barely possible" because "the pin occludes the cervix of the uterus through which the spermatozoa passes" and in so doing would prevent conception. In other words: "At the same time it is dilating the canal from the cervix, it is blocking up the uterus or that canal."[6]

At this point Charles produced a Gold Pin in the Court and stated: "Here is a Gold Pin; it has got a hole right through it." He passed the device to the Lord Chief Justice who asked: "That would not prevent, would it, the entry of spermatozoa into the uterus?"

Young: "It would make it very much more difficult."
Hewart: "It would not prevent it?"
Young: "Not exactly."

Her imprecison drew further questions from the Lord Chief Justice: "If the spermatozoa entered and came into contact with the ovum or ova, might not conception result?"

Young: "It would result."
Hewart: "And if it did result, the continued presence of the Gold Pin would infallibly produce abortion?"
Young: "In course of time."

Again, the Gold Pin had damaged the case of the plaintiff, and had enabled the defence to advance its defence of Justification.

---

[1] Femina Books. (1967). *The Trial of Marie Stopes*. (M. Box, Ed.) London: Femina Books Ltd. Page 174.
[2] *Ibid.*, page 176.
[3] *Ibid.*
[4] Artificial insemination would have been on interest to married couples who were obliged to produce an heir, but who could not conceive on account of a man's infertility. A common cause of male infertility was syphilis.
[5] *Ibid.*, page 177.
[6] *Ibid.*, page 180.

Chapter 24

Testimony of Dr Jane Hawthorne[P]

D r Jane Hawthorne was said to have visited the Mothers' Clinic on a fortnightly basis and accordingly, would have been familiar with its operation.

In the examination by Mr Patrick Hastings KC, Hawthorne confirmed that her rooms were at 150 Harley Street, and that she had largely worked among women in gynaecological cases.[1] She had seen "a considerable number" of patients at the Clinic or sent from the Clinic and had not charged any of them for her services.

Hastings' questions followed the familiar pattern: her opinion of Stopes' writings (the information was of great necessity and there was nothing objectionable in them); whether any part of Stopes' work consisted of making experiments on the poor ("No, not in my opinion; no experiments are made");[2] and whether the occlusive pessary could do any harm ("No harm that I can think of"). Women had been using the pessary before Stopes started her campaign and, according to Hawthorne, no woman had been injured by one.

♦   ♦   ♦

When Mr Charles rose for the cross-examination, he continued on the subject of the cervical cap. Would it be best used under medical supervision, he asked.

Hawthorne replied that she thought a "qualified midwife is quite capable of advising and fitting occlusive pessaries."

Her witness statement said that the method of the cervical cap was "the best one",[3] though she was evasive when answering questions about whether a woman could fit one herself. Given that a wrongly placed cap would not prevent conception, this was key to its effectiveness.[4]

Hawthorne said that a doctor or midwife could fit the occlusive pessary and agreed with Charles' suggestion that "unless you fit the check pessary tightly or unless it fits absolutely accurately, it has a tendency to move." This would not be caused by a movement of the woman's body, but Hawthorne admitted that it might be displaced by the "act of coition".

Charles asked if a midwife was "qualified to recognise any abnormal condition which would make the use of a pessary inadvisable?" Hawthorne replied that a midwife with Hebbes' experience would be able "to recognise any abnormal condition," but conceded that a doctor might discover a condition where a midwife would not.[5]

There followed discussion as to whether the pessary would "impound" discharges from the uterus, whether the cervical cap would stay in place in such circumstances, whether it would move (permitting insemination) as well as the cleanliness of the hands of the poor who were fitting the cervical cap.[6]

Charles told Hawthorne: "I am going to pass to something else" and began his inevitable questions about the Gold Pin:

"What do you think of the Gold Pin; would you advise a person to have a Gold Pin fitted for the purpose of preventing conception?"

Hawthorne replied: "I have very little experience of the Gold Pin."

If not a downright lie, her answer was in sharp contrast to the documentary evidence that is today in the British and Wellcome Libraries. Firstly, Hawthorne's original witness statement had led Stopes' solicitor to remark: "She does not like the Gold Pin",[7] in other words, she had enough experience to form an opinion of it.

Secondly (and as mentioned earlier), Stopes' letter to Hawthorne sought permission to delete the comment about "the fibre being caught in the spring" from her original, settled, witness statement.[8] It was a detail that indicated practical experience.

Thirdly, Stopes had suggested that Lambert send those women who wanted to be fitted with a Gold Pin to Hawthorne.[9] Either Stopes had good grounds on which to make her recommendation, or she was putting these women at risk.

Of course, standing in the High Court in 1923, Mr Charles had not seen the documents that the authors of this book have had access to. He did not know that Hawthorne's witness statement had been altered at the direction of Stopes (or, for that matter, that Stopes had interfered with the evidence of other medical witnesses). Accordingly, he was unable to challenge Hawthorne on this aspect of her testimony.

"Would you, with such experience as you have, advise anybody to use a Gold Pin for the purpose of preventing conception" he asked.

"Well, because I have so little experience of it, I would not advise people," replied Hawthorne.

Charles continued to ask about the Gold Pin and its effects. Would it promote conception, prevent conception or cause an early abortion? He pointed out several times that the effects of the Gold Pin were uncertain and he sought Hawthorne's admission that it was an abortifacient.

Hawthorne's answers were evasive and she only went as far as saying that "if you leave the Gold Pin in, fertilisation may not go any further, the ovum may be thrown off."[10] Charles replied: "It may be, but supposing it is not, then it becomes a simple matter of early abortion, does it not? In one case you throw out the fertilized ova; if it goes a little bit further than that, you have a plain early abortion, that is all."[11]

He asked how frequently Hawthorne attended the Clinic. The distance between Hawthorne's rooms in Harley Street and the Mothers' Clinic was around three and a half miles.

"Well perhaps in the fortnight, but not very regularly, perhaps once a fortnight." She said that around six women per week attended her rooms from the clinic.

During a discussion of Stopes' books, Hawthorne suggested that there was no harm in providing information. When Charles pressed on the suitability of telling a young person about the use of the Gold Pin, Stopes' voice was heard audibly in the Court and not for the first time.[12] Charles protested: "I cannot go on if Dr Stopes keeps on interjecting just under the jury; I would rather she sat on the other side a long way away from the jury. I heard the observations quite clearly where I am."

Hastings said that he "had urged it upon Dr Stopes: I am afraid her enthusiasm runs away with her; [she] will not do it again."

Charles resumed his questions asking what impact the passages about the Gold Pin would have on a fully sexed girl under the age of 16 and whether the information given would be demoralising. Hawthorne saw no reason why the girl should not know about it.

♦   ♦   ♦

Hastings re-examined Hawthorne. Their questions and answers established that there was no reason why healthy minded persons should not get their information from the best sources, that it was desirable that the books were available to the people that sought the information, and that it would not be possible to put the information more simply, straightforwardly or accurately than Stopes had done.

When Hawthorne left the witness box, she was no doubt relieved that her experience with the Gold Pin had not been revealed, and Stopes no doubt pleased that Lambert had not been dragged into the case.

---

[1] Femina Books. (1967). *The Trial of Marie Stopes*. (M. Box, Ed.) London: Femina Books Ltd. Page 180.

[2] *Ibid.*, page 181.

[3] Witness Statement of Jane Lorimer Hawthorne. Wellcome Library. PP/MCS/H/4a:Box72.

[4] Femina Books. (1967). *The Trial of Marie Stopes*. (M. Box, Ed.) London: Femina Books Ltd. Page 184.

[5] *Ibid.*, page 182.

[6] *Ibid.*, page 184-5.

[7] Letter from Braby to Stopes dated 15th January 1923. Wellcome Library. PP/MCS/H/1:Box71.

[8] Letter from Stopes to Hawthorne dated 19th January 1923. Wellcome Library. PP/MCS/H/1:Box71.

[9] Letter from E.W. Lambert to Stopes dated 31st January 1921. British Library: Western Manuscripts MS58638 Vol.CXCII. 1920-1929.

[10] Femina Books. (1967). *The Trial of Marie Stopes*. (M. Box, Ed.) London: Femina Books Ltd. Page 186.

[11] *Ibid.*
[12] *Ibid.*, page 189.

Chapter 25

Testimony of Dr George Jones[P]

The testimony of Dr George Jones was more flamboyant and rhetorical than that of Hawthorne and Young. Nonetheless the damaging revelations about the Gold Pin not only continued, but intensified.

Dr Jones was a registered medical practitioner who had studied at Oxford. He practised as a gynaecologist and venereologist in the East End of London.[1]

Sir Hugh Fraser conducted the examination for the Plaintiff and early in the piece, Jones confirmed that he had read all of the Plaintiff's books and was effusive in his praise: "I say that they are the most excellent books, written in good English, in good taste, and, considering that Dr Stopes has not had a medical education, it is a perfect marvel to me that they are so thoroughly accurate."

He spoke highly of the clinic and of the use of the check pessary. Asked about the danger arising from its use, he answered:

> "There is no possible danger attached to it. The whole thing is moonshine and nonsense — moonshine, that is what it is; how could anyone hurt themselves with a soft rubber thing like that? You have had them in Court; why, it is absurd; Mr Charles knows that it is absurd." [2]

Jones' oratory style might have been effective for audiences in the East-End, but it was not appropriate in Court.

"Now, you must not say that," chided the Lord Chief Justice, explaining: "You are not entitled to make remarks about want of knowledge of the Counsel on the side opposite to you."

"Particularly when it is totally untrue," added Charles indignantly.

"Kindly confine yourself to answering my questions," said Fraser, "I have just one other question. What do you say about the use of the Gold Pin?"

Jones, perhaps a little too predictably by now, said: "About the Gold Pin I know very little."

♦   ♦   ♦

When Charles rose to cross-examine Jones, he began: "Tell me, Dr Jones, do you not know anything about this Gold Pin?" Even through the bland text of the court transcript, one can hear the incredulity in his voice.

Jones replied: "I have had one in my hand, I have examined it very carefully, and I have looked up, as far as I can, what there is which is written about it."

Charles pressed him further. Had he applied it? Had he had a patient to whom the Gold Pin had been fitted? Jones answered "no" to both questions. Then Charles changed tack: "How are you able to say that no harm will result from the wearing of the Gold Pin?"

"I did not say so," Jones replied.

"I thought you said there was nothing harmful in these books," countered Charles.

"There is nothing harmful in the books, because Dr Stopes does not recommend it," said Jones. Charles disagreed. "You know the Gold Pin is recommended in it." Jones contradicted him: "No, it is not; it is criticised adversely."

The answer gave Charles an opportunity to read evidence to the contrary: "… page 36 of *Wise Parenthood*, in the 7th edition; 'The most difficult cases of all, and at the same time those most urgently needing'…"

"Yes, I know the passage quite well," Jones interrupted.

"Please, will you let me complete my observation," said Charles. "'The most difficult cases of all, and at the same time those most urgently needing to exert reliable control over conception are the women who are dissolute, harried, overworked and worried into a dull and careless apathy. Or who are placed that they have neither time nor privacy to take the course recommended. These, too often, will not, or cannot, take the care and trouble to adjust ordinary methods of control so as to secure themselves from undesirable conceptions. For such, there is great hope in the method of the 'Gold Pin,' or 'spring,' sometimes called 'wishbone pessary.' It is, I understand, used by experts in this country and is being widely and successfully adopted in America'. Up to there, for instance, there certainly is not a criticism adverse to the Gold Pin?"

Jones disagreed: "It is a rehearsal, a statement, a recital of what Dr Stopes learned in America, and nothing more; it is neither approval or disapproval."

"'There is great hope?'" suggested Charles.

"Exactly, in the future, not the present."[3]

Jones might not have agreed with him, but Charles' job was not to persuade Jones so much as the jury listening to the cross-examination. Jones' obstinacy enabled Charles to read further testimony from Stopes as author of *Wise Parenthood*:

> "'The method consists in the insertion into the open neck of the womb, the *os*, of a little spring which keeps the mouth of the womb very slightly extended, and thus acts in such a way that it does not hinder the entry of the spermatic fluid but that conception does not take place. The insertion should be absolutely painless and the presence of the spring thereafter should not be felt in any way. The advantages of this method are that all consideration of the subject may be completed once and for all, and the spring should stay in place for years. No further anxiety or trouble on the part of the woman is required, but a visit twice a year to a nurse or doctor to have the spring cleaned or examined. It is, therefore, the one and only method (apart from actual sterilisation) which is applicable and of real help to the lowest and most negligent strata of society. It is therefore a method of the greatest possible racial and social value if its further use proves to be satisfactory. If not, such cases be sterilised'."

Drawing attention to differences between the 7th and 9th editions, Charles added: "... and then she limits it to the women who are C3 women, I think she calls them, or who ought to have no further children too."

He concluded: "Apart from that, is there one word there which is not a word of commendation and recommendation? If so, show me where they are?"

Jones replied: "You have missed the point of the whole thing, Mr Charles: the point is this…"

But Charles had had enough of Jones' verbal diarrhoea and cut him short: "One moment −".

Jones: "I will answer."
Charles: "You must answer my question, first."
Jones: "Yes, I will."
Charles: "Is there one word in that that [sic] I have read about the Gold Pin other than a commendation and recommendation?"
Jones: "You are quite right, but now comes the real point…"
Charles: "What is your answer?"

Jones said that it was not a recommendation and commendation of a method, arguing that because it was expensive to make, it could not be applied to the C3 people.

He used an analogy to support his point: "… you may recommend the Bank of England as a useful place to have an account, but if you have no money to put into it, that recommendation is useless… you might just as well advise extensive investments to a poor person."

Following this speech, Charles asked: "Did she not recommend?"

"She recommends it, yes," replied Jones.

The cross-examination continued, and Jones further irritated Charles by answering a questions with another question and then volunteering irrelevant information: "Shall I tell you when I was a Residential Medical Officer?"

Charles: "No."
Jones: "You have asked me and I will give that to you."
Charles: "I did not ask that."

Jones: "Yes you did; you asked me what it means so I will tell you. I used, when I was Residential Medical Officer..."

Charles listened to his story about the C3s, interrupting it to ask: "Are you a regular know-all?"

Jones continued: "With great respect to you, this Gold Pin Dr Stopes recommended for people who are so hopelessly bad that they ought to be sterilised; if the Gold Pin cannot be used for people, then they are so bad that they ought to be sterilised. Now we have not got to sterilisation yet, but we are not very far off it, but the Gold Pin is a method of perpetual sterilisation without operation, that is all it comes to."

"Perpetual abortions?" asked Charles.

"No. Sterilisation," replied Jones.

This exchange was immensely damaging to the plaintiff's case. The "racial and social" program that underpinned Dr Stopes' work had again been revealed in court, and it exposed her to the horns of a dilemma, for if she knew that the Gold Pin was an abortifacient, she was recommending that the law be broken to achieve her aims and, if she did not know, then surely her work could justifiably be called an experiment.

There followed a to-and-fro discussion as to whether the Gold Pin would promote or prevent conception. Jones was evasive on this point (introducing a red-herring of an "extra uterine foetus", what is known today as an ectopic pregnancy), before the Lord Chief Justice intervened: "I am sure you understand, doctor. It is not suggested that the Gold Pin interferes with conception and the further progress of conception, which it has nothing whatever to do. What is suggested is that, notwithstanding the Gold Pin, conception takes place in the ordinary way."

Jones: "In the uterus?"
Hewart: "Within the uterus, the presence of the Gold Pin will prevent that conception from leading to the natural result, in other words."
Jones: "Yes."
Hewart: "It will prove in that case an abortifacient; that it what is suggested."

Jones: "Yes I think that this is so."
Charles: "That is what I asked you, you know."
Jones: "Yes. I am sorry; it is my stupidity."
Charles: "I would you had honoured me with an answer."
Jones: "I beg your pardon, it is my stupidity."
Charles: "You think it is, so you agree?"
Jones: "I will give one [answer] this time."

Despite his assurance, Jones continued to play games and he quoted Terrence's *Heauton Timouroumenos*.

Charles said: "You must not talk French here," so Jones added that it was Act 1, Scene 2 and he told Charles that he ought to have read it.

Charles passed the witness to Serjeant Sullivan.

♦   ♦   ♦

When Serjeant Sullivan rose to cross-examine Jones for the co-defendant, Harding & More, he started with a question about children in the East End. Did Jones object to boys and girls of the East End talking about sexual matters?

Jones replied that he had "no objection to it" but "regarded it as a state of horror… because their language is foul and filthy and not the English which Dr Stopes writes."

"Their literary style would be improved by talking the same thing a là Dr Stopes?" Sullivan replied.

"No, and the way in which they used it being the way in which…"

Jones was midway through his answer when he noticed that Sullivan had sat down. "That is unfair; you ought not to sit down now; you ought to hear what I have got to say," he protested.

Sullivan did not answer, and it was Charles who spoke: "May I suggest that he ought to?"

The cracks which appeared during the testimony of Young and Hawthorne had now been opened by a wrecking ball. Jones later said that his testimony left him feeling "hopelessly discredited." The following month, he resigned from the CBC[4] and he declined his fee for appearing in Court.[5]

Dr Jones was Stopes' penultimate witness. The last witness, George Roberts MP was not in Court to give testimony. After an adjournment, Mr Charles opened the case for the defence.

----

[1] Hall, R. (1977). *Passionate Crusader: The Life of Marie Stopes*. New York: Harcourt Brace Jovanovich. Page 226.

[2] Femina Books. (1967). *The Trial of Marie Stopes*. (M. Box, Ed.) London: Femina Books Ltd. Page 195.

[3] *Ibid.*, page 196.

[4] Hall, R. (1977). *Passionate Crusader: The Life of Marie Stopes*. New York: Harcourt Brace Jovanovich. Page 227.

[5] Letter from Braby to Stopes dated 2nd March 1923. British Library: Western Manuscripts MS58648 (Jan 1923–Jun 1923) Vol.CCII(ff.124). Jan 1923-June 1923.

Chapter 26

Opening Speech of Mr Ernst Charles[D]

M r Ernst Charles KC spoke for both the Defendant, Dr Halliday Sutherland and the Co-defendant, Harding & More.

Charles began by summing up the significance of the Gold Pin in the case :

> "Can it be said with any element of truth that where the gold pin is recommended, that where the gold pin is so little used, that the evidence before you of doctor after doctor gives no user — they did not know of it, that where it is so uncommon as that, that where it is recommended, that is not an experiment? But, look, what is the nature of the experiment, apart from the actual application to a matter like the gold pin, and indeed the check pessary? This is, according to Dr Stopes, the first, and at the time that this book was written that is complained of, the one and only birth control clinic in England from Land's End to John o'Groats. It is new."[1]

Charles emphasised that the significance of Stopes' clinic was not the introduction of contraceptives, which had after all been in use for many years, but her racial and social aims for the C3s.

> "Hitherto, as was indicated during the course of the case, people have been satisfied not to talk about their

use of check pessaries and contraceptives. No one was very proud, I suppose to voice abroad amongst people in the country that they used these matters. We know there was a certain type of shop where they could be bought — a certain type of shop which I think you will agree — you are gentlemen of business and common sense — is not exactly the sort of shop to which you would have brought your daughter or your sweetheart. Check pessaries have been sold, I have no doubt, so have French letters and other things, in those shops. But here this is for the first time, for a purely experimental reason, the experimental reason being that this lady believes it. Do not think I say she does not believe it, because I believe she is genuine in what she says. I do not profess to use her actual words, but I think it is near enough. She believes she can so control the birth of children at the bottom end of the scale that it will match the diminished output of children at the top end of the scale. She thinks that she can assist to that end by the establishment of a clinic. And who are to be the weapons in her hand which shall assist her towards the successful conclusion, as she believes, of that campaign? Poor, uneducated women."[2]

He said the campaign was likely "to demoralise the whole nature of this nation... increase fornication, debase the family life, and take from us much of that which we are justly proud of in this country of ours. In any case, however conducted, the campaign is a dangerous one. In the way that it is conducted in this case, it is a monstrous one."

Charles used Stopes' high qualifications to argue that Sutherland's remarks were fair comment:

"When a lady like this — and the cleverer she is the more dangerous she is — undertakes, with the best of intentions, it may be, a campaign which appears to be desperately dangerous, she must not any more than a politician, object to strong, firm, hard criticism. She must expect it, and she does expect it. She has been criticised before, she says, by the gutter press. But she takes notice of this book. Why? Because she says people will now be able to say: 'A doctor says that the campaign is a bad campaign.' I would ask you, is it not to the infinite credit of Dr Sutherland that he has stepped forward and criticised frankly and freely that which he honestly and honourably as a man, and as a medical man, regards as a monstrous campaign, which can only end in disaster to the morals and to the life of the nation, if it is allowed to go uncriticised? Is he not right?"[3]

In his speech, Charles again referred to "my friend" which, in the formal courteous language of the Court, meant his opponent, Mr Hastings. "Now my friend, when he was opening this case, occupied a very great deal of time in describing who and what this lady was."

He reminded the Court of Hastings' statement: "… if the verdict is against her in this case there would be no reason at law why she should not be committed at once to take her trial at the Central Criminal Court."

"What rubbish! What stuff and nonsense," Charles exclaimed. He said that while a magistrate might order Stopes' books to be destroyed, it did not follow that Sutherland had said she should be sent to prison.[4] Sutherland's statement was not that she ought to go to jail, but that Bradlaugh had been condemned to jail for a less serious crime.[5]

Charles compared Stopes' books to Bradlaugh's. Hers contained more explicit details including the fitting of the check pessary, the Gold Pin, artificial insemination, a "full description of a man's organ of generation" and its action.

Charles challenged the assertion that Stopes' reputation had been damaged. He said that Sutherland had criticised the campaign, not the campaigner, and that he bore no malice towards Dr Stopes. He said that whilst under cross-examination, Stopes had admitted that she was suing "in the interests of the Society".[6]

He reminded jurors that this was not a state trial of birth control. He turned to Sutherland's book, outlining the sections, and pointed out that a great deal of it could not be said to come within the scope of libel.

Charles then placed Stopes' qualifications into context in relation to her books about sex and contraception: "Mrs Stopes — who is as well qualified but I do assert not better qualified than I myself or any of you. What is the good of saying that she knows more about coal and fossil botany and all sorts of things, as she undoubtedly does, with her brilliant mind? What is the good of saying all that? What is the good of occupying your minds by saying that she has been five times to America or fifty times to America? What is the good of occupying your minds to say she had been to Japan to study coals?"[7]

He made another of his weak jokes: "I thought my friend said 'colds' to begin with, and that would be something, but he says 'coals'".[8]

In his opening speech, Hastings had brought up Stopes' first marriage, perhaps anticipating that the defence would raise it to attack her reputation. Of course, had they done so, they would likely have aggravated the libel, and Charles now threw it back at them:

> "Why on earth would one touch on her unhappy original marriage? What has it got to do with this Clinic, or whether the books are obscene in the eyes of the law or not, that she issues broadcast to the public. It may possibly form some kind of explanation as to the distorted view that she takes of mankind; it may be so, I do not know. I do not know why it was introduced, and there I will leave it. I do not want to speak any more about it. If she desired sympathy, believe me for myself, at any rate, she has it."

He then undermined the notion that Sutherland had defamed Stopes by citing only her German qualification and here he was at his withering best:

> "You certainly cannot say that this woman is not a doctor of Philosophy of Munich. My friend says: 'How on earth can Dr Sutherland have only put that in?' He must have known that she had other degrees. I say with confidence to this Court, that if that is going to be a ground for an action for libel, most of us had better trot round to our solicitors. Do you suppose that one of those of the rank to whom I belong and my friend, suppose I am called 'Mr Ernest Charles, KC.' 'Boo,' I say 'you have not told them I am an MA, I am an Esquire, and all sorts of things.' Off I pop to my Solicitors and drive a Writ into

them. What nonsense, again I say, if I am not imperilling my friendship — what stuff and nonsense."[9]

He explained why Sutherland had written the book. Firstly he wanted "to disclose to the world something that he did not think they knew before… that she was not what we call a woman doctor." Secondly he wanted to make the point relating to the "gross materialism" of German philosophy.

Charles challenged the claims of the plaintiff by posing questions and answering them:

"Is there anything wrong in saying she opened a birth control clinic? — No."

"Where working women are instructed in the practice of birth control? — No, there is nothing wrong with that, it is true."

"Is there anything wrong in saying: 'described by Professor McIlroy' — who is a most distinguished obstetric physician — 'as the most harmful method of which I have had experience'? — No."

He read from *Birth Control*: "When we remember that millions are being spent by the Ministry of Health and by Local Authorities — on pure milk for necessitous expectant and nursing mothers, on Maternity Clinics to guard the health of mothers before and after childbirth, for the provision of skilled midwives, and on Infant Welfare Centres — it is truly amazing that this monstrous campaign of birth control should be tolerated by the Home Secretary. Charles Bradlaugh was condemned to jail for a less serious crime."

He mocked Hastings' opening speech: "I do not know whether my friend would say that the Home Secretary will probably go to jail if this gentleman wins his case, because he has been conniving at that which Charles Bradlaugh was sentenced for."[10]

Charles then drew attention to the attack on the "monstrous campaign," pointing out it was an attack on the campaign and not on the person. Stopes' vision from the Almighty God who: "… must have been a Great Maker singularly acquainted with the public works of Marie Stopes, and who, if you please, she would have you believe, sends down that filthy, beastly message which you find about the priests of the Church. A campaign has come to a great pass when you have to make appeals of that sort to support it."

Charles warned the jury that it would be his duty to ask them to read "filthy passages" in Stopes' books and referred to how Stopes' witnesses had explained it: "And what is the excuse? 'All knowledge is good,' says one of the distinguished witnesses called on behalf of Marie Stopes, 'even if it contains filth'."

Hastings interrupted to clarify a point, namely that Stopes did not advise, nor examine, people who attended the clinic. That done, the first witness for the defence, Professor Ann Louise McIlroy entered the witness box.

---

[1] Femina Books. (1967). *The Trial of Marie Stopes.* (M. Box, Ed.) London: Femina Books Ltd. Page 201. Land's End and John o'Groats are the southernmost and northernmost parts of mainland Britain.

[2] *Ibid.*, page 202.

[3] *Ibid.*, page 203.

[4] One month before the Stopes *v* Sutherland trial, Guy Aldred and Rose Witcop had been prosecuted for selling Margaret Sanger's pamphlet *Family Limitation*. Ruling that the pamphlet was obscene, the Magistrate ordered that it be destroyed, but he did not imprison the defendants. Prior to the trial, Stopes secretly wrote to the Director of Public Prosecutions "condemning Sanger's pamphlet as 'prurient' and the diagrams in it as obscene," an action unlikely to have helped their cause. See Rose, J. (1992). *Marie Stopes and the Sexual Revolution*. London: Faber and Faber Limited. Page 162.

[5] Femina Books. (1967). *The Trial of Marie Stopes.* (M. Box, Ed.) London: Femina Books Ltd. Pages 203-4.

[6] *Ibid.*, page 205.

[7] *Ibid.*, pages 206-7.

[8] *Ibid.*, page 207.

[9] *Ibid.*

[10] *Ibid.*, page 208.

Chapter 27

Testimony of Professor Louise McIlroy[D]

Professor Anne Louise McIlroy was a valuable witness for Sutherland because she embodied many of the different elements contesting the case.

Like Stopes, she was a pioneer. She was one of the first women to become a medical doctor at the University of Glasgow, and the first woman Professor of Obstetrics and Gynaecology at London University, practicing at the Royal Free Hospital for Women.

Like Barr, she was an eminent and distinguished physician, a Dame of the British Empire no less, though she was much closer to the subject at hand than he was. She also had an outstanding war record and had been awarded the Croix de Guerre in 1916.

McIlroy was also central to the case because her words had been quoted in *Birth Control*.

In the examination, Charles went through McIlroy's qualifications before moving to the paper she had read at the Medico-Legal Society on 7th July 1921. She confirmed that she had said that the check pessary — the device in use at the Mothers' Clinic — was "the most dangerous method I know of," and that she still thought that this was the case.

Charles asked her what was bad about the method. McIlroy explained that it "… could not be fitted without a considerable amount of manipulation in the sexual organs… and might induce sepsis or poisoning into the vagina and the canal and if it were possible to fit it on the mouth of the womb (the neck of the womb), then the results... would be very dangerous."

In addition, it would block secretions from the womb. She confirmed that she had examined thousands of women in her time[1] and had made a study into the discharges of the womb some years previously.[2] In addition, any person fitting the device would have to be absolutely sure that the woman was not suffering from venereal disease, which was sometimes difficult to detect without a laboratory test. Then the cervical cap was hard to fit; a woman using it would be unlikely to put it in the right place and, even if it were placed correctly, it would not stay there.

Asked about the Gold Pin, McIlroy confirmed that she had no experience of it, and had never seen one. She nonetheless commented that during pregnancy "… the mouth of the womb wants to be closed. If the mouth of the womb is not closed, abortion will probably take place."[3]

From McIlroy's point of view, the method of artificial contraception that was the least harmful to women was the condom or sheath (vulgarly known as the "French Letter"). She had "come across a great many cases" where women had used contraceptives and subsequently, when they ceased using them because they wanted a child, they could not conceive.[4]

◆   ◆   ◆

Charles sat down and Hastings began his cross-examination.

The brief in relation to McIlroy (possibly written by Stopes) said that she was: "… an unmarried woman of a certain age, and, as I could demonstrate, very ignorant of the subjects she talks about. Nevertheless, she holds an important position, and could certainly say a lot of things which could sound very convincing in one way, therefore, we certainly ought to have her to show that Sutherland was lying when he used her name."[5]

That is where Hastings began his cross-examination. He went to the night that McIlroy delivered her paper at the Medico-Legal Society. He asked a series of questions relating to her paper: "There was nothing in that paper that you read relating at all to this statement about dangerous methods, was there?"

McIlroy: "I did not discuss the methods in the paper."
Hastings: "There was a shorthand note taken, was not there [sic], of all that was said at the meeting."
McIlroy: "Yes."
Hastings: "Have you read it?"
McIlroy: "Yes."
Hastings: "It does not appear in that. This statement that is in the libel, attributed to you does it."

As a trap, it was a good one. If she had said the words, then why were they not in the shorthand note? And if she had not said them, on what had Sutherland based his quote?

Unfortunately for Hastings, the brief had misinformed him and the cross-examination came to a grinding halt.[6] It transpired that the remark had been made during the discussion that followed the paper. Accordingly, it was recorded not in the transcript of her paper, but in the shorthand record of the discussion that followed it, a separate document.

Once the decision had been taken to sue Sutherland, Stopes' solicitor, Braby & Waller, should have verified what McIlroy had said. It was Stopes however, who wrote to McIlroy to ask her if she had made the statement and to which McIlroy replied on 3rd May 1922:

> "You will find my paper in the *Transactions of the Medico-Legal Society* and in it you will see that I have not made the slightest reference to you. At no other time have I mentioned your name and any statements you may have heard have entirely originated from the imagination of your informers."[7]

Notwithstanding that it was Braby & Waller's responsibility, they had likely been influenced by Stopes' assurances (that McIlroy had not said the words) in letters dated 4th May 1922,[8] 11th May 1922,[9] 26th November 1922,[10] and 1st January 1923.[11]

Mr Charles corrected Hastings, saying: "Yes, it is here on page 14; you will find it exactly." [12]

"If it is, I will leave it. I was told it was not. It is my fault for not having read it," replied Hastings, graciously accepting the blame.

"Let me show you it. It is so," said Charles, no doubt in the earnestly helpful tone of a barrister seeking to maximise the embarrassment of his opponent.

"If you say it is so, I really do not mind," replied Hastings, trying to continue with his cross-examination.

Charles was having none of it and, wanting to press the point, he began to read aloud: "'The most harmful method of which I have had experience' etcetera". He handed the document to Hastings who passed it to the (likely red-faced) solicitor.

In his next question to McIlroy, Hastings asked: "Whether you said it or not, you think it?"

"I say it now, yes," she replied.

"Whether you said it or not" prolonged the uncertainty, so the Lord Chief Justice intervened: "Mr Hastings, the gentleman who instructed you thinks verification is not so good as justification by verification."

Hastings conferred with Braby before resuming his cross-examination. He then set about probing McIlroy's attitude to contraceptives. She agreed that medical opinions differed. He asked if she would approve of the use of contraceptives in cases in which women had had a: "… very large number of children and whose health had been impaired?"

> McIlroy: "Yes."
> Hastings: "Women who have had mentally defective children?"
> McIlroy: "Yes."
> Hastings: "Then may I take it that there are cases in which you would approve of contraceptive methods?"
> McIlroy: "I recommend them."

Asked about the number of patients who came to her "for advice with regard to contraceptive methods", McIlroy said that it was "a large number" and added that "they don't come to me for advice directly for contraceptives, but for some medical reason."[13]

The intent behind Hastings' questions was perhaps to whittle down the differences between McIlroy and Stopes and to present McIlroy as someone who, while testifying for the defence, agreed with the plaintiff. Hastings asked if there was a "very large number of people in the country who desire the use of contraceptives". McIlroy did not agree: "there may be," she said, but she did not know the number.

Hastings asked about supposedly hypothetical cases. What would she do, for instance, for the woman who had had three or four children and the children were coming too quickly? McIlroy said that she would advise the women not to have relations with her husband. And if that led to the ruin of their lives? McIlroy said she would advise contraceptive methods.

> Hastings: "You would say to a wife in ordinary language: 'Take my advice and do not sleep with your husband'"
> McIlroy: "I should probably see the husband and put it before both of them."
> Hastings: "That is the advice that you would prefer to give?"
> McIlroy: "I do not know what that means."
> Hastings: "This is the advice you would recommend?"
> McIlroy: "I would advise control before any contraceptive method, if there were no harmful results."[14]
> Hastings: "Have you ever taken into consideration that it may result in the husband going off to some other woman?"
> McIlroy: "Then in those cases I would consider the individual case."

Hastings was likely trying to align McIlroy's reactions with what might have taken place at the Mothers' Clinic. If Hastings could show that Stopes' treatment of the poor was similar to that of Britain's leading female gynaecologist, he could ridicule Sutherland by arguing that McIlroy was exposing the poor to experiment as well. But every time Hastings tried to entrap McIlroy she eluded his attempt. She did this effortlessly because the moral side of the question did not affect her,[15] and she applied her focus to "the individual case that I have in front of me".[16]

McIlroy made it clear that she viewed contraceptive devices as merely one way to help people in their lives. Her approach allowed for the treatment to be nuanced for each person and their spouse.

McIlroy agreed that Stopes was genuinely trying to deal with an important problem of sexual relations between husband and wife and on being asked if there was anything wicked in what Stopes had done, McIlroy said "I think she is misguided."

Hastings changed tack: it was all very well in making recommendations to individuals, he said, but surely she understood that there were "thousands and thousands" who could not "afford to come to you or any doctor for advice".

> McIlroy: "They can come to me perfectly free; I am in the
> hospital the whole day and see patients for nothing."
> Hastings: "Which is your hospital?"
> McIlroy: "The Royal Free."[17]

The name of her hospital put the matter beyond doubt, and Hastings asked McIlroy about her general views on contraception: "I take it you are in principle opposed to the use of contraceptives wherever possible?"

"In general, yes," she replied.

Hastings turned to the pessary. Had McIlroy ever had a case of a woman "who had worn one of these pessaries?" She replied that she had "never met a woman yet who was able to fit on the pessary."

Hastings pressed the point: "I wonder whether you could answer my question: have you ever had a case of a woman who has worn one?"

> McIlroy: "No."
> Hastings: "So that all you have been telling us at some
> length in answer to Mr Charles about the dangers of this,
> is based upon practical experience which does not
> include one single case of that having been worn."

Hastings made his point effectively, but McIlroy stood her ground. Her remarks had been based on her experience of "the occlusion of the womb" and she said that it was not necessary to have observed a single case.

The cross-examination then turned to the problems in the relations between a married couple if they feared conception.

If a woman had had a large number of children and she feared conception, what would McIlroy do? McIlroy said it would depend on the individual case. Pressed for an answer she said that she would advise the woman not to have sexual intercourse. What if that ruined their lives? I would advise contraceptive methods.

Hastings was pressing McIlroy to accept that the language used in *Married Love* was appropriate for the nature of the topic under discussion, given it was "a very delicate matter". He asked if she would deal with it using "plain, outspoken, bald," language and McIlroy agreed: "scientific language is the simplest in the world."[18] and did not agree that romantic language was appropriate.

> Hastings: "Do you think that this is a genuine desire to help in this problem, or not?"
> McIlroy: "I think it is a misguided desire, but I have no doubt it is a desire which I am perfectly sure is perfectly genuine."
> Hastings: "Is it a desire to help?"
> McIlroy: "Yes, but a misguided one."[19]

At the end of the cross-examination, the Court adjourned until the following Tuesday, 27th February 1923 at 10.15 am.

Summary of Day 3

So ended the third day of the Stopes *v* Sutherland libel trial. Of the witnesses for the plaintiff, Bayliss had been the best in terms of his prestige and for his calm and assertive testimony in support of her work. Chapple had avoided making any damaging admissions, but his answers were evasive. Charles had undermined Chapple's credibility by pointing out that his evidence was similar to that of other witnesses.

Young's testimony was very damaging to Stopes' case because she admitted that the Gold Pin would induce an abortion. The many different outcomes of the Pin — said to promote conception, prevent conception, hinder fertilisation and produce an abortion — brought it into the realm of an experiment.

Hawthorne's experience of the Gold Pin had been concealed from the Court and Stopes would have been pleased that Lambert had been kept out of the case. On the other hand, her answers in relation to whether a woman could fit a cervical cap herself, and on its tendency to move, undermined her assertion that it was the best method. Then there was her admission that while a midwife might recognise an abnormal condition, she was not able to recognise disease to the same extent as a doctor.

Jones' testimony had been disastrous. He had not merely contradicted himself, but gave Charles an opportunity to read out damaging passages from *Wise Parenthood*.

To these successes, the defence was able to add the testimony of Professor McIlroy who embodied all of the desirable qualities of a witness in this trial. Hastings' assertion that Sutherland had falsely quoted McIlroy in *Birth Control* had not only been defeated, but had stalled his cross-examination of this key witness.

Under cross-examination, McIlroy had admitted that she did not have practical experience of the cervical cap. While this was in the plaintiff's favour, McIlory had said that her statement was based on the occlusion of the womb.

While the impact that all this had on the minds of the 12 men of the jury is not recorded, Stopes' realisation that she might lose the case was. Her letter to Mr Braby the following day included: "… suggestions which I want you particularly to hand on to both Mr. Patrick Hastings and Sir Hugh Fraser for the Cross-examination... Do, for God's sake get Mr Patrick Hastings to study them and to use all the technical questions especially. If he does not, particularly on that question of the Gold Pin use absolutely all I have put in we shall simply lose the case."[20]

Both sides stood down until 10:30 am on Tuesday, 27th February 1923 when the battle would resume.

---

[1] Femina Books. (1967). *The Trial of Marie Stopes*. (M. Box, Ed.) London: Femina Books Ltd. Page 213.

[2] *Ibid*., page 214.

[3] *Ibid*., page 213.

[4] *Ibid*., page 215.

[5] Documentary fragment headed "Name of witness" and "Type of evidence" (archivist has written in pencil at the top of the page: "Dec 22?"). British Library: Western Manuscripts MS58647 (1913-1922) Vol.CCI(ff.170). 1913-1922.

[6] Brief on Behalf of the Plaintiff, page 12. Wellcome Library. PP/MCS/H/4a:Box72.

[7] Letter from McIlroy to Stopes dated 3rd May 1922. Wellcome Library. PP/MCS/H/4a:Box72.

[8] Letter from Stopes to Braby dated 4th May 1922. Wellcome Library. PP/MCS/H/1:Box71.

[9] Letter from Stopes to Braby dated 11th May 1922. Wellcome Library. PP/MCS/H/1:Box71.

[10] Letter from Stopes to Braby dated 26th November 1922. Wellcome Library. PP/MCS/H/1:Box71.

[11] Letter from Braby to Stopes dated 1st January 1923. British Library: Western Manuscripts MS58648 (Jan 1923–Jun 1923) Vol.CCII(ff.124). Jan 1923-June 1923.

[12] Femina Books. (1967). *The Trial of Marie Stopes*. (M. Box, Ed.) London: Femina Books Ltd. Page 216.

[13] *Ibid.*, page 217.

[14] *Ibid.*, page 218.

[15] *Ibid.*, page 219.

[16] *Ibid.*, page 218.

[17] *Ibid.*, page 220.

[18] *Ibid.*, page 223.

[19] *Ibid.*, page 224.

[20] Letter from Stopes to Braby dated 24th February 1923. British Library: Western Manuscripts MS58648 Vol.CXCII. 1920-1929.

DAY 4

Tuesday, 27th February 1923

Chapter 28

Testimony of George Roberts MP^P

T he Right Honourable George Roberts was a Member of Parliament, a former Minister for Labour and member of the Privy Council. He was also a vice-president of the CBC. Aged in his fifties, he was distinguished by a thick moustache drawn out to thin points on both sides of his face. He had been unable to testify the previous Thursday, so had been allowed to testify on a day otherwise set aside for the defendant's witnesses.

In the examination, it was revealed that Roberts had chaired the Stopes' rally at the Queens Hall in 1922, which he described as a "pleasure and privilege". He had taken an interest in Stopes' work on birth control and had read some, but not all, of her works. He: "… appreciated the fact that this subject was one that ought to be treated with tact and delicacy, and I have felt that Dr Marie Stopes and those associated with her have done so."[1]

◆   ◆   ◆

Hastings passed the witness to Charles for cross-examination. Charles asked Roberts if he had read *Married Love* and, in particular, the pages "devoted to the minute description of the act of copulation?" What about the part that spoke of "inseminating women with other men's seed who they have not seen?" Did Roberts really think this was suitable to be broadcast to old and young alike?

Roberts replied that the book should be taken as a whole, and Charles asked for "a simple answer to a simple question".

Roberts said it was "… far better that a girl should be informed from a decent source than to acquire the knowledge, which is undoubtedly in it, by surreptitious methods."

"We have heard that answer almost in the same words from other witnesses," said Charles.

Charles asked if *Wise Parenthood* should also be broadcast, to which Roberts replied that both sexes should be educated in the subject. Charles said that there were two subjects, not one — sex and contraception. Was it advisable that a young girl, 16, but fully sexed, should know?

Roberts said that all girls should be educated in such matters though "whether it is abused or not, I cannot say."[2]

Charles then turned to the Gold Pin, no doubt expecting that Roberts' answer would match the answers of other witnesses for the plaintiff.

> Charles: "Supposing it is established that for certain purposes, Dr Stopes did not know it, but supposing it is established that the Gold Pin is an instrument which produces early abortion, do you think that a young girl fully sexed should be introduced to an article of that sort?"
>
> Roberts: "I think you are asking me a question which really ought to be addressed to some well qualified man."
>
> Charles: "I am asking you the question of these books. As I gather, you say you think that any young girl or young boy might properly have this book put before her or him or be able to buy it anywhere, *Wise Parenthood*?"
>
> Roberts: "As I understand, you were putting to me that question if it is widely established; whereas it is well known that medical opinions differ widely on this subject."
>
> Charles: "On the Gold Pin?"
>
> Roberts: "You put it yourself, if it is established, which implied in itself that there is a wide difference of opinion. As I understand, there is a wide difference of opinion; if it is established, then, of course, nobody would recommend the use of it."

On hearing "nobody would recommend the use of it," Charles asked: "You were not here on the last occasion when the Plaintiff and others were giving evidence?"[3]

"I have to earn my living elsewhere. I should like to have been here," said Roberts.

"Do you say you would very much have liked to be here?" asked the Lord Chief Justice, perhaps thinking that the Houses of Parliament were the better option.

"Yes," replied Roberts.

Charles used the opportunity to quote yet again from *Wise Parenthood*. In the final questions, Roberts gave evasive answers to Charles' next questions and, having not read *The New Gospel to all Peoples*, was not able to answer questions about that either.

♦   ♦   ♦

Serjeant Sullivan's first question was: "Will you tell me, are there indecent books circulated among the working-classes?"

Sullivan was likely trying to draw Roberts into a discussion on features that might lead him to conclude that a book was indecent or obscene, and then point out that these features applied to Stopes works as well. The aim was to verify Sutherland's assertion that Bradlaugh had been imprisoned for a lesser crime.

Roberts replied that it was a matter of opinion. He continued to avoid answering questions in keeping with the best traditions of British politicians before and since.

Having twice asked: "can you answer yes or no?" Sullivan said: "Can you answer yes or no to any question, Mr Roberts?"

"I believe I might put a question to you which you could not answer aye or nay," he replied.

When further pressed for an answer, Roberts said: "If I am to answer as I like —" but Sullivan interrupted him: "That is one of the things, in this system of jurisprudence we do not allow; you have to answer as you are prescribed here." Roberts told him that he was treating the matter from his political experience, and that he had "always declined to be bound down to an answer yes or no, according as was desired by my opponents."

> Sullivan: "Are you afraid to give a plain answer to the extremely plain question I put to you; can you answer yes or no to that?"
> Roberts: "I think I have given you an intelligent answer."
> Sullivan: "As you will not, I will press you no further."

Roberts was Stopes' last witness in the trial.

---

[1] Femina Books. (1967). *The Trial of Marie Stopes*. (M. Box, Ed.) London: Femina Books Ltd. Page 228.
[2] *Ibid.*, page 229.
[3] *Ibid.*, page 230.

Chapter 29

Examination of Dr Halliday Sutherland

Dr Halliday Sutherland followed Roberts into the witness box for one of the key exchanges that would determine the outcome of the trial.

The evening before, an incident had occurred in the office of Sutherland's solicitor, Charles Russell & Co, that would help him in the witness box. As he would write ten years after the case:

> "Every afternoon when the Court rose all our counsel met in conference at Sir Charles Russell's office to discuss the evidence from day to day. At these conferences I was present. I had the whole case from A to Z in my mind, and if any of the leaders made the slightest unimportant slip I immediately corrected him. This annoyed Sir Charles Russell, and on the eve of my going into the witness-box there was nearly a scene. It was Mr Charles, KC, who made peace. "Leave him to me, Russell, if you get him upset to-night there's no saying what will happen to-morrow morning"; and to me: "Now, Dr Sutherland, I know exactly what the trouble is. You're attempting to carry every detail of this case in your head. You forget that you are not defending yourself, and that I'm here to defend you. Why not leave it to me? Very well, to-morrow I'll be able to help you in your evidence-in-chief and in re-examination, but I can do nothing when Pat Hastings is cross-examining, and whatever he says, don't lose your temper." "Ha!" said

Sir Charles, clenching his fists, "if he dares to lose his temper, he'll never enter this office again."[1]

The admonishment and the advice of Mr Charles would have been fresh in Sutherland's mind the following morning. As with the other witnesses in the trial, the examination began with his resumé. Sutherland lived in Over, Gloucestershire. He was a Bachelor of Medicine and Bachelor of Science, with Honours and a Doctor of Medicine with Honours at Edinburgh University. During the war, in 1916, he had discovered the aetiology of cerebro-spinal fever.

Aged 40, Sutherland had been married for 2½ years and had three children, one girl and twin boys.[2] He had attended the meeting at the Medico-Legal Society and confirmed he had heard Professor McIlroy say: "The most harmful method of which I have had experience is the check pessary" followed by an explanation of why she had said that.

Remarking that the plaintiff had said a good deal in her evidence about Roman Catholics, Charles asked if Sutherland was a Roman Catholic — he was — and whether he had written the book at the behest of the Roman Catholics — he had not. He had written it to "make known to the public certain arguments against artificial birth control."

They turned to the "campaign", the prominence given to contraceptives in general, and Stopes' books in particular. They discussed the publication of *Birth Control*, that he had been challenged to a debate in a letter from Stopes' husband Humphrey Roe, and that he had not replied to the letter because he "did not want to do anything to further advertise the campaign".

Charles referred to page 101 of *Birth Control* (the page on which Sutherland had written "Exposing the Poor to Experiment") and asked him what he had meant by "experiment"? Sutherland explained that it was: "The indiscriminate distribution of contraceptives amongst the poor for the purpose of attempting to redistribute the birth rate by means of artificial contraceptives and contrary to the law of nature."

In subsequent answers he added that it was "a social experiment" and "a bad experiment".[3]

Charles asked Sutherland if he knew that the Mothers' Clinic "was the only clinic of the sort," to which he answered "yes". Did he have knowledge of the effect of contraceptives in other countries? Sutherland replied: "I knew what has happened in France. I knew that France was and is dying owing to the use of contraceptives."[4]

By this he meant that the French birth rate had declined at an alarming rate. Although the evidence relating to France had been struck out in one of the pre-trial hearings,[5] Charles asked Sutherland if he was "aware that a law had been passed in France forbidding contraceptives…"

Hastings objected on the grounds that Charles was "leading the witness", in other words, asking the question in such a way as to indicate what the answer should be. There was discussion between the barristers for both sides and the Lord Chief Justice, following which France was not mentioned again.

Charles turned to the dangers of a woman fitting the check pessary to herself. Sutherland had based his views on McIlroy's concern that occlusion of the womb might cause medical danger to the user and that a dirty finger or a scratch might cause a "good deal of harm".[6]

"Is that in the Particulars?" asked the Lord Chief Justice. The "Particulars" was a legal document that contained information that Sutherland had provided in the pre-trial exchanges. The Lord Chief Justice had asked because the defence was not allowed to introduce anything new into the trial at this stage.

It was Hastings who answered the Lord Chief Justice's question. "No, not a word of it," he said. "I have looked and I cannot find it."[7]

"I am sure my friend should not say this; it is not so," replied Charles.

"I am asking for information," said the Lord Chief Justice.

Sutherland said: "I think the word 'endometritis' [inflammation of the inner membrane of the womb] would cover it."

Hastings' knowledge of his brief had been deficient, and Charles wanted to rub it in: "It was alleged absolutely in these Particulars, but if my friend is desirous of objecting —"

"I have told you I would not object," said Hastings. "Surely we may go on."

The examination continued, guided by the allegedly defamatory words in *Birth Control*. Sutherland confirmed that, as a doctor, he believed that his statement: "the ordinary decent instincts of the poor are against these practices" was true. Asked if he still believed it to be true, he answered: "I do, most emphatically."

Asked why he described Stopes as a doctor of German philosophy, Sutherland explained that he wanted to make it perfectly clear that Stopes: "was not a doctor of medicine, and moreover, that she had no scientific degree which qualified her by knowledge to teach these methods." He did this because he believed that the public had mistakenly thought that she was "a woman doctor in the popular sense".

His term "German philosophy" was shorthand for the philosophy of materialism.

By "monstrous campaign," Sutherland explained that he had already given the medical objection, and that he wanted to add a new one: "I say morally it is a bad thing, because if you broadcast indiscriminately, information throughout the community, as to how people may have sexual intercourse without the risk of pregnancy, I think it is inevitable that you are going to lower public morality."[8]

Charles asked him why he had made a reference to Bradlaugh. Sutherland replied that it was because he had been sentenced to prison for "having indiscriminately distributed information on contraceptives."

Finally, he said that he had not spoken to Dr Stopes and bore no malice against her.[9]

---

[1] Sutherland, H. (1934). *A Time to Keep*. Geoffrey Bles. Page 251.

[2] They were the authors' aunt, Jane, and uncles, John and Peter.

[3] Femina Books. (1967). *The Trial of Marie Stopes*. (M. Box, Ed.) London: Femina Books Ltd. Page 238.

[4] In *Birth Control*, Sutherland drew on the relative populations of France and Germany to refute Malthusian arguments that over-population leads to war: "Malthusians may inveigh against wars waged to achieve the expansion of a nation, but so long as international rivalry disregards the moral law their words will neither stop war nor prevent a Malthusian country from falling an easy prey to a stronger people. On the contrary, a low birthrate, by reducing the potential force available for defence, is actually an incentive to a declaration of war from an envious neighbour, because it means that he will not hesitate so

long when attempting to count the cost beforehand. In 1850 the Population of France and Germany numbered practically the same 35,500,000; in 1913 that of France was 39,600,000, that of Germany 67,000,000. The bearing of these facts on the Great War is obvious. In 1919 the new Germany, including Silesia, had a population of just over 60,000,000; whereas, in 1921, France, including Alsace-Lorraine, had a population of 39,200,000. Thus, despite her victory in the war, the population of France is less to-day than it was seven years ago."

[5] Order dated 24th October 1922. Wellcome Library. PP/MCS/H/4a:Box72.

[6] Femina Books. (1967). *The Trial of Marie Stopes*. (M. Box, Ed.) London: Femina Books Ltd. Page 239.

[7] *Ibid.*, page 240.

[8] *Ibid.*, page 241-2.

[9] *Ibid.*, page 242.

Chapter 30

Cross-Examination of Dr Halliday Sutherland

Mr Patrick Hastings KC rose for the cross-examination. It was one thing to write a book arguing a point of view, but an entirely different thing to come face-to-face with your accuser and to hear the testimony of the eminent people who supported her.

Up to the trial, argument had been conducted in carefully written legal documents, in the pre-trial exchanges, and in the trial by his barrister, Mr Charles. Now, alone in the witness box, Sutherland faced Stopes' barrister and would be subjected to the intense scrutiny of the Court.

Difficult questions from a hostile barrister causes confusion in the witness. They make mistakes and contradict themselves so that, if they are not actually lying, they might appear to be. Sutherland was aware that his testimony might lose the case, let down his many supporters and throw him into ignominy and financial ruin.

Mr Hastings had been given a list of questions for Sutherland by Stopes' solicitor, Mr Braby, and it indicated where and how he might be trapped into admissions, or to contradict himself. The preamble to the questions read: "I hear from someone who knows him that Sutherland is very highly-strung, nervous, irritable and loses his temper very easily if opposed, and when thoroughly roused completely loses his head and his temper and slashes about. He would, therefore make a very bad witness if subjected to a very long and persistent cross-examination of a hostile nature."[1]

For his part, Sutherland was well prepared for the cross-examination. He had fortified himself by praying to St Thomas More, the Lord Chancellor of England who had been beheaded for adhering to his Catholic faith in defiance of a tyrannical King.

In addition, he had also exposed himself to Hastings' methods of cross-examination, as he explained in a later memoir: "For a week before the trial I was taken to the Law Courts every morning to the court where Sir[2] Patrick was pleading. Sir Patrick did not know me in the witness-box, but I knew him, his inflections of voice, and his methods in cross-examination."[3]

Hastings began by asking Sutherland about the last time he had attended a woman in childbirth − 1907 − to draw attention to his lack of recent practical experience and expertise in the area.

They then discussed the writing of the book *Birth Control*, when he began writing it, and when it was published.

"What sort of a book did you intend it to be?" asked Hastings.

"A popular social book," replied Sutherland. He said he intended it be polemic, controversial, but nonetheless fair.

Hastings turned to Lord Dawson of Penn, whom readers will remember was the King's physician who had addressed the Birmingham Congress of the Anglican Church in October 1921.

Hastings' intent was to show that not only had Sutherland defamed his client with his book, but that he had defamed the head of the medical profession as well.

> Hastings: "I suppose you would agree that amongst the head is the present Lord Dawson?"
> Sutherland: "Undoubtedly."
> Hastings: "You would not think it was fair discussion of the subject to suggest he was lying in what he said, would you; I use the word lying deliberately?"
> Sutherland: "I think it is a perfectly fair thing to point out that Lord Dawson in the particular article to which you refer, had misrepresented."
> Hastings: "Lied. Lord Dawson of Penn had lied?"

Calling any person a liar was a strong insult and, moreover, Dawson was a peer of the realm and the head of the medical profession. In his book, Sutherland had not said that Dawson had lied; "giving a person the lie" was an idiom to point out the falsity of that person's statement, not to call them a liar. Given that the passage had not been read out in Court, the jury were none the wiser. Hastings was creating the impression that Sutherland had tossed out libels like a farmer's muck-spreader, had been lucky to have received only one writ for libel, and needed to be punished for it.

Sutherland said: "May I say this?"

Hastings replied: "I am coming back to it; I shall not forget it."

"Let him answer," said Charles. His intervention was timely and likely reminded Sutherland of his words the previous evening: "… you are not defending yourself… I'm here to defend you."

Sutherland spoke: "Since you have drawn attention to the fact that I have attacked Lord Dawson's views on a particular matter, may I point out that I made no personal attack whatever on Lord Dawson."[4]

Hastings asked Sutherland if his book was a fair discussion of birth control. Lord Chief Justice Hewart intervened to clarify whether "some eminent persons in the medical profession took one side and some took another" to which Hastings replied that he intended "to ask [about] birth control generally".

"Does that mean artificial birth control?" asked Hewart.

"Yes," replied Hastings.

"Would you tell me this?" asked Sutherland.

"Birth Control" was a broad term and its meaning would depend upon the context in which it was discussed. It could include many things from abstinence from sex, the "safe period" advocated by Sutherland, the contraceptive devices advocated by Stopes (which were, strictly speaking, the prevention of conception), to abortion.

Hastings resumed the cross-examination: "Listen to me for a moment. When you speak of 'birth control,' you realised, did you not, that what I was speaking of, was artificial birth control?"

Sutherland: "If you say artificial control."

Hastings: "Had you any doubt when I was talking about birth control that I referred to artificial birth control; had you the slightest doubt when you asked that question? You knew I was referring to artificial control, did not you?"

Sutherland: "Yes, I know; I have no doubt."

Hastings: "No doubt whatsoever?"

Sutherland: "No."

Hastings: "Your answers to my question were given upon the understanding that the questions related to artificial birth control."

Sutherland: "I really do not know what my answer was."

Sutherland was later to write:

"…that no witness has a chance unless he tells the truth. If his mind is occupied in guarding a lie, he cannot give his full attention to the questions, and will make mistakes about the simplest matters. In all probability most judges can tell instinctively whether a witness is nervous or lying."[5]

This was such a moment and it revealed the pressure he was feeling. Hastings said that he would ask his questions all over again, from the beginning, and he then quoted one of the more offensive parts of Sutherland's text:

"During the decline of the Roman Empire, men gorged themselves with food, took an emetic, vomited, and then sat down to eat again. They satisfied their appetite and frustrated the object for which appetite is intended. The practice of birth control is parallel with this priggishness."

He finished with a question: "That is the sort of birth control with which a large number of eminent men in your profession disagree?"

Hastings' implication was that Sutherland said that the eminent men who disagreed with him were akin to the degenerates of the Roman Empire. Again Charles interrupted to point out Hastings' sleight-of-hand: "You superimpose that they disagreed with that. He never said what the eminent men disagreed with."

When Hastings resumed, he listed the eminent men: Lord Dawson, Sir James Barr, and when he added Sir William Arbuthnot Lane, Sutherland replied: "Very eminent on another subject altogether."

Hastings: "Do you realise you are speaking about eminent doctors? What eminence have you got on the subject of birth control, seeing that since 1907, you have had no gynaecological experience?"

Sutherland replied: "I do not claim to have; all I claim to do is to have studied the question and written a book."

In cross-examination, a great deal of pressure is placed on the witness and it is difficult for them to think clearly. Sutherland's last answer, however, indicated that, if he had been flustered before, he was not now.

Sutherland said: "All I want to say, if you will allow me to do so is, you are making it appear as if, because a doctor is distinguished in one subject, he is distinguished in others, and it does not follow, therefore, that everything he says is to be accepted on birth control."

Hastings denied the assertion: "I am not suggesting that for a moment and, if it had not been for the interruption, we should not have had any trouble." He asked Sutherland to confirm that he was "trying to give fair discussion of a subject which you agree is one of great importance, birth control — you agree it is of great importance, either way."

"I do; the birth rate last year was the lowest in the history of England," Sutherland replied.

Hastings asked if this justified making "a violent attack on the Protestant Church in order to arrive at that?" Sutherland said that he did not think that he had made a violent attack on the Protestant Church. Hastings read two sentences from page 127 of *Birth Control*: "Birth control condemned by Protestant Churches. The Protestants at the time of the Reformation, retained and even exaggerated certain beliefs of the undivided Catholic Church."

He added: "I need not read any more of that paragraph unless you wish me to go to the bottom." Sutherland replied: "I would rather you read the whole paragraph."

"Yes, certainly," said Charles, needling Hastings who replied: "You need not make any unnecessary observations. I told the witness if he wanted it read, I would read it."

"I think it would be better if you did," said Mr Charles.

Hastings, perhaps stung by Charles' implication that he was being unfair, made a more generous offer: "If, in reading your book, I omit anything, any passage that you want read, please tell me and I will read it at once."

Hastings began to read passages from *Birth Control* which put Sutherland's words into context and revealed the statistics used to support his arguments.

Sutherland had time to compose himself and his answers included uncontroversial responses including: "Thank you"; "Will you please continue to read"; "I do, if you please" (in answer to "Do you want me to read on?"); "Will you please read on," and "Thank you".

For his part, Hastings' questions framed *Birth Control* as a sectarian attack: "Do not you think that was likely to cause grievous offence to members of the Protestant Church?" and "What was the reason of putting in this matter of birth control, this, which I suggest is a violent attack upon people who believe in the Protestant faith and are not Catholics."[6]

This sectarian appeal was made to what was likely to be a majority Protestant jury, and Hastings' aim was to stir up Protestant indignation against Dr Sutherland.

The Lord Chief Justice thought that Hastings had gone too far, and said: "It is well I should point out to you now, as I shall have to point out, it is very clear, to the jury later on, that the likes and dislikes about Protestantism and Roman Catholicism are not relevant to any issue in this case. Nothing could be more unfortunate than that, even indirectly, it should be suggested to the jury that Protestant and Catholic likes and dislikes are to influence their judgement in the smallest degree; nothing could be more unfortunate."[7]

Hastings implied that the fault was with Sutherland's book rather than his descriptions of its effects. "I propose, unless your Lordship rules that it is inadmissible, to go through this book with a view of showing that this gentleman's views are violent in every direction."

"Very well," replied the Lord Chief Justice, "you take what course you think fit. It may be my duty from time to time to state to the jury what is relevant and what is not."

Hastings returned to Lord Dawson, repeating that he was a very eminent physician. He asked questions relating to Dawson's statement in favour of birth control at the Lambeth Conference.

Hastings asked Sutherland if he thought that Dawson was being honest in his view. Sutherland said he was. Then passages from *Birth Control* were read out to show that Sutherland had intended "to attribute dishonesty to Lord Dawson".

Sutherland denied that he had sought to show that Lord Dawson was dishonest, adding "that things a hundred times stronger are said every afternoon in the House of Commons."[8]

"That is what we are complaining of you in this action," replied Hastings. They discussed the availability of information about contraceptives, and Hastings challenged his view that: "no person ought ever to have the means of knowing of such things as contraceptives except through a doctor."

Sutherland said: "That is the official opinion of the British Medical Association," and added that it was one with which he agreed.

Next Hastings led Sutherland through the ready availability of contraceptives and their use by members of the public for many years. If contraceptives were dangerous should the public not have it pointed out to them which ones were dangerous and which ones were safe? Sutherland agreed. Hastings told him to leave aside the question of him being a doctor for a moment.

> Hastings: "Do you see any objection to that information being spread amongst people provided it is accurate?"
> Sutherland: "Yes I do,"
> Hastings: "What is your objection to it?"
> Sutherland: "Well, I thought I had already given my objection; it is this: I say that the indiscriminate broadcasting of information on contraceptives throughout the country will undoubtedly lead to a decline of public morality."

Changing tack, Hastings drew from Sutherland that he did not know of a woman who had used contraceptives, nor one whom had been injured by contraceptives. Sutherland agreed that there was "a number" of lives (although he declined Hastings' suggestion that it was a large number) in which husband and wife were estranged "on the subject of intercourse", such as, for instance, if "a woman says she does not feel able to have any more children."[9]

When Hastings suggested that the only thing the woman could do would be to keep her husband away from her, Sutherland disagreed, suggesting they could use the "safe period".

"Would you have any objection to every married woman knowing that?" asked Hastings.

"I would not," replied Sutherland.

Hastings asked if he would have "any objection to a book being circulated telling her in the plainest, simplest, most straightforward language?"

"No."

Ignorance on sexual issues was discussed, as well as the proper way in which to educate children on such matters. Sutherland said that children should be informed individually, not in groups, and that they should be instructed at the age of puberty. In relation to his own children, Sutherland said: "First of all, they should be allowed to see a hen hatching eggs, after that they can keep rabbits. I think before anything else was done, that gets the idea into the minds of children what sex is; after that the mother can tell them."[10]

The questions led into why Sutherland could have any possible objection to *Married Love*. "Do you think that Dr Stopes is dealing with [the subject of sex] very simply and straightforwardly?" asked Hastings.

Sutherland replied: "I think in her writings on the subject of sex, she was most unfortunate, and she was unfortunate for this reason, that her writings contained a mixture of physiology and emotion, and I say if you are going to write of sex at all, there are only two ways in the world it can be decently written about: one is the cold language of physiology and by cold language, I mean language that contains no emotional adjectives; the only other way in which you can deal with sex is the way the greatest poets have dealt with it, such as Shakespeare, but for an ordinary person to write on sex, I think they should use the cold language of physiology."[11]

He continued: "I think the good in *Married Love* — the good idea in the book — is absolutely spoilt by the details which follow. The good idea in *Married Love* is this, that a man should not be selfish, that he should woo his wife after marriage, as much as before, and should be considerate of his wife's feelings. I say this is a good idea — it is not a new idea."[12]

Hastings quoted the preface of Father Stanislaus St John from one of the earlier editions of *Married Love* which praised it: "as a piece of thoughtful scientific writing, I find it admirable throughout, and it seems to me that your theme could not have been treated in more beautiful or more delicate language, or with a truer ring of sympathy for those who, through ignorance or want of thought, make shipwreck of their married happiness."[13]

Hastings sought to get Sutherland's agreement that ignorance would lead people to make shipwreck of their married happiness. He asked: "Do you think this book is a piece of thoughtful writing, *Married Love*?"

"Would you mind telling me what you mean by thoughtful?" Sutherland asked. "I am going to say straight away I believe the book was written with the best intentions in the world; I am sure of that." In saying this, Sutherland indicated that he did not view the activities of those who disagreed with him as entirely without merit.

Hastings tried again: "Would you mind telling me what harm you think that book could do to any living soul who wanted to be benefited by it?"

"I say that book has indiscriminately distributed throughout the country an unnecessary knowledge of sex, including many rather unpleasant things, and also the other book [*Wise Parenthood*], a knowledge of contraceptives; and I say these things are utterly unnecessary to the purpose of a book; they should give a simple account of sex and possibly touch on some of the other things," Sutherland replied.

"Is that really what you mean?"[14] said Hastings "... your complaint of *Married Love* is that it has given unnecessary knowledge of these matters to people throughout England?"

Charles interrupted to point out that Sutherland had said more than that, and the witness was given an opportunity to clarify what he had said: "I say the book is extremely unfortunate, because it is a mixture of physiology and emotion, which, frankly, is nauseating."

In supplementary questions, Sutherland said that Father St John had "made a very serious mistake of judgement" in allowing his letter to be published at the front of the book.[15]

Hastings moved to Bradlaugh's tract. He read from *Birth Control*: "Charles Bradlaugh was condemned to jail for a less serious crime."[16] This was a key moment in the trial, because the reference to the crime of Bradlaugh had been one of the stings of the libel.

Hastings: "Did you mean, first of all, to impute to Dr Stopes that she had committed a crime?"

Sutherland: "I said she had committed a more serious crime than Charles Bradlaugh, who was sentenced to jail."

Hastings: "Did you mean she had committed a crime?"

Sutherland: "In my judgement, yes."

Hastings: "What crime had she committed?"

Sutherland: "Two, because it was the two things that made me say what I did say."

Hastings: "Tell me what they are?"

Sutherland: "I say that Charles Bradlaugh was sentenced to jail for a less serious crime."

Hastings: "What crime has this lady committed?"

Sutherland: "May I just tell you. Charles Bradlaugh, I knew, was sentenced to a term of imprisonment for having indiscriminately distributed information on contraceptives in a pamphlet. This lady has not only indiscriminately distributed the same information, but she has also started a clinic where special instruction in these methods are given. I say this is a more serious thing than Charles Bradlaugh did."[17]

In his reply, Sutherland had stated the case for Justification. Further, he had corrected the heuristic error that he had said that Stopes should be imprisoned. He replaced it with two statements: firstly, that he thought she had committed a crime and, secondly, that Charles Bradlaugh had been imprisoned for a lesser crime. Hastings' next questions ostensibly aimed at clarifying what Sutherland had said.

> Hastings: "Then, may I take it that describes the crime which you intended to impute to this lady?"
> Sutherland: "Yes."
> Hastings: "Do you agree, then, in my summing it up in this way, that she had spread knowledge about contraceptives and also started a clinic?"
> Sutherland: "Yes."
> Hastings: "Was there any other crime that she had committed except that?"
> Sutherland: "Do you mean in my mind at the time?"
> Hastings: "Yes."
> Sutherland: "No."
> Hastings: "That was the crime that you meant to impute to her, that she distributed knowledge of contraceptives and started a clinic?"
> Sutherland: "Yes."

When a barrister summarises information it may be to clarify it, or to emphasise a point so that the jury would remember it. Again, Hastings had not summarised what Sutherland had said, and the Lord Chief Justice said: "He put in, Mr. Patrick Hastings, the word upon which he has laid stress again and again, the word 'indiscriminately'."

Hastings said that it had been inadvertent: "Yes, I did not mean to eliminate that from my question – indiscriminately – I did not mean to leave the word out."

"No," Sutherland said.

"I hope you will not think that I am endeavouring to paraphrase any of your answers, or that I am trying to trick you or, indeed, say something that you did not say?" Hastings replied.

"May I say, Mr Hastings, I think you have been most fair to me," said Sutherland.

When Hastings had asked Sutherland about Stopes' crime, it would appear he had anticipated that it would relate to criminal obscenity, because he now asked Sutherland about the mention of aphrodisiacs in the Bradlaugh tract.

There was a small delay while the Bradlaugh tract was passed to Sutherland, and he read the passages marked by Mr Hastings which related to aphrodisiacs. Then Hastings asked: "Does it seem to you that those passages are advocating the use of aphrodisiacs?"

Sutherland: "Yes, certainly."
Hastings: "You have read all Dr Stopes' pamphlets?"
Sutherland: "Yes."
Hastings: "Am I right in saying that you can nowhere find any such reference or suggestion as that?"
Sutherland: "To a mechanical aphrodisiac or a chemical one?"
Hastings: "I am speaking of the mechanical aphrodisiac?"
Sutherland: "No."

Hastings turned to the subject of Stopes' qualifications. Sutherland agreed that the number of qualifications was large and that the lady must be exceptionally distinguished.

"Do you agree with me that there is nothing practically nothing which, to the mind of the public, could be so injurious as to describe a person as a German Philosopher, or a Doctor of German Philosophy?" said Hastings.

Sutherland did not agree, saying he had drawn attention to "her highest academic distinction". While he was not able to answer why he had not called her a Fellow of the Royal College of Literature, he did explain that he did not refer to her as a Doctor of Science, London, because: "... it was intended, in the first place, to make it perfectly clear to the readers of my book that she was not a Doctor of Medicine and, moreover, she had no scientific qualifications to enable her to teach this subject."

Hastings asked: "Was it not deliberately intended as far as possible to make people think that she was nothing but a German charlatan?"

"No," Sutherland replied.[18]

Hastings then turned to the differences between Stopes and the Malthusians – after all, the full title of Sutherland's book was *Birth Control: A Statement of Christian Doctrine Against the Neo-Malthusians.*

Hastings: "Have you dealt with the differences between the Malthusian doctrines and this lady's doctrines; have you studied the difference between this lady's views and Malthusian views?"

Sutherland: "I know, roughly, what the differences are."

Hastings: "There is very great distinction between them?"

Sutherland: "Yes."

Hastings: "You know she does not advocate the limitation of birth in the sense of restricting the population?"

Sutherland: "She wishes to restrict the population amongst the poor."

Hastings: "She wants to get healthy children at the best times; you know that?"[19]

Sutherland: "Yes, but you cannot do it, of course, that is the matter."

Hastings: "Now about exposing the poor to experiments, were you, in that, aiming at the Clinic? You see, we have got the words here…"

Hastings quoted the words of the libel in *Birth Control* and asked: "Do you mean by that, the experiments upon these poor victims took place at the clinic?"[20]

"No," replied Sutherland, "the first part of it is a general thing; I did not mean experiments, if you mean by experiments, a surgical experiment."

They discussed the passage in which he had said: "In the midst of a London slum, a woman has opened a birth control clinic".

Hastings: "Why did you say, instead of a woman in the midst of a London slum, a woman who is a Doctor of German Philosophy; why did you not say something to show that she was a lady of very great distinction, but not a doctor?"

Sutherland: "I do not know. I take it that what was in my mind was this, in a very short phrase, to convey certain impressions, and I told you what the impressions I wanted to convey were: (1) That she was not a doctor; (2) That she had no scientific qualification to be teaching this topic; (3) I thought the whole philosophy of the movement was analogous to the philosophy of materialism associated with Germany."[21]

Next, they discussed "this monstrous campaign" which, Sutherland said, did not specifically refer to Stopes' books, nor her clinic, but to the whole campaign for birth control.

Hastings: "Do you suggest that at this Clinic any experiments are made upon the poor?"
Sutherland: "I say that at this Clinic, poor working-class women to the number we have heard, 1,700, are being fitted out with a contraceptive described by Professor McIlroy as 'the most harmful method of which I have had experience.'"
Hastings: "You were in Court and I suppose you heard Dr McIlroy say, if I remember rightly, that she had never herself had a case of a woman who had been injured by the use of one of these pessaries; did you hear her say so?"
Sutherland: "Yes, but I heard her say more, too."
Hastings: "Of course you heard her say more, too, but did not you hear her say that?"
Sutherland: "Yes."
Hastings: "Do you suggest that there is any other experiment at this Clinic, except fitting women with this pessary?"
Sutherland: "Yes, I say that the whole thing is an experiment."
Hastings: "What is there done, or what do you suggest is done, at the Clinic, other than that?"
Sutherland: "The distribution of this knowledge and these contraceptives among the poor is an attempt to redistribute the birth rate. I say that is a social experiment, and I think it is a harmful one."

A few further questions, confirming the books that Sutherland had read before he wrote his article — *Married Love* and *Wise Parenthood* — Hastings concluded his cross-examination.

♦   ♦   ♦

Mr Charles stood up to re-examine Sutherland.

Charles referred to the "long cross-examination concerning what you have said about a distinguished gentleman, Lord Dawson."

> Charles: "Has he ever made a complaint to you about what you wrote in the book?"
> Sutherland: "He has made no complaint whatsoever. As public attention has been drawn to my attack on Lord Dawson's views, I should like to say that I do not know whether Lord Dawson has read my book, but I am perfectly certain if he has read my attack on his views, he would accept it as a sportsman."

In further discussion, Sutherland opined that Lord Dawson, like himself disapproved of the indiscriminate broadcasting of information about contraceptives.

With that, Charles sat down and Dr Halliday Sutherland left the witness box. He described the moment in a later memoir:

> "The well of the court was crowded with barristers, and as I went back to my seat beside Sir Charles Russell, some of them congratulated me. As I sat down Sir Charles squeezed my hand and whispered: 'Excellent'."[22]

---

[1] "Dr Sutherland" undated briefing to legal counsel, presumably written by Dr Stopes. Undated. Wellcome Library. PP/MCS/H/4a:Box72. Stopes and Sutherland had not met before the trial and it is not known how she came to form this view. The name of the source was not disclosed, but there were many possible sources for this information. For instance, Dr Norman Haire knew Stopes and rented consulting rooms from Sutherland. Further, Dr Charles Porter — Medical Officer for Health of St Marylebone — was a member of the National Birth Rate Commission with Stopes and was on the Executive Committee of the St Marylebone Dispensary for the Prevention of Consumption which employed Sutherland as Medical Officer in 1911. The note is not to suggest that these two gentlemen were likely sources so much as to point out that it was the proverbial "small world".

[2] As mentioned, at the time of the trial "Sir" Patrick Hastings K.C. was still "Mr". Sutherland's memoirs were published in 1934, after Hastings had been received a knighthood.

[3] Sutherland, H. (1934). *A Time to Keep*. Geoffrey Bles. Page 253.

[4] Femina Books. (1967). *The Trial of Marie Stopes*. (M. Box, Ed.) London: Femina Books Ltd. Page 244.

[5] Sutherland, H. (1934). *A Time to Keep*. Geoffrey Bles. Page 253.

[6] Femina Books. (1967). *The Trial of Marie Stopes*. (M. Box, Ed.) London: Femina Books Ltd. Page 248.

[7] *Ibid.*, page 249.

[8] *Ibid.*, page 251.

[9] *Ibid.*, page 256.

[10] *Ibid.*, pages 257-8.

[11] *Ibid.*, page 259.

[12] *Ibid.*

[13] *Ibid.*, page 260.

[14] *Ibid.*, page 261.

[15] *Ibid.*

[16] *Ibid.*, page 262.

[17] *Ibid.*

[18] *Ibid.*, page 267.

[19] *Ibid.*, page 264.

[20] *Ibid.*, page 265.

[21] *Ibid.*, page 266.

[22] *Ibid.*

Chapter 31

Testimony of Dr Arthur Giles[D]

Sutherland was followed by Dr Arthur Giles, Senior Surgeon at the Chelsea Hospital for Women, Consulting Gynaecologist to the Prince of Wales General Hospital at Tottenham, the Sutton Hospital and the Passmore Edwards Hospital, Wood Green. His books included *Diseases in Woman* and *Sterility in Women* and he had published the results of 1,000 abdominal operations.

Giles was examined by Mr Rabagliati, one of the friends with whom Sutherland had met when he received the writ, who was now acting as his barrister. He began by reading from page 12 of Stopes' *A Letter to Working Mothers* which instructed women how to fit the cervical cap themselves.

> Rabagliati: "In your opinion, Dr Giles, if those instructions were carried out, would there be any danger to the woman who carried them out?"
> Giles: "If it were done effectually there might or might not be danger, according to the condition of the woman at the time."
> Rabagliati: "Would you explain that a little further?"
> Giles: "If there was any unhealthiness in the woman leading to unhealthy secretions, the covering for any time, say a day or two, by such an implement would tend to cause the secretions, instead of finding their natural outlet, to be drawn back into the system, and there is a harm great inflammation might result."[1]

Giles said it would be "most unwise" to keep the pessary in position for seven days.[2] Asked if a nurse or midwife was capable of saying whether a woman ought to use a check pessary or not, Giles answered: "Certainly not" and he could think of "several" diseases that a woman might have, that could not be detected by a midwife in making an examination.[3]

Giles was passed an instrument which he identified as "the Gold Pin, sometimes known as the wishbone pessary." When Rabagliati asked Giles to "explain exactly what the action of that implement is," the Lord Chief Justice interrupted: "Has that not been sufficiently done?"

"If your Lordship thinks so," replied Rabagliati and he continued with his examination.

Rabagliati asked if the Gold Pin was a contraceptive. Giles replied it was not and said that it was advertised as favouring conception. Left in, however, "a miscarriage would be the almost certain result."[4]

> Rabagliati: "Do you think that, apart from the question of abortion, it is safe for a woman from the point of view of her own health, to wear that pin for any length of time?"
>
> Giles: "No, I think it is dangerous."
>
> Rabagliati: "What special dangers do you think of?"
>
> Giles: "May I say that this type of thing is by no means new; a form of instrument like this has been in use for certainly 20 or 30 years, and has been used occasionally for other purposes, to check pain with menstruation, and the effect of leaving such a pin in the womb is to favour inflammation spreading from the vagina right up to the tubes. I have seen one case in which it was used for an innocent purpose like that, and the patient got a very violent attack of inflammation with abscesses internally, and that was in a very serious condition."

◆   ◆   ◆

Mr Hastings rose to cross-examine Giles. He asked about the difficulty of anyone who was not a doctor in using the Gold Pin. Giles answered that it would be very difficult.

Hastings: "For practical purposes impossible?"
Giles: "It is difficult to say anything is impossible, but I should have thought very difficult."

The cross-examination led to a discussion of the difference between fertilisation and conception. Giles said he regarded them as identical: "conception consists in the union of the two elements."

Hastings said: "I see, but there are two stages, there is the fertilisation of the ovum, then a loose substance, and it subsequently become[sic] adherent, does it not, in fact, become the child till it has become adherent, does it?"

It begins to develop almost from the moment of fertilisation," replied Giles.

Hastings then wrapped up with a question as to how long the check pessary had been in use and suggested 50 or 60 years.

Giles: "That may be; I have no knowledge as to how long"
Hastings: "For a very long time?"
Giles: "Possibly."
Hastings: "And bought at all sorts of shops, chemists and so on?"
Giles: "Probably."
Hastings: "Somebody must have put them in?"
Giles: "Yes."

Hastings sat down and the Lord Chief Justice addressed Giles: "You know do you not, from Criminal Courts and otherwise, that there are a great many women in this country who practice abortion professionally?"

Giles: "Yes."
Hewart: "And in the course of that traffic they acquire very considerable skill in dealing with the particular parts of a woman?"
Giles: "Yes."
Hewart: "They procure abortion, for example, with instruments?"
Giles: "Yes."

Hewart: "With sounds and the like?"

Giles: "Yes."

Hewart: "Do you think a woman of that kind would have any difficulty in inserting a Gold Pin?"

Giles: "She might. Many of these women, although they are supposed to be practised at that kind of thing, are likely to do great damage by the insertion of these instruments; they perforate the womb."

Hewart: "Do you suppose that a skilled female abortionist could not insert the Gold Pin?"

Giles: "I should think she could."[5]

---

[1] Femina Books. (1967). *The Trial of Marie Stopes*. (M. Box, Ed.) London: Femina Books Ltd. Page 270.

[2] *Ibid.*, page 271.

[3] *Ibid.*

[4] *Ibid.*, page 272.

[5] *Ibid.*, page 273.

Chapter 32

Testimony of Dr Frederick McCann[D]

The next witness was Dr Frederick McCann, an expert in gynaecological medicine who was vastly experienced in dealing with women's diseases, including almost 30 years at the Samaritan Free Hospital for Women (where he was surgeon), as well as a large private practice. He was also consulting gynaecologist to the West End Hospital for Nervous Diseases.

Mr Charles began his examination by asking McCann about artificial contraceptives: "I want to ask you generally from your experience, what is the general effect of artificial contraceptives upon women?"

McCann's view was that they were "contrary to the best interests of the woman's health"[1] and were "injurious to health".[2] He said: "It naturally depends upon the sexual feeling of the individual in question, and that, in my opinion, is the reason there is so much difference of opinion. If a woman of the highly sexual type has an interrupted or prevented orgasm, it is only a question of time when she suffers greatly in her general health; on the other hand, if sexual feeling is negative, the direct effect on her general health is proportionately diminished, but there is a local effect through the use of a medical contraceptive or chemical contraceptive."[3]

He thought that the pessary, over time, would cause a general effect and a local effect. Asked to clarify, he said: "Assuming that the pessary was efficacious, and I mean by that properly placed and doing its work, the work for which it is intended, then there is a chronic congestion produced of the womb, which would be evidenced by increased loss at the monthly periods, backache and bearing down pains, and an obscure subtle effect on the general health. Many of these patients feel ill, yet they do not know why they are ill, and unless the matter is gone into often, the real secret of their illness is not discovered, and the longer I practice, the more I am impressed by the serious influence that this is coming to have among patients."

McCann viewed the use of quinine in a pessary as dangerous and that the broadcasting of such methods as "most injurious, and it seems to me would lead to an amount of immorality in this country."[4]

Asked about the Gold Pin, McCann said: "It hinders conception, but it does not stop it. You can readily understand any foreign body in the womb must exert a certain retarding influence, but its chief action is as a stimulant to the womb, causing it to contract and expel any growing ovum which may be found inside; it is really, in medical language, an abortifacient; it is a method for procuring abortion."

Asked if he had had experience of the Gold Pin, McCann produced one and handed it to Charles, saying: "This was 15 months in the cavity of the womb and one of the limbs of the divergent blades has become eroded and detached in the same way as a gold wire connected with your teeth sometimes does. The limb had become embedded in the substance of the womb and caused considerable difficulty in its removal; it was causing a free discharge. Happily, the patient survived after this was taken out, and the womb disinfected, but she was running a very, very considerable risk, not only to her health, but to her life."[5]

◆　　　◆　　　◆

When Hastings rose to cross-examine McCann, he asked: "I rather gather that you take a strong view against the use of contraceptives altogether?"

"I do, except for medical reasons — except for reasons of health," replied McCann, though he agreed with Hastings' suggestion that he personally knew a great many members of his profession who took a strong view on the other side.

Hastings' next questions related to McCann's statement during the examination that the "mere fact of the interrupted or the unsatisfied union of husband and wife causes ill will to the wife."

> Hastings: "When you have one of these cases of which you told us, where the nervous system of the woman becomes affected, what remedy do you suggest?"
> McCann: "That this method of preventing contraception should be stopped."
> Hastings: "You mean to say the use of contraceptives is affecting her nervous system."
> McCann: "Yes, the effect of it."
> Hastings: "I thought you told us — it must be my mistake — that there were cases in which the woman's nervous system was affected and therefore you prescribed contraceptives?"
> McCann: "No."

The Lord Chief Justice clarified McCann's answer: "What the doctor said was that the use of contraceptive devices on the sexual woman, or woman of a highly sexual type through the interruption of the orgasm is serious to her and leads to results."[6]

> Hastings asked: "What do you mean by the interruption of the orgasm?"
> McCann: "If such a pessary is used, the orgasm obviously cannot be so complete as if nature is uninterrupted."
> Hastings: "Do you really mean that? — What do you mean by 'Orgasm'?"
> McCann: "By 'Orgasm' is meant the discharge of fluid on the part of the female from the uterine glands; it is connected with a definite movement on the part of the womb which becomes more erect and goes a little downwards; that discharge of the fluid is prevented if this check pessary fits accurately; the congestion is so that it may be thrown back, and it exerts a permanent influence on the womb in proportion to the time and number of times it is repeated."[7]

It was exchanges of this type that made the Stopes *v* Sutherland libel trial of enormous interest to the press, the public and the prurient alike.

Hastings was either surprised, or he affected surprise: "Did you say then, that in those cases the use of the contraceptive is bad, but in other cases it is not?"

> McCann: "In cases in which the woman's sexual feelings are practically nil, there is obviously no harm; therefore the effect is only one of local infection as the result of putting a dirty thing into the vagina."[8]
> Hastings: "I do not follow…"
> McCann: "There is another very important question — that the womb is prevented from the value of the absorption of the spermatozoa fluid; it is more than a fertilising agent, it exerts an extraordinary and far reaching effect on the female body."[9]

In this view, McCann had similar views to Stopes, though Stopes would argue that her "Prorace" cervical cap did not prevent the absorption of seminal fluid.

> Hastings: "I did not appreciate it the way you put it. Do I take it you never consider it permissible, the use of contraceptives?"
> McCann: "I did not say so."
> Hastings: "I am asking you. Do you say or do you not?"
> McCann: "In certain cases of disease it is essential. Because, of two evils, you must choose the lesser."[10]

McCann said he would advocate contraception in the cases of "advanced tuberculosis", "insanity" and in cases in which conception would be dangerous to the health of the particular woman. Outside of these limited cases, he said, contraception was "a national sin". The sin was against the state, not the church, for as he put it: "Of all the countries in the world, Britain is the last to think of using birth control, when we have so many colonies crying out for population."[11]

Later the questions discussed how effective the check pessary was in preventing conception.

Hastings: "One would imagine that women have found their use effective, otherwise they would not have been employed?"

McCann: "As a matter of fact, in many of those cases, if the patient who successfully prevents, or the woman who successfully prevents pregnancy with such pessaries, would probably have been sterile without them and a woman who is prolific, becomes pregnant in spite of them."

Hastings: "That is a matter of surmise. Do you really mean with all your experience, you think that those who bought these pessaries were effecting no result at all by buying them?"

McCann: "In the majority of instances, certainly."

Hastings asked if all pessaries, bought "in many shops and in considerable quantities a long time ago" were useless.

McCann: "I do not know that this particular type of pessary has been in use a long time, but one somewhat similar."

Hastings: "The same sort of pessary?"

McCann: "Yes."

Hastings: "Have they been useless?"

McCann: "Some of them may have been useless — some useful."

Hastings: "Any useful and effective?"

McCann: "Yes."

Hastings: "Do you suggest the useful pessaries were put in by doctors and the useless ones not?"

McCann: "No, it is a matter of chance. I quite admit a woman may acquire such proficiency; she would be able to introduce this effectively, but I should say that in most women, it is just a piece of chance whether it is effectively placed in the exit of the womb or not."

Hastings turned from the effect on women in general to particular cases, and he asked McCann when he had last seen a woman injured by use of the occlusive pessary. When he replied that he saw these cases "every day", Hastings asked for a particular case: "What was the nature of her injury?"

McCann: "She had a free bleeding at her monthly periods."

Hastings: "And that was caused by an occlusive pessary?"

McCann: "Yes."

Hastings: "When did you see her?"

McCann: "I think it was two months ago."

At this point, Hastings said: "let us leave her for a moment: I shall come back to her".[12]

Pressed for other cases, McCann provided a case of a woman who had had a miscarriage who protested that because she had been to a birth control clinic, she could not have been pregnant. This instance was discarded because McCann could not confirm that the check pessary had been the cause. It was further irrelevant because, when Hastings asked: "Is that a woman whom you have had under your own personal hands?" McCann replied: "No a colleague of mine."

Hastings chided Dr McCann: "Really, doctor, you do realise it may be rather disadvantageous to this lady if you introduce matters of that sort that you have not seen. I purposely asked you for cases you have known. Would you mind restricting yourself to that—under your own personal hand."[13]

In his next question, Hastings said: "Would you mind answering the questions I put to you. Except the one you have mentioned two years ago, have you any others?"

McCann corrected him: "Two months ago."

"Yes, I meant two months ago," replied Hastings. They discussed a private patient who had suffered increased bleeding at her monthly periods.

Hastings: "How are you able to attribute that to the use of this particular pessary?"

McCann: "Because it is a common consequence of interfering with the sexual organism."

Hastings: "You told me you had never seen another case, or had no details of another case, which you were able to attribute to the use of this pessary. How do you mean it is a common cause?"

McCann: "Would you repeat your question?"

Hastings: "I thought you said you were able to attribute this excessive haemorrhage to the use of this particular occlusive pessary?"

McCann: "Yes, I did."

Hastings: "How were you able to attribute it to that?"

McCann: "Because of it causing congestion of the womb."

Hastings: "Did you ask her whether she had ever used any preventatives."

McCann: "I did, yes."

Hastings: "Did she tell you she had or had not?"

McCann: "She told me she had."

Hastings: "What did she say she had been using?"

McCann: "A rubber check pessary."

Hastings: "Anything else — a quinine pessary?"

McCann: "No."

Hastings: "Nothing else?"

McCann: "No."

Hastings: "And you attributed this excessive haemorrhage to that?"

McCann: "I did."

Hastings: "Were you able to give any reason, or can you give us any reason why you attributed that effect to that cause?"

McCann: "Because of the chronic congestion of the womb."

Hastings asked how many patients McCann had seen in the course of the last 12 months. They agreed on "a very large number".

Hastings: "Have you any doubt that many of them have used these occlusive pessaries?"

McCann: "I do not know they have used those occlusive pessaries, but they have used methods to prevent conception, as I said. I did not enquire as to the particular preventatives."

Hastings: "The only case you are able to give is this lady you saw two months ago."

McCann: "Yes."

In the course of the next few questions, Hastings asked about whether certain eminent men were among the large number of doctors whom he knew disagreed with him about contraceptives, but McCann would not be drawn. Then Hastings tried to create a scenario in which McCann would advise the woman to use contraceptives, but again he would not be drawn. In closing Hastings asked who had inserted the Gold Pin which McCann had removed. "Did you find out the name of the doctor who had put it in for her?"

McCann: "I did not enquire."
Hastings: "It was a doctor, no doubt?"
McCann: "I understand so; It was."

Hastings inquired if it was a professional abortionist and whether anyone other than a doctor could insert the Gold Pin. McCann said that anyone who had enough practice could learn how to do it. A professional abortionist, a midwife or a nurse.

Hastings asked: "A person could not do it for herself; ordinary persons without skilled training could not do it for themselves, could they?" Hastings presumably asked this question to ensure the jury did not think a woman had inserted a Gold Pin into herself after reading *Wise Parenthood*.

McCann replied: "It is possible. Women have done extraordinary things; they have introduced..."

Hastings interrupted, perhaps worried as to what might follow: "Still, with a desire to part on the best of possible terms, we know women have done extraordinary things, but you are not suggesting that an ordinary woman could put a Gold Pin into herself?"

McCann: "But women have introduced knitting needles and procured abortion."
Hastings: "I will leave knitting needles."[14]

Hastings sat down and the next witness, Dame Mary Scharlieb, entered the witness box.

---

[1] Femina Books. (1967). *The Trial of Marie Stopes*. (M. Box, Ed.) London: Femina Books Ltd. Page 274.
[2] *Ibid.*, page 275.

[3] *Ibid.*, page 274.
[4] *Ibid.*, page 275.
[5] *Ibid.*, pages 275-6.
[6] *Ibid.*, page 277.
[7] *Ibid.*
[8] *Ibid.*
[9] *Ibid.*
[10] *Ibid.*, page 277.
[11] *Ibid.*, page 278.
[12] *Ibid.*, page 279.
[13] *Ibid.*, page 280.
[14] *Ibid.*, page 283.

Chapter 33

Testimony of Dame Mary Scharlieb[D]

The examination of Dame Mary Scharlieb began with a summary of her qualifications, a Doctor of Medicine and Master of Surgery and a CBE. She was the consulting gynaecologist for the Royal Free Hospital and consulting surgeon for the New Hospital for Women. She was 77 years old.[1]

Scharlieb and Stopes were acquainted through their participation in the National Birth Rate Commission and, in addition, Scharlieb had reviewed the manuscripts of some of Stopes' books.[2]

The examination was carried out by Mr Harold Murphy, a junior barrister representing Dr Sutherland. Scharlieb confirmed that she had read *Wise Parenthood*. She had, in fact, revised the proofs when the book was being produced,[3] and was familiar with the passages in it that related to the check pessary.

Scharlieb thought that the check pessary would damage the health of women because it "would restrain the natural secretions of the part and lead to a mild continuous sepsis if it were retained."[4] She believed it that the device would be deleterious to wives as well as husbands and, if used in the early days of married life, could lead to problems with infertility after they had ceased using it. She went on to say that there were "very few women who would be able to adjust it themselves." She thought that a woman was liable to inflict some injury upon herself when fitting it on her own.

Her view of the Gold Pin was that it was not a bar to conception and that it was likely to cause an early abortion. She added: "…we are told in the book that the pessary, the wishbone pessary, may be retained for months and even for a year. If that so does, and therefore, it is a danger, a real danger. Should a woman have an abortion it is too likely [sic] that it might prove to be a septic abortion."

The examination had been short and to the point, and Hastings began the cross-examination.

◆   ◆   ◆

Hastings' instructions from Braby & Waller on the cross-examination of Scharlieb had said: "In cross-examination of Dr Scharlieb remember she is old, hostile and very muddle-headed [and] could easily be made to contradict herself."[5]

Accordingly, the cross-examination took the form of a memory test. Hastings cited material that Scharlieb had written years before and quoted the parts that seemed at odds with what she was saying now.

He asked if Stopes had done useful work by publishing her views. Scharlieb replied that Stopes had "not done any useful work by publishing these books," but she thought that she was sincere in her views. When asked which book she objected to, Scharlieb said it was all of them.

> Hastings: "You don't agree then that it really is imperative that people should be enlightened on these matters."
> Scharlieb: "No; a certain amount of enlightenment, I think, is essential, but not conveyed in that manner."[6]

Hastings raised Scharlieb's revision of the manuscript for *Wise Parenthood*, written five years before. Had she expressed: "the slightest opinion against the wisdom of publishing that book of which you corrected the proof?"[7]

Lord Hewart asked Scharlieb what she had done, and she told the Court she had written to the publisher, Putnam's, saying that she could not agree with the views expressed in the book. She "differed from the author entirely in this matter" and that the author's work had been honest, but mistaken.

Hastings produced two letters, including a copy of Scharlieb's six-page letter to Putnam's, and began to question her about them. Had she really thought, when she had been reading the proofs and making suggestions, that "Dr Stopes was doing a wicked act in publishing this book?"

"I thought that it was very indiscreet; I thought it was more calculated to do harm than good," Scharlieb replied.

He quoted her as having said: "As to the enlightenment of the public in sexual matters, that is imperative: people are destroyed for want of knowledge."

This question revealed the trap that had been laid in the last question because, had Scharlieb said that Stopes writing the book had been a wicked act, she would appear to be contradicting herself. She said to Hastings: "No sir, I did not mean that, because in my view, the enlightenment of the public should be undertaken in perfectly simple and non-provocative-language; it should not be emotional and should make no appeal to passions."

Charles asked to see the letter.

"You shall see it," replied Hastings, but he did not hand it over.

Hastings said that she had allowed her name to appear in the foreword. Scharlieb said she had disagreed with Stopes, and that Stopes had acknowledged this disagreement in her foreword to *Wise Parenthood* when she said that Scharlieb (and another) "have also very kindly read the proofs, and I have benefited by their suggestions, although we disagree on fundamental principles".[8]

Hastings quoted Scharlieb as having said that *Wise Parenthood* had offended her less than the style of *Married Love*, "but the thing that offends me is the purely materialistic view…"

"What is that?" he asked.

"Looking upon married relations simply from the material and carnal point of view and not seeing the spiritual side of it at all," Scharlieb replied.

"I am glad that you mentioned that; I am coming to that in a moment. 'It is pure hedonism.' What do you mean by that?" asked Hastings.

"Pleasure," Scharlieb replied.

Hastings handed the letters to Charles and asked about the harm that would occur to married people if they were to abstain from their ordinary relations. Scharlieb said she did not think that it would be harmful to abstain for some time.

Hastings quoted a published interview — *The Declining Birth Rate* — in which Scharlieb had said: "I think that as long as a man is single or as long as a woman is single, not the slightest harm is done by continence. On the contrary it is a perfectly right state, and in my opinion no harm is done in such cases. But directly a couple are living together in the intimacy of marriage, abstension appears to have a very deleterious effect."

But Scharlieb's recollection was sharp, particularly for someone supposedly so "old" and "very muddle-headed": "I do not think that that is the whole of the passage, is it?" she said.

Hastings handed her the book and asked her if she could see anything better, and he continued reading extracts from the book. He repeated a question that had been asked in the interview:

"'Have you come across many cases in your practice in which women have apparently become nervous wrecks from this cause?'" She replied: "That was from the use of douches, pessaries and mechanical contrivances."

Hastings quoted a passage which linked: "'hysteria at forty or fifty years with abstention at an earlier period of life',," adding: "I think that makes it quite plain?"

Scharlieb was having none of it. She pointed out that he should go further on in the book to where she had specified that "'The couple should abstain for a few months.' There is no harm whatever in that; it is the prolonged abstention extending over many years that does harm; but that has nothing to do with Dr Stopes' methods."

She agreed with Hastings' suggestion that marital relations were of great importance, that women were made miserable by excessive childbirth, but said that contraceptives would lead to the husband making excessive demands on his wife.

Scharlieb confirmed that she had read *Married Love* and described it as a "dangerous book — dangerous not only to married people, for whom it is intended, but dangerous also for others for whom it is not intended, but into whose hands it must necessarily fall." She said that the danger was that it was "calculated to rouse passion and to lead people to hold wrong views as to the purpose of the married state. I think it is extremely likely to make people look only to the pleasures and comforts of married life and to neglect its duties."[9]

She repeated this view and added that the book was "written in an exceedingly emotional and sentimental manner" which was "liable to cause passion and desire in the hearts of people who ought not to have those passions and desires."

Hastings sat down.

◆　　◆　　◆

Charles stood to re-examine Scharlieb on matters arising from the cross-examination. His first question suggested her letter to Putnam's was a criticism of the check pessary, "in almost the same words you have used today, as to the danger of it." Scharlieb agreed.[10]

He quoted the other letter stating that the thing that also grieved Scharlieb was the "purely materialistic view throughout." Again, she agreed.

Scharlieb left the witness box. Her testimony had been clear and she had demonstrated a good recall of the things she had written.

---

[1] British Medical Journal. (1930, November 29). *Obituary of Dame Mary Scharlieb*. British Medical Journal, 935-937. Retrieved January 29, 2019, from https://www.ncbi.nlm.nih.gov/pmc/articles/PMC2451802/?page=1.

[2] National Birth Rate Commission. (1920). *Problems of Population and Parenthood. Being the Second Report of and the chief evidence taken by the National Birth-rate Commission, 1918-1920*. London: Chapman and Hall, Ltd. Page viii. Retrieved January 28, 2019, from https://archive.org/details/problemsofpopula00natiuoft/page/n8.

[3] Femina Books. (1967). *The Trial of Marie Stopes*. (M. Box, Ed.) London: Femina Books Ltd. Page 285.

[4] *Ibid.*, page 284.

[5] "Dr Mary Scharlieb" undated briefing to legal counsel. Undated. Wellcome Library. PP/MCS/H/4a:Box72.

[6] Femina Books. (1967). *The Trial of Marie Stopes*. (M. Box, Ed.) London: Femina Books Ltd. Page 285.

[7] *Ibid.*

[8] *Ibid.*, page 287.

[9] *Ibid.*, page 290.

[10] *Ibid.*

Chapter 34

Intermission

At this point, the reader is perhaps overwhelmed trying to keep track of the case, amidst all of the minutiae of the examinations, cross-examinations and re-examinations. If you consider the twelve men of the jury, it is not far-fetched to imagine that they felt the same way.

Over the trial, the number of witnesses giving testimony each day had increased: one on the first day, three on the second and six on the third. On this, the fourth day, Scharlieb was the fifth witness of the eight scheduled to appear.

By now Mr Hastings' opening speech was perhaps a distant memory, and the jury were fairly taxed to keep track of the threads that had been introduced into the trial. The trial was appeared as an amorphous mass of information which they would somehow would use to decide the case. The barristers for both sides would use their powers of persuasion to get them to see it in a way that was favourable to their client.

For instance, had Sutherland accused Stopes of performing human experiments, or merely that she was engaging in a social experiment?

Had Sutherland said that she should be jailed, or had he merely opined that Bradlaugh had been imprisoned for a less serious crime?

Were the changes in Stopes' books simply clarifications of earlier statements? Or were they the inclusion of new facts that had come to light as her "experiment" unfolded? Were Stopes' books wholesome sources of knowledge for young people, that they might otherwise learn from disreputable sources, or would the juxtaposition of technical facts and emotive descriptions lead them astray?

Barr's testimony on the first day had been undermined when gaps in his knowledge were revealed. Stopes' unnecessary appearance in the witness box on the second day had undermined Hastings' opening speech. The third day had brought troubling admissions from Dr Young, and the testimony of Dr Jones — the last witness before Mr Charles' opening speech — was disastrous. Sutherland's first witness, Professor McIlroy, had validated the words that Sutherland had written in *Birth Control* and was a credible medical expert in the area that Stopes claimed as her own.

Today they had heard Roberts — a man who had held high office — take a politician's approach to answering questions by not answering them. While Charles was able to remind the Court of the recommendation of the Gold Pin in *Wise Parenthood*, Sullivan had failed to get Roberts to admit that *Married Love* had the qualities of an indecent book or a racy romance novel. The next witness, the defendant Sutherland, had given a good account of what he had meant when he wrote *Birth Control*.

Next Giles and McCann — experienced doctors who worked in the area of medicine under examination — had given testimony that was damaging to the Plaintiff. Giles had produced a corroded Gold Pin in Court which, he said, had threatened the life of the user, and McCann had questioned the efficacy of the check pessary as a contraceptive device.

Then Scharlieb had appeared. She had sat on the National Birth Rate Commission with Stopes and had revised proofs for *Wise Parenthood*. She had said that the Gold Pin was a dangerous instrument, and thought that the use of contraceptives in the early years of marriage was detrimental to later fertility.

The use of the Gold Pin to procure an abortion, or the exhibition of a corroded device might have shocked the Court, but the astute juror would detach his reaction to those incidents and consider whether this had anything to do with Stopes. They would have to remember that the issue at hand was whether Sutherland had been entitled to criticise her work in the way that he had, and whether he could support his defence of Justification.

Then there were the appeals to sectarian subtexts, such as Catholics criticising the established Protestant church which, while not ostensibly part of the trial, was central to the plaintiff's efforts to influence the jury against the co-defendants.

The following day, the jury would be asked for their decision, but for now, still on the fourth day, they were to hear the testimony of Dr Norman Haire.

Chapter 35

Testimony of Dr Norman Haire[S]

D r Norman Haire was unlike other witnesses in the trial in that he was aligned neither to the plaintiff, nor to the defendant. He attended under subpoena, in other words, his presence in the witness box was compelled by law.

While in this sense Haire was a neutral witness, the subpoena had been served by the defence and they would not have done this unless it was advantageous to their case.

Like Stopes, Haire was a birth-controller, an admirer of her work and he had visited the Mothers' Clinic.[1] He had set up the Walworth Women's Welfare Centre for the Malthusian League which, when it opened in November 1921, was Britain's second birth-control clinic. Like her, he advocated compulsory sterilisation,[2] though he went further to advocate infanticide "on those who at birth are obviously below a (variable) minimum standard."[3]

Like Sutherland, he was a medical doctor and they had been landlord and tenant as well.

Haire was examined by Mr. Rabagliati, a junior barrister for the defence. Haire was a Master of Surgery and Bachelor of Medicine at the University of Sydney, and was currently an obstetric and gynaecological surgeon practicing at 90 Harley Street.

He had established a birth control clinic in Walworth in late 1921 on behalf of the Malthusian League.[4] The Walworth Clinic offered advice in each case by a doctor, and a later answer from Haire revealed that he did not think that a midwife would be competent to make an examination of a woman to see if she was "a proper subject for the fitting of a check pessary".[5]

Questioned about the Malthusian League's *Hygienic Methods of Family Limitation*, Haire answered that the pamphlet would be provided only after the receipt of a signed declaration that the applicant was over 21 and was, or was about to be, married. This contrasted with the "indiscriminate" dissemination of contraceptive information published by Stopes.

The examination established that Haire had visited the Mothers' Clinic in February 1921 and that the Gold Pin had been discussed. Haire said that Stopes had asked him if he would be willing to fit it to patients sent to him for that purpose. While he had agreed, he later learned that the Pin was a dangerous method.

At this point, Hastings intervened: "This is just a little bit inconvenient, because it would have helped if these matters had been put to the plaintiff." It seemed a fair point: the plaintiff should be able to see the testimony on which the defence would draw, and vice versa.

Charles replied that it: "… was quite impossible. This gentleman is here upon subpoena; he is not here by way of supporting one side or the other; if I had known of all the letters and the details of it, I should, of course, have put it. I put it as generally as I could to her because I knew, generally, what the effect of his evidence was to be."

The Lord Chief Justice said, no doubt in the interests of fairness: "If Mr Patrick Hastings thinks it right it would, of course, be right that Dr Stopes should come back into the witness box and deal with it."

"That was not what I wanted. I wanted the letters," replied Hastings. He perhaps felt that the reappearance of Stopes in the witness box would do more harm than good.

The examination continued and it was revealed that on 8th June 1921, two women had presented themselves to Haire to be fitted with the Gold Pin. Haire refused to fit the Pin, telling the women that it was unreliable and dangerous. He did not charge either patient.

Readers will recall Stopes' testimony in which she said she had: "… received from unknown correspondents letters asking me to give them the addresses of medical persons and have given, on two or three occasions, the address of a gynaecologist and an obstetrician."[6]

Rabagliati read Stopes' letter to Haire on 5th June 1921 to the Court, and it revealed that her involvement had been more than merely administrative.

> "'I am interested in what you say about the women who are keen on birth control and quite unbiased. Are they themselves speaking from personal knowledge of their own use of it [ie. the Gold Pin], because I hear from American women it is entirely satisfactory. I should therefore, like very much for you, if you do not mind, to take on two or three cases, which you could watch carefully and if these yielded unsatisfactory results, we will drop it. On the other hand, if it does have, as reported, so many advantages, I should be sorry to discard it without proper investigation. I have now on hand two or three people who desire its insertion. May I send these to you definitely? I expect you would rather these were sent to New Cavendish Street than to trouble you to come up to the clinic to meet them. Some time back, relying on your kind offer to do one or two of these cases, in order to study them, I told a woman that there would only be a small charge of, say 5/-s., and Mrs. X.'
> ...... 'these two seem to be suitable cases, that is, women who ought not to have any more children and who have asked themselves to have the spring. In corresponding with these two women, I have stated as follows: 'I would warn you that the method being a new one, we are not yet quite sure whether the result would be entirely satisfactory, but Dr Haire will watch the case carefully and remove the spring if it seems advisable, and recommend some other method."[7]

The letter came as close to an admission of an experiment as the defendants were likely to get. It was very damaging to Stopes' case, for not only did it reveal that she had lied during her testimony, but that her standards of care fell below those expected of a medical doctor. As Germaine Greer wrote in *Sex and Destiny: The Politics of Human Fertility*, it made clear: "... her utter disregard for the rights of others and her total ignorance of a code of ethics which binds those doctors who deal with living human flesh instead of fossil plants."[8]

The examination concluded with Haire's condemnation of the Gold Pin:

"I regard it first of all unreliable as a contraceptive. I understand that it was first introduced to facilitate impregnation in some cases of sterility where the neck of the womb is tightly closed and it is difficult for the woman to become pregnant. This instrument is sometimes used by doctors to keep the neck of the womb open long enough for conception to take place, and it is then removed. That is the first reason I regard it as unreliable as a contraceptive, and, secondly, I think if it is left in after contraception has taken place, it would most probably give rise to abortion; thirdly, it keeps the neck of the womb open and leaves free passage for septic germs to get in from the outside, and may give rise to various diseased conditions; it may give rise to inflammation of the womb, of the ovaries and of the tubes, and even, I believe to peritonitis."[9]

Rabagliati sat down and passed the witness to Hastings.

◆   ◆   ◆

Hastings began by asking Haire when he had met Stopes and asserted more than once that Haire had been canvassing for patients. Canvassing for patients was not permitted by the standards expected of medical doctors and Haire denied this assertion each time.

Haire could not recall if his visit to the clinic arose from his request to Stopes or her inviting him.[10] He said that Stopes' books were "serving a very useful purpose," although he had not read all of them. He had given away "50 or more of her *Letter to Working Mothers*[11] because [he] thought at that time that it was the best thing available." In addition, he thought that her books were excellent and that they served the purpose of giving "knowledge of sex to women who otherwise cannot get it."

Hastings asked if he had any criticism of Stopes' clinic. Haire replied that he had: "… found it out myself that the method of the check pessary is an unsatisfactory one, and that anyway it would be much wiser to have every patient seen by a doctor, rather than by a nurse" adding "that is the only criticism I would pass."

Asked to detail his objection to the check pessary, Haire replied: "Well, first of all, I think it is utterly unreliable. I have notes, careful notes of 29 cases, of which 25 became pregnant in spite of using it, and only four succeeded in avoiding pregnancy. I think it is unreliable."[12]

While it was not a statistically sound sample size, it was a large failure rate.[13] Other criticisms included that women could not fit it on their own. Haire explained that he had recommended this pessary until he had discovered a better method. When he had recommended it, he advised women not to leave it in longer than 24 hours, and that, once out, "women were unable to use it properly; generally they could push it in, but they did not manage to push it in properly, so they became pregnant; so I gave up using it."

Asked if he knew of any harmful result because of the use of the pessary, Haire said that he had seen harm but could not determine that the pessary had been the cause.

Haire was a birth controller, yet here he was in Court affirming McIlroy's statements about the cervical cap and questioning its efficacy.

Hastings asked about the discussion of the Gold Pin between Haire and Stopes — had not Stopes made it clear to Haire that it was only to be used in cases as an alternative to sterilisation?

Haire said he could not remember. He conceded that he "did not make strict enquiries as I should have done before giving consent." He confirmed that the President of the American Birth Control Society told him that "in an audience [at a conference] of nearly 400 medical men, only one spoke in favour of the Gold Pin pessary and that all the others condemned it".

Haire's testimony had been extremely damaging to the Plaintiff's reputation and valuable in advancing the defence of Justification.

---

[1]   Visitors   Book   of   the   Mothers'   Clinic.   Wellcome   Library. PP/MCS/E/10:Box62.

[2] Wyndham, D. (2012). *Norman Haire and the Study of Sex*. Sydney: Sydney University Press. Page 104. Professor Wyndham quotes Haire's statement published in *The Sun* (a Sydney newspaper), "that there was a growing realisation of the need for 'sterilisation of the unfit in the interests of the race' and that soon 'all but the very lowest would practice birth control' and, when this happened, citizens would turn on the reckless breeders and insist on compulsory sterilisation."

[3] Ludovici, A. M. (1925). *Lysistrata or Woman's Future and Future Woman*. London: Kegan Paul, Trench, Trubner & Co., Ltd. Page 7. Retrieved September 30, 2019, from
https://archive.org/stream/lysistrataorwoma00ludouoft#page/6/mode/2up.

[4] Femina Books. (1967). *The Trial of Marie Stopes*. (M. Box, Ed.) London: Femina Books Ltd. Page 291.

[5] *Ibid*.

[6] *Ibid*., page 95.

[7] *Ibid*., page 294.

[8] Greer, G. (1985). *Sex and Destiny: The Politics of Human Fertility*. London: Picador (in association with Martin Secker & Warburg Limited). Page 315.

[9] Femina Books. (1967). *The Trial of Marie Stopes*. (M. Box, Ed.) London: Femina Books Ltd. Page 294.

[10] Stopes' letter to Haire dated 3rd April 1921 would suggest that she had invited him. Letter from Stopes to Haire dated 3rd April 1921. Wellcome Library. PP/MCS/B.12.

[11] Femina Books. (1967). *The Trial of Marie Stopes*. (M. Box, Ed.) London: Femina Books Ltd. Page 296.

[12] *Ibid*., page 297.

[13] The success rate of Stopes' contraceptive devices has since been called into question. Historian Deborah Cohen wrote that in the first official report of the Mothers' Clinic, *The First Five Thousand*, Stopes claimed that only 31 had become pregnant while using the device recommended by the clinic, results that Cohen described as "impossibly spectacular". (Cohen, D. (1993). *Private Lives in Public Spaces: Marie Stopes: the Mothers' Clinics and the Practice of Contraception*. In History Workshop (No.35 Spring 1993). Pages 95-116.) These results were achieved by counting women who did not return to the clinic as a success.
In the 1996 Galton Lecture, historian Richard A. Soloway said: "Stopes' efforts to sustain her pre-eminence and establish her scientific credibility in the field of birth control were increasingly compromised in the 1930s by her exaggerated claims of success, rejection of improvements in contraception and refusal to co-operate with others. Despite her husband's hesitant warnings that she needed to be careful not to inflate the number of patients who visited the clinic and overstate her successes, Stopes' claims of failure rates of somewhere between 0.52 and 2.5 percent in anywhere from 5,000 to 10,000 cases was met with some scepticism, particularly when it was learned that she counted as a success any woman who did not return to the clinic or did not complain." (Soloway, R. (1997). *The Galton Lecture 1996: Marie Stopes, Eugenics and the Birth Control Movement*. In R. Peel (Ed.), *Marie Stopes Eugenics and the English Birth Control Movement*. London: The Galton Institute. Page 49.)

Chapter 36

Testimony of Dr Agnes Saville[D]

Saville was a doctor who specialised in the treatment of girls with nervous afflictions. She had had experience of women who had "injury to physical health brought about by the reading of books of a stimulating sex character."[1]

In the examination, she confirmed that she had two cases: a woman aged "just over 40" and another aged 25, both of whom were unmarried.

Saville's testimony related to her two patients and the impact that *Married Love* had had on them, presumably to justify Sutherland's reference to the jailing of Bradlaugh on the charge of criminal obscenity.

Both women were unmarried and had been profoundly disturbed by the book. The one "sleeplessness and nerves wrecked; thin, loss of health, and self-abuse" and the other "in a highly neurotic condition; sleeplessness was one thing, nervous, jumpy, [and] uncontrolled".

◆　　◆　　◆

In his cross-examination, Hastings dealt with the older of the two first. Saville could not testify that her condition was entirely due to her reading *Married Love*.[2]

He then dealt with the 25 year old, asking about her circumstances such as work, her mode of travel, and whether she would pass any bookshops? Saville knew of the change caused by *Married Love* because she had known her for many years as a friend.

"She came to me suffering from sleeplessness and run-down nerves. I used all the usual methods of treatment for a month. There was no result and, therefore, in the usual way in which one does in one's profession, I taxed that girl with some grave worry. I said: "You have a love affair on your mind, or some business financial loss?" Bursting into tears, she told me she had read *Married Love*; she could not get it out of her mind day or night; it had been a horrible revelation to her."

In subsequent questions, Saville said that she did not like the book and that she thought it had a bad effect on people, though she did concede that she didn't think it could do any harm to married people.

She said: "it is making a natural function like eating and drinking a high art form. It is like a gourmand with food. What is a simple thing is made an art; it makes married people think too much about it, and all the details of it. When they read this book it stimulates passion. Of course, if you want me to, I can say what other doctors have said; I could go on indefinitely."

Hastings pointed out that other doctors might come and say what other doctors have said. "I am only asking what you say. That is the two; the girl 25, and the woman of 40." He concluded the cross-examination by pointing out that there were only two patients, undermining any suggestion that Saville's evidence had wider application.[3]

---

[1] Femina Books. (1967). *The Trial of Marie Stopes*. (M. Box, Ed.) London: Femina Books Ltd. Page 301.

[2] *Ibid.*, page 302.

[3] *Ibid.*, page 303.

Chapter 37

Testimony of Dr William Falkner[D]

D r William Falkner was the physician to the out-patients department of the Paddington Green Children's Hospital, Harrow Road, from where he had "a good deal of experience" in working amongst poor mothers and poor women.

Charles asked him about the contraceptives advocated by the Plaintiff, and Falkner said: "I dislike them all very much." He did not like the Gold Pin; he regarded it as an abortifacient. His experience of the Gold Pin occurred when a woman came to see him, presented one to him, and asked that he implant it in her uterus. Falkner warned her of the dangers and refused to fit it.

Falkner was asked where the woman had got the Gold Pin from and began his answer: "She handed me —"

"I do not know. My Lord, it is no use objecting afterwards," said Hastings, preventing the possible disclosure of hearsay testimony.[1]

The Lord Chief Justice intervened, and Charles explained that what Falkner was going to say was that the woman "handed me a book." Falkner confirmed that the book was *Wise Parenthood*.

◆　　◆　　◆

Hastings' cross-examination was a single question: "From what you understood, she quite gathered it would require a doctor to insert the Gold Pin?"

"I take it so," said Falkner.

If the defence were going to assert that *Wise Parenthood* was the reason the woman wanted to use the Gold Pin, then Hastings was going to assert that Stopes' instructions that it be fitted by a medical doctor was appropriate.

Perhaps cognisant that the trial was due to be completed the next day, Hewart asked Charles if the evidence would last much longer. Charles confirmed it was almost done and would take only 30 minutes more.

The case was adjourned until 10.15 am the following day.[2]

Summary of Day 4

So ended the fourth day of the Stopes *v* Sutherland libel trial. The only witness for Stopes that day, Roberts, had neither added nor detracted from her case. Sutherland had acquitted himself competently and had provided a credible explanation for what he had written in his book. Giles, McCann and Scharlieb's testimony provided a coherent criticism of Stopes' work, and the testimony of Saville and Faulkner had rounded out the evidence for the defence.

The testimony of Dr Norman Haire had been very damaging to Stopes not least because, as a birth controller, he might have been expected to support her. While he had spoken favourably of her books, his testimony that the cervical cap had failed in 25 out of 29 cases and that the Gold Pin was likely to cause septic abortion was damning. Further, the reading of Stopes' letter to the Court revealed that the standard of care she applied to women who came to her for help was below that of the medical profession.

The impact all this had on the minds of the 12 men of the jury was not recorded, but it would not be long before the Court would find out.

In addition to the burden of the trial, Stopes was taxed further by the death of her younger sister, Winnie, at the age of 38.

---

[1] Femina Books. (1967). *The Trial of Marie Stopes*. (M. Box, Ed.) London: Femina Books Ltd. Page 304.
[2] *Ibid.*, page 305.

DAY 5

Wednesday, 28th February 1923

Chapter 38

Testimony of Sir Maurice Anderson[D]

O n the third day of the trial, Mr Charles had received a note that one of the witnesses for the defence, Sir Maurice Abbott Anderson was ill with phlebitis (inflammation of the veins) and would not be able to attend the Court to give evidence. With the permission of the Lord Chief Justice, both sides agreed that Anderson would give evidence in front of an Examiner.

The Examiner was appointed by the Court and was authorised to administer an oath and take testimony. In this way, Anderson could testify at a place convenient to him; his evidence was recorded by a shorthand writer and verified by the Examiner. The testimony, given on 26th February 1923, was submitted to the Court when proceedings began on Day 5.

One thing that the barristers for both the plaintiff and the defence agreed was, as Sir Hugh Fraser put it: "we all know this witness is a very distinguished man."[1] As an inspector appointed by the courts in suits for nullity, Anderson had signed the report (relating to Stopes' virginity) that had led to the annulment of her first marriage (on the grounds of non-consummation).[2]

Mr Victor Rabagliati, performing the examination, asked Anderson about his general opinion in relation to contraceptives. Sir Maurice said: "Broadly speaking, I am in favour of contraception up to a point; in other words I feel that it is wrong that a poor man should be open to have a family of say 16, 17, 18, 20 children when he has about £2 10s 0d to keep them on."

The best and proper methods were the condom, the quinine pessary and douching. None of these methods was absolutely safe. Asked how well developed the science of contraception was, he said: "… it is all experimental. There is no definite statement made by anybody anywhere, either by personal experience or in any book, that this or that method is a certain contraceptive; they are seeking after it and looking for it."

Of these, the check pessary was: "… not only not satisfactory in that it may not perform its supposed duties, but in my opinion it is absolutely dangerous."[3]

> Rabagliati: "Before you go into the dangers, will you tell us what you mean by saying it will not perform its supposed duties?"
> Anderson: "Well, it has to be placed in proper position, which is not an easy thing to do."
> Rabagliati: "Now to its actual dangers?"
> Anderson: "May I say that it has to be placed round the *os*, and that it has a firm ring, a strong ring — two words which are used in her book — and that it acts by suction; that it has to be placed right over the *os*, and that it is not an easy thing to do. As regards danger; you see, there is absolutely no suggestion anywhere either of asepsis or of antisepsis. The whole practice is a dirty practice. I mean 'dirty' from a surgical point of view."[4]

Anderson had little to say that was positive about the cap, not least of the ability of women to fit it themselves. He did "not care if it is a working woman or any other woman; I think 19 out of 20 would not be able to effect this." Anderson was asked about the Gold Pin. He was acquainted with it, in that he had seen it and had read about it, but he had never had a case. He said: "As a doctor of my experience, I should say it is a barbarous instrument."

Like others he recognised that it helped conception and it acted as an abortifacient.

> Rabagliati: "Apart from its action as an abortifacient, in your opinion is the Gold Pin when inserted, an

instrument which can be worn by a woman with safety?"
Anderson: "No not unless it is under the immediate care of her doctor, and that frequently."

He later explained that the woman should visit her doctor at least fortnightly. Rabagliati quoted from the 7th edition of *Wise Parenthood* which stated that "all consideration of the subject may be completed once and for all, and the spring should stay in place for years". Sir Hugh Fraser insisted that Rabagliati read the next part, which he did: "No further anxiety or trouble on the part of the woman is required, but a visit twice a year to a nurse or doctor to have the spring cleaned and examined."
"No, I do not agree with that — at least once a fortnight," said Anderson.

◆　　◆　　◆

Cross-examined by Sir Hugh Fraser, Anderson admitted that he took the view that contraceptives did more harm than good.
Anderson confirmed that he had heard the evidence of Sir James Barr and he said that his impression was that Barr did not understand the check pessary at all. Anderson objected to the cap on the grounds it was "dirty inasmuch as it dams back the natural outflow from the uterus."
The next questions dealt with the tightness of fit between the check pessary and the *os*, and the ability for secretions to pass the seal of the pessary. Then to the Gold Pin. Anderson agreed that a woman could not fit it herself.

Fraser: "I do not want to prolong this, but that really means that your view is that it ought really to be used and used only — I want to put it fairly to you — under the supervision of a medical man?"
Anderson: "I do not think it should be used at all."
Fraser: "But if used at all, only under those conditions?"
Anderson: "Absolutely and by the advice of."

◆　　◆　　◆

In re-examination, Rabagliati questioned Anderson about the cap. A tight fit meant that the spermatozoa could not get in and therefore the secretion could not get out – they were two sides of the same coin, so that if the secretions could get out, then the cap would not be effective because the sperm could get in.

On completion of Anderson's testimony, the Examiner and his witness signed the transcript as a true and proper record and it was presented to the Court.

Sir Maurice's testimony was the last to be heard in the trial. Neither Lord Dawson nor Beatrice Parkinson testified in the case.

The trial moved into the next phase in which the barristers would make their closing speeches — their last chance to influence the jury. This would be followed by the Judge's "summing up" — his summary of the case and the issues to be considered by the jury. Then the jury would withdraw to discuss their decision, which they would deliver to the Judge.

---

[1] Femina Books. (1967). *The Trial of Marie Stopes*. (M. Box, Ed.) London: Femina Books Ltd. Page 306.

[2] Hall, R. (1977). *Passionate Crusader: The Life of Marie Stopes*. New York: Harcourt Brace Jovanovich. Page 211.

[3] Femina Books. (1967). *The Trial of Marie Stopes*. (M. Box, Ed.) London: Femina Books Ltd. Page 307.

[4] *Ibid*.

Chapter 39

Deciding the Questions to be Put to the Jury

First however, a decision had to be made as to the questions to be put to the jury. A jury, made up of laymen, is tasked to make a complex decision. To give them a framework for their deliberations and to ensure that their decision is intelligible and useful to the Court, questions are set. Each question must be answered "yes" or "no" or, if a decision as to damages is required, a monetary sum.

Compared to the drama, noise, conflicts and tensions of the last four days, this part appeared to be a calm backwater. It was, however, a critical part of the trial.

Charles said that Sullivan and himself had discussed the questions to be put to the jury. The Lord Chief Justice asked Charles if he had discussed the questions with Hastings. He replied that he had, and that both of them had thought "the proper way" was to consider the questions independently and then ask "your Lordship to indicate what questions first were in your Lordship's mind."[1]

The Lord Chief Justice said: "The plan which appealed to me was this. Of course, it is for the jury to say what these words mean. I thought the first question might probably be: Were these words defamatory of the plaintiff — or some such question — a question raising that point."

He continued: "It is also admitted that the matters which were being referred to amounted to a matter of public interest. Then there are the two ingredients which may be severed or taken together. One is whether the statements of fact are true in substance and in fact; and the second is whether the comment is fair comment."[2]

When the elements of "whether the statements of fact are true in substance and in fact" and "whether the comment is fair comment" were combined within a single question, it was known as the "rolled up" plea.

"But inasmuch as a question of fair comment does not arise unless the statements are true in substance and fact," said the Lord Chief Justice, "it might be proper to leave the question of fair comment with a direction as to the circumstances in which and which alone fair comment arises. So that upon what view of the matter the first question would be: Are these words defamatory of the plaintiff? (2) Are they fair comment? (3) If not, damages."

Hastings asked his Lordship "to leave a specific question as to whether these words are true."[3]

The Lord Chief Justice asked Charles what he thought. It was Sullivan who replied. In contrast to the Lord Chief Justice, he said that the questions of truth occurred "after fair comment" and that there were "two different matters of truth involved". The first of these concerned the factual parts of Sutherland's statement and whether these were true. The second part was "whether the libel — that is to say fact plus deduction — was true in substance and in fact." "I have no objection to that going to the jury," said Sullivan, and Charles concurred.

The Lord Chief Justice had asked Hastings and Fraser to indicate to him what they considered to be statements of fact and of opinion, and Hastings now proposed to tell him.

"Have you written them down?" asked the Lord Chief Justice.

"No, My Lord, I have not," replied Hastings.

"Then I will make a note of them," replied the Lord Chief Justice.

Hastings indicated that the "first statement of fact [was] that the plaintiff exposed poor people to experiments." Sullivan said that this passage was not a fact but an innuendo. The Lord Chief Justice replied that members of the jury would make that decision. He told Hastings: "the better thing would be if you would kindly put them into writing," otherwise it would delay proceedings.

Hastings said that he would, but that he could not do it in time for Sullivan's closing speech. The case was running behind time and the Judge had not received questions in writing from any of the barristers representing the parties. Presumably to avoid the prospect of further delay, the Lord Chief Justice decided to set the questions himself.

"Well as far as the questions to the jury are concerned, I propose, therefore, to leave these questions: "(1) Were the words complained of defamatory of the plaintiff? (2) Were they true in substance and in fact? (3) Were they fair comment? (4) Damages, if any."

The Lord Chief Justice had recognised Hastings' request "to leave a specific question as to whether these words are true," meaning that "truth" and "fair comment" would be considered separately, rather than "rolled up" in a single question. The jury's answers to these questions would decide who would win in Stopes *v* Sutherland.

---

[1] Femina Books. (1967). I. (M. Box, Ed.) London: Femina Books Ltd. Page 317.

[2] *Ibid.*, page 318.

[3] At this point in the typed court transcript (held today in the Wellcome Institute) Stopes wrote in the margin: "The source of all our trouble." Given that many other issues contributed to her loss (such as, for example, the Gold Pin) attributing *all* of her troubles to this single moment overstates the case.

Chapter 40

Closing Speeches

Serjeant Sullivan, K.C.[D]

ullivan rose to close the case for the co-defendant, Harding & More. He had previously discussed his speech with Charles to ensure that they did not go over the same ground.

Sullivan told the jury that "The Courts of Justice do not hire themselves out for persons to debate matters of public interest for the purpose of securing approbation on one side or the other." His implication was that the case had arisen when Stopes had failed to provoke public controversy with her review of Sutherland's book in her magazine, *Birth Control News* rather than her being genuinely offended.

> "Is this, as we call it, a libel? That is to say, has she suffered damage by having her personal character reflected on in such a manner as would expose her personally, apart from her public propaganda to (in the old phrase) hatred, ridicule or contempt?"

In Sullivan's opinion, Stopes' claim to have been personally offended and damaged by Sutherland's book did not hold water: "If a person chooses to take an active part in public life, to advocate views which were matters of public controversy, everybody is entitled to attack those views in any terms that are not outside the bounds of reason and fair play."[1]

According to Sullivan, the defamatory passage had been "mutilated"[2] in order to transfer the last words of the paragraph to the clinic."[3] By changing the text, Sullivan said, "experiments" had become linked to a plea for Stopes' imprisonment, making a connection that had not made in the book and which made it worse than what Sutherland had intended. [4]

He went through the defamatory words, phrase by phrase. "Exposing the poor to experiment" — he told the jury that "every new gospel, gentlemen, is an experiment, above all this new doctrine that the ills of the poor will be remedied by contraceptives. Who is going to tell what the result of that is going to be?"[5]

> "The effect is not going to be seen today or tomorrow or next year. How will it affect, first, the morality of the poor? Then consider, because even in the 20th Century perhaps some of us still survive who think that that is the first consideration you might think of: how may it affect the morality of the poor. How will it affect their well-being? How will it affect their position in the social order? How will it affect the state? Who knows that?"

He then referred to Stopes, and said: "The prophet of God may perhaps know it, but if one is not the Prophet of God, which of us, who make no claim to that, can forecast what will be the effect of this new gospel for all peoples?"

Given that "the whole thing is an experiment," Sullivan respectfully submitted that Sutherland had as much of a right to express an opinion as the plaintiff.

He referred to the next section: "the ordinary decent instincts of the poor are against these practices and indeed they have used them less than any other class." This was something, Sullivan suggested, that there was common agreement on.

"Whether or not that is because their ordinary decent instincts are against it," and whether they were "the natural victims of those who sought to make experiments on their fellows" were matters of opinion as well.[6]

The passage: "In the midst of a London slum, a woman, who is a doctor of German philosophy (Munich), has opened a birth control clinic, where working women are instructed in a method of contraception described by Professor McIlroy as 'the most harmful method of which I have had experience'." ... was, he said, "a statement of fact and every word of that is true."

"It is said it is not in good taste to refer to her as a Doctor of German Philosophy. May I ask in what other capacity has she opened this clinic and taught this new gospel of the new revelation? She is not a medical doctor. There is nothing so deceptive to the poor as to 'Doctor Stopes' recommending this and 'Doctor Stopes' recommending that."[7]

The clinic was, Sullivan said, only a part of the wider campaign which included books, papers, press interviews, public speeches and debates and these were: "a greater crime against society than that for which Bradlaugh was sentenced to jail."

Sullivan told the jury: "the next matter that my Lord is leaving to you, I think, is fair comment."[8] Hewart intervened to say: "No, I think logically the other question comes first: true in substance and in fact."

Sullivan explained that the plea of Justification went to the whole matter, that "taking that paragraph as a whole it is true, taking both the innuendo… that she seeks to ascribe to it as a personal reflection on herself, that it is true in substance and in fact — both statement of fact and statement of opinion."[9]

Whether Bradlaugh's offence was greater or less than "the monstrous campaign conducted by these books and publications" was a matter of opinion. Here Sullivan was indicating which parts of Sutherland's statement should be considered as facts and which as opinion and, in doing so, was determining whether they would come under the defence of Justification or fair comment.

Sullivan continued to address the jury: "The next matter my Lord is leaving to you, I think, is fair comment."

Of course, the Lord Chief Justice's questions were in a different order, and the defence of fair comment was addressed in the third question. Hewart interrupted again and, following a brief exchange, Sullivan continued.

Sullivan explained that the plea of Justification (that the words were true in substance and in fact) was "a little technical" in the sense that it dealt with the words themselves and their meaning, as well as "the meaning that is put upon the whole paragraph".[10]

"You plead Justification not only in respect of your plain statement of fact, but also in respect of your inferences both of fact and of opinion. It is perhaps a little metaphysical. I am trying to make myself plain. Now, take this statement and look at it again, and now let us see. Is there any falsehood to be found in it, whether in opinion, whether in deduction, or whether in statement of fact?"

Sullivan said that he had already covered the statements of fact and the statements of opinion.

"I have pointed out to you already what I conceive to be one plain statement of fact and apart from matters of opinion; but here are clearly expressed in that paragraph and in the context in the book the strongest criticism and objection to the whole of the plaintiff's doctrine and the plaintiff's propaganda. There is expressed an opinion and a deduction from the facts that she is conducting experiments on the poor; that what she is doing is experimenting on the poor in a way that anyone can forecast what the result would be; and there is a statement that the methods of her propaganda are methods compared to which the offence of Bradlaugh and Besant was a less serious crime; and in that fullest sense of fact and opinion I most respectfully submit it is proved that the whole statement of fact and opinion is true in substance and fact."[11]

Sullivan urged the jury to: "Listen to her own written word," and he read out the letter that Stopes had sent to Haire in relation to the Gold Pin. At various points while reading the letter, he pointed out the experimental nature of what she asked him to do.

He then quoted the letter that Stopes had sent to warn the women: "I would warn you that the method being a new one, we are not quite sure, whether the result could be entirely satisfactory; but Dr Haire will watch the case carefully and remove the spring if it seems advisable, and recommend some other method."[12] Sullivan said: "This is an experiment; we do not know how it is going to turn out, but you need not be afraid, because the doctor will watch it carefully."[13]

Sullivan compared it to an older experiment: "Just look at your Bradlaugh pamphlet. It is forty years old. Look at the forecast of what was to be the position of workers in England if Bradlaugh and Besant failed in this campaign which this lady has revived."[14]

To emphasise the point, Sullivan drew on the dire predictions made in the tract, few of which had come to pass.

> "It is true in substance and in fact that she is experimenting on the poor — experimenting in two different ways, each of them, at all events in the opinion of many qualified to judge, most dangerous. She is introducing a philosophy which is foreign to their natures; she is teaching that the child is or may be a curse. That is a dreadful thing. You have heard the opinion of many distinguished ladies carrying on professional practices among the poor; they do not agree with that. The child is the real foundation of the home. The position of the child in the home is of as much importance to any nation as the position of the highest statesman in the land."[15]

Sullivan turned to the "monstrous campaign". Regardless of "whether you agree or disagree with her Malthusian doctrines, and the desirability of righting the affairs of the state by checking the production of children by the only class that is now producing children to maintain the strain of population", the fact remained that Stopes herself had said that it would be an outrage to read her publications aloud in Court. He pointed out that her sincerity had nothing to do with it:

> "No one was more sincere than Charles Bradlaugh, and the jury that tried him found: 'we are unanimously of opinion that the book in question is calculated to deprave public morals, but at the same time we entirely exonerate the defendants from any corrupt motives in publishing it'."[16]

He reminded them that because Stopes was "a distinguished scientist" it did not give her a right to publish these books any more than they had.[17]

Sullivan then turned to the issue of whether Sutherland's remarks were "fair comment" which was, he explained: "... the protection of the individual from having his honest and conscientious opinions overborne by legal process because he ventures to express them on a matter of public concern. It is a great weapon of personal liberty."[18]

He explained that when dealing with fair comment, "you are not dealing with matters of deductions from the fact; you are dealing with the fundamental facts as stated."[19] He repeated the fundamental facts relating to the birth control clinic and the campaign. Stating that it was an experiment was opinion, but "if that was a statement of fact you would have no difficulty at all in finding it, because everybody has described it so."

Sullivan took the opportunity to remind the jury of Dr Haire's testimony: "Dr Haire, with regard to the plaintiff's own method of contraception, told you he took 29 cases and kept under observation and 25 of them were failures."[20]

The Lord Chief Justice corrected him: "Twenty-four."

"Twenty-four was it?" replied Sullivan, "I thought it was twenty-five. Twenty-four were failures. So is it not experimental when you do not know the proportion of twenty-four to five, whether your object is to be attained or not."

Sullivan concluded by telling the jury: "Do not penalise a man because [of] what he feels sincerely. Remember that you are asserting a great principle of personal liberty in a verdict of fair comment. It is a most essential portion of the law to be upheld and maintained; and, remember this: that it is only the protection for one who, feeling deeply and sincerely in his heart that he may have the means of saving his own people from something that is most detrimental and harmful to them and cannot remain silent, but feels in good conscience bound to deliver to them whatever good is in him."

Mr Ernst Charles, K.C.[D]

Mr Ernst Charles KC began with the question of why they were there, asserting that: "... never once before she issued this writ did she complain one word in one sentence written or spoken that anything in this libel, so alleged as a libel, affected her personally at all." According to Charles, the reason they were there was because "she was afraid" because a medical doctor had written a book which attacked her propaganda as "a danger to society, a danger to the nation, a danger to health and a danger to the whole morality of married life." That is why she wanted to make use of his book to debate him at Essex Hall and to gain publicity from this trial. Citing her words, he said that Stopes had brought the action "in the interests of the Society".

Charles reminded them that this was not a state trial of birth control. He outlined the campaign which he called a "preparation by books". *Married Love* was purely a sex book "stimulating the sex passions" and that "having stimulated the person strongly and cultivated their tastes in this matter", was followed by *Wise Parenthood: A Practical Sequel to Married Love* which went on "to show how you can enjoy all that you find in *Married Love* without the responsibilities of children."[21]

He said: "It is an experiment; you know it is an experiment. You have never heard of it being tried before." By this he meant the experiment of trying to distribute and arrange population, "lopping off those at the bottom and encouraging those at the top. That has never been tried before; that is an experiment, and some people think a hideously dangerous experiment."[22]

Stopes, "an amateur — well meaning, but an amateur" had exposed people to the dangers of the check pessary. The plaintiff had argued that it was not an experiment because it had been tried in rubber shops for many years, yet "what harm it has done to them I do not know; you do not know." He pointed out the great experience and expertise of those who testified to the Court that it was dangerous, and according to Professor McIlroy was the most dangerous method of which she had had experience.

No check was made on the women who attended the clinic. "If their experience is that of Dr Haire's, goodness alone knows what has happened to them."[23]

And then there was the Gold Pin. Charles referred to Stopes' letter to Haire and called it "a damning letter... and indeed one hopes that it is a damning letter in one way: that this lady did not know what she was doing," for, he said, she was recommending a method of procuring abortion – early abortion.

The abortifacient effects of the Gold Pin were one side of the pincer, and now Charles deployed the other: "Do you believe that she knew it? I do not. I do not suppose many would think that if she had a true appreciation of this beastly pin, she would ever have recommended it at all. I do not suppose she would. She is not that sort of lady I hope and believe. But is it not an experiment?"

Witness after witness, called by both the plaintiff and the defendants said that they had practically no experience of the method "and yet it is calmly recommended as a 'great hope to women who are dissolute, harried and overworked.'"

In referring to Stopes' work as an experiment, Sutherland could have said: "It is an amazing thing that the Home Secretary allows this monstrous campaign... This lady advises openly in thousands and tens of thousands of copies all over England that poor women, dissolute, harried and overworked, shall use an instrument which inevitably will produce abortion. He might have said that, and it would have been absolutely and entirely true."

And in spreading the message she received from God, were the jury really to believe the "horrible message about boys"?[24] Was this whole book not drawn not from God but from her own works? After all, Charles said, "one smells singularly like the other."[25]

> "Is not it a simple bit of propaganda dressed up to the infinite discredit, I say, of her who is responsible for it, dressed up in the garb of a message from the Almighty God, direct from his chosen servant, Marie Stopes, Doctor of Science, Doctor of Philosophy, Munich, and of other earthly distinctions."

Charles referred to the plaintiff's witnesses as "a circle". In other words, they were not independent agents who had decided to support her, but were all connected in some way to her Society. By contrast, the defendant's witnesses were all detached, and all were unanimous in saying that the method recommended by Dr Stopes was a dangerous method and that the Gold Pin was not only a dangerous method, but also unlawful as an instrument for procuring early abortion.

Mr Patrick Hastings, K.C.P

Mr Patrick Hastings KC had opened the case and his speech was to be the last. In the best parts, his speech was short and to the point, but more than once his meanderings, qualifications, and sub-clauses made him difficult to follow. Persuading jurors in Court was one thing; it was quite another to give members of the jury memorable points and arguments that they could take into the jury room to win over their fellows. For example, he said:

> "I want to point out to you, if I may, the difference which exists, not in my position, because, of course, that it quite immaterial, but the position of Dr Marie Stopes in this matter. It is much easier, you may think, to obtain the evidence of men or women in this country, who, if they are asked to give evidence, know that they are going to the witness box to assume a high moral tone in every sense, and particularly when you find upon one side a professional man, and a doctor; you may think that it would be rather difficult or might be rather difficult to get other medical men willing to give evidence against a brother professional, who, after all, as Mr Charles has told us, is doing his duty to his profession, and it seems to me that it hardly lies in the mouth of Mr Charles to comment contemptuously on the fact that two, perhaps, of the greatest doctors in England, as I suggest you may think they are from what you have seen, Dr Chapple, the gynaecologist of one of the biggest London hospitals, and Sir William Arbuthnot Lane, that those two are called, and the only thing that Mr Charles is able to say against them is that one married the daughter of the other."[26]

He went on to say that asserting that *Married Love* was a "bundle of muck" was unfair, but the impact of this point was lost when placed in passages like the one below:

"Now I am afraid I must ask you to allow me, quite shortly, to consider with you one or two of the things which have been said in this case, and members of the jury — may I say this? — which I really want to say dispassionately, and I hope in a way that will give no offence to anybody; there is no doubt, and there can be, I think, no doubt in your minds, that not only people outside this Court, but people inside this Court may form a view — I am, of course, eliminating yourselves from this — may form a view of their own, and it is impossible to prevent it."[27]

Hastings reminded the jury to dismiss from their minds the part "when I was cross-examining this gentleman [and] I asked him some questions which drew from his Lordship an observation." He was referring to his suggestion that Sutherland's writings were a grievous attack on Protestantism.

"May I say at once, directly his Lordship makes any suggestion to me at all, I would unswervingly adopt it. Therefore, upon that portion of the cross-examination, which was not quite perhaps directed to the ends which might, owning to my clumsiness, have been thought; but whatever ends it was directed to, I dismiss it at once from my part of the case and from your minds."

Of course, by raising the issue, Hastings had reminded the jury of what it was he wanted them to forget. Lest that make him seem insincere, he insisted: "I say no more about it. If it had not been for that, I might have said something on the subject, but now I am not going to ask you even to consider it and I am not going to say anything more about it."[28]

And he didn't until, a few moments later, he did.

"… I should not like to have you think that I, in cross-examining this gentleman, was trying to introduce a topic of which you would not have approved. Therefore, I mention that to show you what my object was in going through this gentleman's cross-examination. I should not like any one of you gentlemen to leave the box with the slightest feeling on your mind that I cross-examined this gentleman in order to put before you topics of any sort which you might not think either desirable, or material to the question."

Hastings reminded the jury that Dr Sutherland had last attended midwifery cases or woman's cases since "1897" an error that was corrected by Mr Charles to "1907".

Hastings then proceeded to remind the jury that Sutherland had criticised Lord Dawson and that he was entitled to do so, "just as he is entitled to criticise this lady."[29] But had Sutherland been fair in attacking Dawson or Stopes? Sutherland chose to: "… ignore every one of her high qualifications, her remarkable qualifications, and say she is a Doctor of German Philosophy. Does that strike you as either the act of a gentleman, or of a fair gentleman, or of a reasonably-minded man?"

He said that the rubber pessary had been available "in shops for innumerable years."[30] He listed the eminent men and women who testified for Stopes and asked: "Can you have any doubt, therefore, that there is an immense body of people in this country — serious reasoned people — who believe that? Whether or not this birth control is desirable, those gentlemen whom I have called believe it is desirable. They believe above all, that it is right nowadays that every thinking man and woman should have the opportunity of making up their own mind."[31]

"I have tried to count how many times you have had one sentence put before you in this case; 'A fully-sexed girl of 16.' You can say that in a loud tone or in a gentle tone, and you can thump the desk when you say it, but it is the same old sentence; and it is very much easier to stand up purporting to represent the interests of the fully-sexed girl of 16 in this country of ours, than it is to stand up and be pointed at as those who are attacking that person. But you know that, in my suggestion, it is not fair; it is not right, and it is not the proper way in which nowadays these things should be discussed. We have got to face the world as it is."

Reasonable words and well put, but then Hastings over-reached to the point of absurdity: "I am going to point out to you here that this lady is charged with a crime. It has got to be proved by the man sitting there just as fully as if she were standing in the criminal dock upon her trial."[32]

Hastings turned to the evidence of harm from contraceptives and referred to the evidence of Sir Maurice Abbott Anderson: "He is a gentleman, of course, known to everybody practicing in these Courts. You have heard his evidence; as I understand, as far as contraceptive methods are concerned, the only difference between Sir Maurice Abbott Anderson and this lady is that he says his methods are better than hers... Supposing Sir Maurice Abbott Anderson had written a book advocating the quinine pessary, would you have suggested that he had been guilty of an obscene libel because another lady said she did not like quinine pessaries, and that, perhaps, some other one was a better one than his"?[33]

Hastings drew attention to the failure of the defendants, who had been: "… unable to give us one single case of anybody who suffered any injury, however remote, at whatever time, in whatever way, from the use of this pessary."[34]

"In my submission to you, it just shows how wise Mr Charles was to talk glibly in this case about the filthy passages in the bundle of muck, because it is the best thing he has got. When you come to look at the case, it is the best thing he has got."

Hastings spoke of the admirers of Stopes' works, pointing out that it came from unlikely quarters. Haire had said he had "admired them intensely" as well as the Roman Catholic priest who had written a foreword to *Married Love*; he "must have been very courageous, because here he was advocating apparently this bundle of muck". Then there were the people, "professional honest men…the heads of their profession, people of all grades, who come and say: 'We think it is a beautiful book, we think that the work this lady has done is serving a very useful purpose.'"[35]

Hastings had gone over time and indicated that he was about to summarise the case so as not to delay the adjournment. The Lord Chief Justice intervened: "Please do not omit anything. I am sure the jury will not mind sitting a little longer, nor should I," he said.

The jury had to ask whether Sutherland's words were true and he suggested that: "… the most and by far the most important thing is to say that you have to be satisfied by the evidence on that side of the Court, that this lady has committed a crime far more serious than that for which Charles Bradlaugh was condemned to jail."[36]

Further, Hastings said, the defence had to prove it all: "They cannot pick out little bits of the libel and say: 'we may fail in proving you are a criminal; we may fail to prove that you in fact use this most harmful method; but in point of fact we can prove that you are a Doctor of German Philosophy.' You have to prove it all."[37]

He reminded the jury that in their pleadings the defence had said that they were going to rely on the testimony of Beatrice Parkinson "who was going to give some evidence as to what had happened to her at the clinic" yet Parkinson had not appeared in the trial. He said that: "out of all the 1,700 patients there is not one who has ever expressed the slightest dissatisfaction, disappointment, or injury that has ever been done to her." He asked why the defence had they not brought such persons before the Court, and then answered his own question: "They could not find one because there is not one."

And what if this lady thought she had a divine message and it had been wrong? It was only sent to the Bishops after all.[38]

He then dealt with the Gold Pin. He said that "they did have an extraordinary stroke of luck, and that was a letter from Dr Haire". While the Gold Pin was "fairly obviously a thoroughly unsatisfactory method," he said:[39]

> "Is it not perfectly obvious that all this lady has said to any one of them is: If anybody wants this, they must go to a doctor and see him about it. Can you think that any person of the sort who is so poor — 'owing to their poverty, lack of learning, and helplessness' — do you think those are the people who can go and buy Gold Pins?"

His reference to the libel led him to ask rhetorically:

> "Can anyone suggest that this is making experiments of the poor within the meaning of those words? What this means is that this lady started a Clinic in the East End of London, not out of charity, not out of a proper idea, not in order to do good; but in order to make unworthy experiments upon poor people."[40]

He continued:

"I put this lady before you as a lady who believes that she is doing an important public service. She is trying to do it in the best way that a woman can; she is doing it honestly and straightforwardly and she is supported in her views by some of the greatest minds in this country — people eminently qualified to judge, surgeons who have been in hospitals, and who have told you that their hearts have been touched by the misery which they have seen."[41]

And having emphasised the virtue of the plaintiff's side of the case, Hastings over-egged his point by suggesting that their opponents were equal and opposite:

"Against them you have had surgeons who perhaps, owing to their lack of sympathy, have never been approached by poor people as they told us — who have never been told by poor people of their miseries and their sufferings; and who, perhaps, have gone there solely for medical reasons and possibly have been glad when they could leave. You do not see misery and suffering unless you want to; you can avoid it easily if you wish to. This lady had done neither. She has done this out of her own pocket, not for her own purposes, but solely in the interests of what she believes to be just."

It was an unnecessary contrast, and it was hardly as if the heartlessness of the eminent doctors on Sutherland's side had arisen, let alone been proved. Hastings closed by again referring to whether:

"… this lady in your opinion has been guilty of a crime, and has written a book which is fairly described as containing filthy passages which can be found in a muck heap, then she ought to be hounded out of decent society; but if the view that you see fit to take is that these people have failed to prove that she is a criminal, that she has written foul and disgusting books, and that she has sunk so low as to make helpless victims of people who are too poor to be able to defend themselves... you are the judges of whether this libel is true, or not — I ask you to say that it is neither fair nor true, and that this lady should leave the Court at least as honoured, if not more honoured, than she was when she came into it"[42]

---

[1] Femina Books. (1967). *The Trial of Marie Stopes.* (M. Box, Ed.) London: Femina Books Ltd. Page 321.
[2] *Ibid.*
[3] *Ibid.*, page 325.
[4] *Ibid.*
[5] *Ibid.*, page 322.
[6] *Ibid.*, page 323.
[7] *Ibid.*
[8] *Ibid.*, page 325.
[9] *Ibid.*, pages 325-6.
[10] *Ibid.*, page 326.
[11] *Ibid.*
[12] *Ibid.*, page 327.
[13] *Ibid.*
[14] *Ibid.*, page 328.
[15] *Ibid.*, page 328-9.
[16] *Ibid.*, page 330.
[17] *Ibid.*, page 331.
[18] *Ibid.*, page 332.
[19] *Ibid.*, page 333.
[20] *Ibid.*, page 334.
[21] *Ibid.*, page 337.
[22] *Ibid.*, page 338.
[23] *Ibid.*, page 339.
[24] *Ibid.*, page 341.
[25] *Ibid.*
[26] *Ibid.*, page 343.
[27] *Ibid.*, page 344.
[28] *Ibid.*, page 346.
[29] *Ibid.*
[30] *Ibid.*, page 347.
[31] *Ibid.*
[32] *Ibid.*, page 349.
[33] *Ibid.*
[34] *Ibid.*, page 350.
[35] *Ibid.*, page 351.
[36] *Ibid.*, page 353.
[37] *Ibid.*
[38] *Ibid.*, page 354.
[39] *Ibid.*, page 355.
[40] *Ibid.*, page 356.
[41] *Ibid.*
[42] *Ibid.*

Chapter 41

Summing up and the Jury's decision

The trial was well behind time when the Lord Chief Justice began to deliver his summing up speech at around two o'clock, and it lasted for two hours.[1]

In it he urged the jury to "an instructed and informed impartiality" and "to have your mind open to all the evidence and, having come to your conclusion honestly and fairly, to act upon it fearlessly."[2]

Hewart summarised the events that had led to the case, concluding with the Statement of Claim on behalf of Dr Marie Stopes.

> "To that claim in due course the defendants put forward their defence. Publication was admitted, but they said, if I may leave out matters of less importance, two things, and they say them still; and these are the real issues in the case. They say: so far as statements of fact in which is complained of are concerned, those statements of fact are true statements. So far as regards what is expression of opinion, that expression of opinion is fair comment."[3]

And later on: "And so, apart from the initial question, whether these words were defamatory, and defamatory of the plaintiff, the questions which remain are, so far as statement is concerned: Was the statement true? And so far as comment is concerned: Was the comment fair?"[4]

At this point the reader might recall that this was one of Sutherland's alternative defences, and that his primary defence was: "The said words in their natural meaning are true in substance and in fact."[5]

Hewart explained that when they dealt with the questions they should ignore their personal views on the matters under discussion.

"Gentlemen, that what is important here is the evidence. Your duty is — and your oath as Jurors enjoins that you should — to give a true verdict according to the evidence. Once you depart from the admitted truth that it is well that young people should learn the first elements of sexual matters from a good and pure source, and not from a dirty source, you get at once into the region of controversy."[6]

"It is not suggested that the defendant has a personal animus against the plaintiff; they have never met, they are strangers; but it is said these are defamatory words, defamatory about her, which are neither true in fact nor fair in opinion."[7]

He then took them through Sutherland's book *Birth Control*. He read the defamatory passage in full and drew attention to the different meanings that each side attributed to the reference to "experiments".

The plaintiff said this meant "that at her clinic surgical experiments are made upon poor persons",[8] while the defendant said "that is not what I meant... by experiment I meant the indiscriminate distribution of knowledge of contraceptives among the poor for the purpose of redistributing the birth rate according to the use of contraceptives and contrary to the laws of nature. I say this is a social experiment, I think it is a bad experiment."[9]

"Now, of course, you are not primarily or ultimately concerned with what the plaintiff says that word means or with what the defendant says that word means. The question is: what is the meaning likely to be conveyed to the reasonable reader of this book?"[10]

Hewart discussed the check pessary, the Gold Pin and the controversy over whether the latter was a contraceptive or an abortifacient. He listed the views of the various witnesses for both sides.[11] He instructed the jury: "You will not, of course, exaggerate the part which the Gold Pin plays in this matter, or the part which any particular thing plays in this matter."[12]

He covered the assertions relating to the "monstrous campaign" and the Bradlaugh case, and he concluded by reminding the jury of the four questions that they were to answer:

"(1) Were the words complained of defamatory of the plaintiff?

"(2) Were they true in substance and in fact?

"(3) Were they fair comment?

"(4) Damages, if any."

A trial involves an immense amount of work. The researching of evidence, studying case law, dealing with the responses of the other side, meeting court deadlines and organising witnesses to attend the trial. Then there is the invisible informal side: the arguments, sleepless nights, worries about legal bills, strained relationships and articled clerks berated for producing sub-standard work. All that was now past. The piles of paper and voluminous words. All of it had, it seemed, evaporated and the only thing that remained were the 24 words on the piece of paper that the Lord Chief Justice handed to the foreman of the jury.

The foreman thanked him and, at eight minutes past four in the afternoon,[13] the jury withdrew to the seclusion of the jury room for deliberation. The most critical exchanges of the trial took place in secret.

Dr Sutherland described the scene in the Court Room in a memoir of the trial:

> "The jury retired at four o'clock, and Lord Hewart went into his room at the back of the bench. In the court there was a buzz of conversation. Half an hour later the bell from the jury room rang. They had come to a verdict! They were only sending a written question to the judge. The slip of paper was taken to the judge, and the messenger returned with the answer and pushed it under the door of the jury's room. Soon it began to get dark, and people were leaving the court. The electric light was switched on, and the court was only half-full.

"Again the jury's bell rang. Another question was sent to the judge. At six o'clock the only people in court were the litigants, their friends, the junior solicitors, and the most junior barristers. A cheerless scene. At seven o'clock it was said that Lord Hewart had given up a public engagement and was prepared to stay in his room if necessary, until midnight. We sent out for sandwiches, but they were not very good. At five minutes past eight the bell rang, the jury returned and took their places. The Lord Chief Justice returned to the Bench and read aloud the answers to the four questions left to the jury."[14]

"Gentlemen of the jury, are you all agreed?" The foreman answered: "We are." The paper containing the jury's answers was passed to the Judge who read them out.

"(1) Were the words complained of defamatory of the plaintiff? — Yes.
"(2) Were they true in substance and in fact? — Yes.
"(3) Were they fair comment?..."

The Lord Chief Justice paused, and passed the paper to the foreman of the jury. "Would you look at that, Mr Foreman?" he asked, "Two words have been written: which is the final one?"[15] The foreman marked the paper, handed it back, and the Lord Chief Justice continued:

"(3) Were they fair comment? — No.
"(4) Damages, if any? — £100."

Sir Hugh Fraser, junior barrister for the Plaintiff, stood and announced: "My Lord, in that I ask for Judgement."
"Well, I think it must be argued, Sir Hugh Fraser," replied the Lord Chief Justice, explaining a few moments later: "the jury have found that the plea of Justification is right."
At this, Mr Harold Murphy and Mr Theobald Mathew, for Sutherland and Harding & More respectively, also asked for judgement.
"Very well," said the Lord Chief Justice, "I will not give judgement now. The argument on these findings will take place tomorrow morning."

Summary of Day 5

So ended the fifth day of the Stopes *v* Sutherland libel trial. The view of the 12 men of the jury was now known and had been expressed in the answers to the four questions. Despite this, and despite five days of a bitterly fought trial, their answers led both sides to claim victory.

The plaintiff sought judgement on the grounds that the jury had said that the words complained of were defamatory, that they had not been fair comment, and that the jury had awarded damages of £100.

The defendants said that judgement should be given to them. The words complained of were defamatory, however, the jury had ruled that they were true in substance and in fact, meaning that their defence of Justification had worked.

Readers will remember that, in the defence of Justification, if the statement were true then, in the eyes of the law, Stopes was not entitled "to recover damages in respect of an injury to a character which [she] either does not or ought not to possess."[16] Further, according to the author of those words, Justification was a complete answer to the action and the end to the matter.[17]

The participants would have to wait until the next day to find out what the result would be.

---

[1] Femina Books. (1967). *The Trial of Marie Stopes*. (M. Box, Ed.) London: Femina Books Ltd. Page 380.

[2] *Ibid.*, page 357.

[3] *Ibid.*, page 359.

[4] *Ibid.*

[5] Defence of the Defendant dated 31st July 1922. Wellcome Library. PP/MCS/H/4a:Box72.

[6] Femina Books. (1967). *The Trial of Marie Stopes*. (M. Box, Ed.) London: Femina Books Ltd. Page 362.

[7] *Ibid.*, page 364.

[8] *Ibid.*, page 366.

[9] *Ibid.*

[10] *Ibid.*, page 367.

[11] *Ibid.*, page 369.

[12] *Ibid.*, page 371.

[13] *Ibid.*, page 378.

[14] Sutherland, H. (1934). *A Time to Keep*. Geoffrey Bles. Page 234.

[15] Femina Books. (1967). *The Trial of Marie Stopes*. (M. Box, Ed.) London: Femina Books Ltd. Page 379.

[16] Salmond, J. W. (1916). *The Law of Torts: A Treatise on the English Law of Liability for Civil Injuries (Fourth ed.)*. Temple Bar: Stevens and Haynes. Page 464. Retrieved January 18, 2019, from https://archive.org/details/cu31924022354173/page/n5.

[17] Odgers, W. (1897). *An Outline of the Law of Libel: Six lectures delivered in the Middle Temple Hall during Michaelmas Term 1896*. Macmillan and Co., Limited. Page 95.

DAY 6

Thursday, 1st March 1923

Chapter 42

Legal Argument and Judgement

When proceedings commenced the following morning, Mr Patrick Hastings KC was not in Court.[1] Sir Hugh Fraser was the first to speak, on behalf of the Plaintiff. Fraser was author of *The Law of Libel in Relationship to the Press* and *Principles and Practice of the Law of Libel and Slander*,[2] so was an acknowledged expert on defamation.

He said that firstly, the jury had found the words to be defamatory ("there is no doubt about that"), secondly, that the statements of fact in the libel were true in substance and in fact, thirdly that the expressions of opinion in the libel were not fair comment and fourthly that damages of £100 were awarded. Notwithstanding the answer to question two had been that the statements were true in substance and fact, the case should be awarded to the plaintiff.

> "My submission to your Lordship is this," said Fraser, "and I ask your Lordship in dealing with this matter, if I may respectfully say so, to bear in mind not only, as I have stated, the way in which the case was fought, but what your Lordship said to the jury about the vital distinction between statements of fact and expressions of opinion."[3]

Hewart confessed that it was not easy for him to recollect the whole of his summing up, but his recollection was that "the defence of fair comment must be based on an accurate statement of fact. You cannot have fair comment upon things which are said to be facts, but which are not real facts."

Fraser had likely anticipated that the defendants were going to ask for judgement on the basis of legal precedent. By referring to the Lord Chief Justice's summing up speech, Fraser's aim was to make that speech the basis on which the case would be decided. At this time though, Fraser did not have the transcript from the day before. If he had had it, he would likely have read the relevant parts to the Lord Chief Justice. Without it, however, he remained dependent upon his Lordship's recollection. As Fraser acknowledged: "I am within your Lordship's recollection, and if I am mistaken there is an end of it."[4]

Fraser submitted that: "having regard to the way in which your Lordship charged the jury, these findings mean this: that the whole of the words were defamatory, that the words fall into two classes — one, statements of fact; two, expressions of opinion; that as regards the statements of fact, the defendants, according to the findings of the jury, have made out their defence; but as regards the expression of opinion the defendants have failed to make out their defence; and I ask your Lordship to bear in mind the way in which the jury have answered your Lordship's questions. They have answered them in such a way, I submit, as clearly goes to show that that was their way of dealing with the subject — that they were dealing with two separate things. Well, if that be so, I submit that it is really not arguable whether I am entitled to judgement on the findings. I submit it is clear, if my contention is sound, and if I am right in saying that is the way the jury dealt with the matter, I am entitled to judgement for £100."[5]

"What do you say, Mr Charles?" said the Lord Chief Justice.

Charles' answer related to Sutherland's primary defence of Justification, that the words were true in substance and in fact. He reiterated the questions set by the Lord Chief Justice:

"Were the words complained of defamatory to the plaintiff?" and then answered: "Yes."

"Were they true in substance and fact?" and he again answered: "Yes."

Charles then argued that the answer to the second question had concluded the matter. Once it had been answered "yes", the defence of Justification had succeeded. In other words, Sutherland had won the case and the answers to questions three and four were superfluous. He said: "My Lord I submit that by every rule of law, and, indeed, I think my friend, with his very great knowledge, and I will say unequalled knowledge of this particular subject, could not point to a case where the conclusion which has been arrived at by the jury that the words complained of were true in substance and in fact does not conclude the matter."[6]

The differences between the two sides can be explained by analogy: to win the case and to gain damages of £100, the plaintiff would have to proceed through locked gates. Each gate would be unlocked by an answer in favour of the plaintiff. The first gate (the question "Were the words complained of defamatory of the plaintiff?") was unlocked (when the jury answered "yes"), and she moved along the path. The second gate (the question "Were they true in substance and in fact?") remained locked (when the jury answered "yes").

To Charles, the four gates were placed in sequence and that, blocked by gate two, the plaintiff could not proceed to gates three and four. To Fraser, the gates were not in sequence and gates two and three were placed side by side. While gate two remained locked, gate three provided an alternative route. Given gate three (the question "Were they fair comment?") was unlocked (when the jury answered "no"), the plaintiff could proceed to gate four (the question "Damages, if any") which was unlocked (when the jury answered "£100").

Charles backed up his statements with legal opinion and case law:

> "They have found that it was true, and I submit that by every rule of law, and by every decided case, only one verdict can follow from that finding, and that is a verdict for the defendants."

Sullivan added a comment relating to his closing speech in which he: "… told your Lordship and the jury in the plainest of plain terms that this was an issue of Justification, and I used the word Justification, and that under it we undertook to prove not only the simple allegations of fact contained in the publication, but whatever meaning you think should be ascribed to it, and your Lordship told them that it was their duty to find it afterwards."

He cited further legal precedent for the plea of fair comment not arising if the plea of Justification is made good.[7]

Fraser said that he would have liked to have looked at the transcript of the shorthand notes,[8] and that without them he could not add anything usefully, though he did ask his Lordship if he had asked the jury to consider the questions relating to the statements of fact and the statements of opinion separately.[9]

Hewart replied that his recollection was that he had asked counsel on both sides to agree the questions to be put to the jury. When these were not forthcoming from either side: "… I then indicated that I thought it would be sufficient to ask the jury, first, whether the words were defamatory, and secondly, whether the words were fair comment, because that would involve the two things, whether the expressions of opinion were fair, and whether the allegations of fact upon which they purported to be founded were real facts. But it was said on the part of the plaintiff, by your learned leader [Hastings], that it would be more satisfactory if the two question were put separately, and thereupon the three questions were made into four, and that it was expressly at the invitation of the learned counsel for the plaintiff that, instead of putting the whole matter in one, what I think is sometimes called the rolled-up plea, I adopted a specific question upon the plea of Justification. That is my recollection."[10]

Hewart said that there was no course open to him other than to give judgement for the defendants. Charles asked if the judgement for the defendants included costs, in other words, that the legal costs of the defence would be paid by the plaintiff. The Lord Chief Justice replied: "Yes."

The co-defendants, Sutherland and Harding & More had won and Stopes had lost… for now.

Cardinal Bourne wrote to Sutherland on 2nd March 1923 to tell him: "Monsignor Coote has just telephoned to me the result of the action and I hasten to send you my heartiest congratulations. May God bless and reward you for your plucky and persevering fight for purity and morality."[11]

---

[1] Hall, R. (1977). *Passionate Crusader: The Life of Marie Stopes*. New York: Harcourt Brace Jovanovich. Page 225. Hall remarked that Patrick Hastings "after a brilliant opening speech… appeared to lose interest; so much so that he was not even in court to hear the verdict." This is perhaps unfair to Hastings. In respect

of the jury's verdict, neither Charles nor Sullivan were in Court either, according to Sutherland's account in his memoir *A Time To Keep*. This was as it should be: no one knew how long the jury would take to deliver the verdict and the barristers knew they would have to be in Court the following day. In respect of the Judge's verdict on 1st March 1923, Hastings' absence did not necessarily mean that he had lost interest, because the trial was supposed to have ended on the fifth day, and he may have been booked for another case. For the legal arguments, Stopes was ably represented by Sir Hugh Fraser, an acknowledged expert on the law of libel.

[2] Fraser, S. H. (1898). *A Compendium of the Law of Torts*. London: Sweet and Maxwell. Frontispiece. Retrieved March 28, 2019, from https://archive.org/details/compendiumoflawo00fras/page/n3.

[3] Femina Books. (1967). *The Trial of Marie Stopes*. (M. Box, Ed.) London: Femina Books Ltd. Page 380.

[4] *Ibid.*, page 383.

[5] *Ibid.*, page 381.

[6] *Ibid.*, page 382.

[7] *Ibid.*, page 383.

[8] Fraser referred to the transcripts on three occasions: (1) "Unfortunately I have no transcript of the shorthand notes of my learned friends' speeches, or indeed of your Lordship's summing up, otherwise I venture to think that I should not have much difficulty in finding passages bearing out that contention in regard to what your Lordship said, but in any case I can put my contention quite shortly." (*The Trial of Marie Stopes* Femina Books, 1967, page 381) (2) "I do not think I can add anything usefully to what I have said except this: I hardly like to refer to it. I wish that one had a transcript of the shorthand notes. I venture to ask your Lordship whether, considering what questions should be left to the jury, your Lordship did not say this: I propose to ask the jury whether statements of fact were not true and whether the expressions of opinion were not fair comment." (*Ibid.*, page 383) (3) "If your Lordship pleases, I do not think that without a transcript of the shorthand notes I can carry the matter any further. I have made my point clear to your Lordship." (*Ibid.*, page 384).

[9] Femina Books. (1967). *The Trial of Marie Stopes*. (M. Box, Ed.) London: Femina Books Ltd. Page 383.

[10] *Ibid.*, page 384.

[11] Letter from Cardinal Bourne to Dr Halliday Sutherland dated 2nd March 1923. Sutherland family archive.

Dr Halliday Sutherland in 1920.

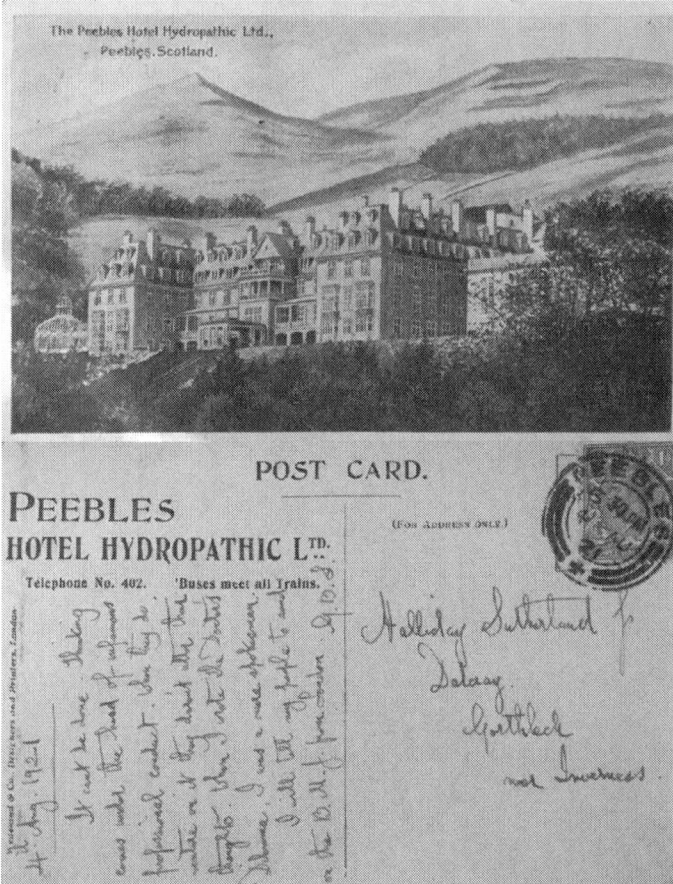

Picture postcard from George Bernard Shaw to Dr Sutherland dated 4th August 1921. At the time, Sutherland was writing *Birth Control* and may have used excerpts from the British Medical Journal sent by Shaw in his book.

The moral support of Cardinal Bourne, Archbishop of Westminster, enabled Dr Sutherland to properly defend the libel action. This letter was sent by Bourne to congratulate Sutherland on his win in the High Court.

PART 3

AFTERMATH

Chapter 43

Fallout

Some newspapers erroneously reported that Stopes had won in the High Court. This is perhaps unsurprising. The jury's verdict had been delivered after 8 pm on the previous evening, and reports had to be written, edited, typeset and printed, among the many other things that were required to produce a newspaper for the next day. A reporter knew that the case would be awarded to either Stopes or Sutherland, so if they reported a Stopes win, they had a fifty percent chance of being right. The jury's answers to questions three and four seemed to increase their chances.

Stopes received letters of support including one from Alfred Goodman, KC, who wrote on 1st March:

"After such a summing up as the jury listened to I cannot for a moment think it was their intention to decide otherwise than that you had been unfairly treated."[1]

In reply, she sent a form letter which read: "The result of the trial is indeed remarkable, but I feel absolutely vindicated as I obtained a clear finding for damages from the British public as represented by a jury, though this is withheld as a legal technicality. Even this has worked for good and led to many public expressions of sympathy and indignation..."[2]

Aylmer Maude's biography *Marie Stopes: Her Work and Play* published in 1933, purported to give the inside story of the discussion that took place in the jury room:

"More than one member of the jury had come to hear the judgement, and they informed Mr Percy Braby (Dr Stopes' solicitor) that the intention of the jury had been to find in her favour, the only difference of opinion among them being whether to award her heavy damages as eleven of them wished to, or to give her only one hundred pounds they eventually agreed on. Having been dismissed the day before the judge gave his decision they were deprived of the power — usually exercisable by juries — of correcting his misunderstanding of their meaning and of seeing that judgement was given in accordance with their intention. "The point of misunderstanding, as explained by members of the jury to Mr Braby and subsequently by him to Dr Stopes, lay in the fact that Dr Sutherland's statement that the methods used at her clinic were harmful and her propaganda criminal, were not considered by the jury as being matters of fact, but as unfair comment for which they awarded her damages: the true statement in the libel being that she had founded a clinic and given information to the poor."[3]

At first sight, Maude presents a plausible account, but how much reliance can be put on it? Firstly, and as mentioned earlier, it was not an objective biography.[4]

Secondly, there is the discrepancy in the way in which the numbers in Maude's account were expressed. For instance, the number of jurors wanting to award heavy damages was clearly expressed as "eleven". This is in contrast to the number of jury members who attended the Court on 1st March and who spoke to Mr Braby, which was expressed as "more than one". Had Mr Braby spoken to four, five, six, or even all twelve jurors, it is not unreasonable to suppose that Maude would not have written "more than one".

Thirdly, while Maude's account gave an impression that the disclosure of the jury's deliberations was spontaneous, a letter from Braby to Stopes on 2nd March 1923 suggests it may not have been. It said: "… in response to your enquiry, the name of the foreman of the jury was Mr Maurice Spencer," and he told her: "Please, however, on no account attempt to communicate with any of the jury, as this would be quite irregular"[5]

If contacting the jury was irregular, then informing his client was as well, because it is hard to see for what other purpose Stopes would have sought this information. Braby's actions were in keeping with his passive complicity when Dr Hawthorne's settled witness statement had been altered. Telling her not to contact jury members shows that he knew there was a chance that she would. His instruction was little more than a cover to absolve himself of blame if the Court found out.

Around one month later, on 11th April 1923, a "certain gentleman" met a representative of Braby & Waller to give information about how the jury arrived at their decision and what they intended by their answers.[6] Whether this was a coincidence, or was the result of his being contacted, is not known. Likewise, the man's name, or if he was a member of the jury, is not known. That said, "a certain gentleman" is precisely singular.

Later in the year, in June 1923, Stopes' book *Contraception* was published. Contrary to the impression given in Court (and, for that matter, in her biographies), Stopes continued to endorse the Gold Pin as:

> "… the best available pessary which being once inserted by a doctor secures a contraceptive means which is out of the control of the patient. Therefore, at present, it should be valuable if properly used, because it might be applied to one of the greatest problems for those advocating a racially valuable practice of contraception, namely, to secure freedom from conception on the part of the degenerate, semi-feeble-minded or carelessly drunken women who are incapable of giving the necessary thought or care to the use of contraceptives themselves, and who ought on no account from a racial point of view to bear further children."[7]

In the book, she also took the opportunity to personally attack Dr Sutherland:

> "'Once pregnancy is abolished there is no natural check on the sexual passions of husband or wife.' This low-minded statement is made by Halliday Sutherland, MD, who proceeds to glorify Ireland and Spain as models for us to copy! Such a statement as this is based on a confusion between lust and true love, and can only be made by one who is ignorant the latter, and who

ignores not only physiological laws but also forgets the instincts of human refinement and restraint which characterize love as distinct from lust."[8]

Shortly after the Judgement in the High Court, Stopes instructed Braby to commence proceedings to appeal. In preparation, she arranged for Braby & Waller to contact the clerks to the Judges of Appeal to learn their religious denomination. She was no doubt pleased to hear that none of the Judges were Catholics.

---

[1] Hall, R. (1977). *Passionate Crusader: The Life of Marie Stopes*. New York: Harcourt Brace Jovanovich. Page 237.

[2] *Ibid.*, page 238.

[3] Maude, A. (1933). *Marie Stopes: Her Work and Play*. (2nd ed.). Pages 196-7. Covent Garden: Williams & Norgate. Retrieved April 2017, 17, from https://archive.org/details/in.ernet.dli.2015.176142.

[4] Hall, R. (1977). *Passionate Crusader: The Life of Marie Stopes*. New York: Harcourt Brace Jovanovich. Page 262.

[5] Letter from Braby to Stopes dated 2nd March 1923. British Library: Western Manuscripts MS58648 (Jan 1923–Jun 1923) Vol.CCII(ff.124). Jan 1923-June 1923.

[6] Braby & Waller documentary fragment. Wellcome Library. PP/MCS/H/1:Box71. The document, a slip of paper likely used by Braby & Waller for billing purposes, reads: "WEDNESDAY 11.4.23. DR STOPES re Sutherland. Attdg the clerks to all the Judges of Appeal and ascertg that they were all members of the Church of Eng. Attdg a certain gentleman on his giving us infmrn as to how the Jury arrived at thr decsn and what they intended by thr answers. Attdg Mr H.V. Roe on the telp requstg him to call when we could give him this addnl infmn. Attdg Mr Roe on his callg fully infmg him as to the above facts."

[7] Stopes, M. C. (1923). *Contraception (Birth Control): Its Theory, History and Practice*. London: John Bale, Sons & Danielsson, Limited. Page 174. Retrieved March 28, 2019, from
https://archive.org/stream/in.ernet.dli.2015.94163/2015.94163.Contraception #page/n5/mode/2up/search/sutherland.

[8] *Ibid.*, page 206.

Chapter 44

The Court of Appeal

The role of the Court of Appeal is to review the decision of a lower court. It would not re-try the case that had been in the High Court, so much as to see if there were grounds for an appeal and, if there were, to decide how to fix it (such as, for instance, by reversing the decision or ordering a new trial).

Compared to the drama of the High Court the hearing in the Court of Appeal was an astringent legal affair. Both sides were represented by their legal counsel, but witnesses were not required.

The judgement of the Court of Appeal was delivered on 20th July 1923. It ordered that the decision of the High Court (in favour of the Defendants) be reversed, that the Plaintiff be awarded £100, one-half of the costs of the action and the costs of the appeal.

The three Judges made their decision by a margin of two to one. Lords Justices Bankes and Scrutton found for the plaintiff, while Lord Justice Younger dissented.

Bankes opined that it was "impossible to ignore any of the answers of the jury or to deal with the case as the Lord Chief Justice dealt with it by entering judgement for the defendant, because the jury found in the defendants' favour upon what the Lord Chief Justice, in the course of the argument as to how judgement should be entered, described as the main issue. If there was a subordinate issue, and the jury decided in the plaintiff's favour on that issue, she is entitled to the benefit of that decision."[1] The jury had considered the issue of fair comment separately and had found in her favour. The remedies considered by Bankes were to order a new trial or to reverse the Judgement of the High Court in Stopes' favour.[2]

Lord Justice Scrutton concurred adding, amongst other things, "I do not think it was seriously argued that we could disregard the third answer of the jury because there was no evidence on which the jury could find the comment unfair: if it was, I think the argument fails."[3]

Lord Justice Younger dissented from the judgement of his fellows: "By their first answer the jury found that the words complained of were defamatory; by their second, they found that these words, that is to say, the words which they had characterised as defamatory, were true in substance and fact. On these findings, construed according to their terms, no course, it would appear, was open to the Lord Chief Justice other than that which he took. The jury in one of their answers had, in terms and with sufficient clearness, found that the words used of the Plaintiff were defamatory of her, were all of them — not merely some of them but all of them — true. In an action for libel such a finding was a verdict for the Defendants; as to that there can, I conceive, be no question."[4]

Two judges against one meant that Stopes had won the victory she sought and she decided to try to recoup her legal fees from public donations. On 28th July, an advertisement in the *Westminster Gazette* announced an "Appeal for a £10,000 Fund" for the Mothers' Clinic, in part to cover "the heavy expenses incurred in the recent lawsuit".[5]

At the time, Dr Sutherland was at a spa in the French Pyrénées. Afflicted with toxic myocarditis, he was unable to walk a hundred yards without being short of breath.[6] The treatment included drinking and bathing in sulphurous and radium water, which led to a case of colic. He described receiving the news in his memoir:

"In the afternoons at the casino I played boule [an old French roulette-based casino game], but always stopped when I had lost twenty francs. It is a foolish game, so foolish that I was the only person in the spa who played it. The true odds are 6 to 1, and you are paid 4 to 1 when you win. A certain money-loser for the gambler, and a mug's game. Yet I was trying a system, and was annoyed one afternoon when my wife appeared and said. 'You've lost.'

"No man likes to be interrupted when he is at work, and I said: 'Of course I've lost. I've lost fifteen francs; I always lose.'

"'You've lost more than that. You've lost in the Court of Appeal. It's on the *News Bulletin* outside.'"

"The news of the disaster saved me five francs. Rising from the table I said: 'I hate this place. Let us go to Spain.'"[7]

---

[1] Femina Books. (1967). *The Trial of Marie Stopes*. (M. Box, Ed.) London: Femina Books Ltd. Page 387.

[2] *Ibid.*, page 388.

[3] *Ibid.*

[4] *Ibid.*, page 388-9.

[5] *Work of the Mothers' Clinic. Appeal for a £10,000 Fund*. Newspaper cutting from the Westminster Gazette. Westminster Archdiocese Archive. BO5/59 Birth Control 1921-26.

[6] Sutherland, H. (1934). *A Time to Keep*. Geoffrey Bles. Page 276.

[7] *Ibid.*, page 278.

Chapter 45

The House of Lords

At this point, Sutherland appeared to have lost the case and, unless there was a successful appeal to the House of Lords (at that time Britain's highest court), the decision of the Court of Appeal was final.

An appeal to the House of Lords would cost money and, once again, money was a problem. On 7th August 1923, Sir Charles Russell wrote to Monsignor Jackman, Secretary to Cardinal Bourne in Westminster, to advise: "The position at the moment is that we strongly advise Dr Sutherland to appeal to the House of Lords, but this is not possible without funds. Even so far, we ourselves are well over £1,000 out of pocket."[1]

By October, Edward Eyre of the Catholic Federation was organising the fund raising.[2] He arranged a meeting of around 30 people at *Pagani's* in Great Portland Street — a bohemian restaurant associated with artists and musicians — on 15th November. When, inevitably, the issue of illegal maintenance was raised, Mr Oddie of Charles Russell & Co assured those present that it did not apply to coreligionists and that, even if it were to, the liability of each person would not exceed £4,000.[3]

The prospects for raising money were dire. The Catholic Union and the Saint Vincent de Paul Society declined the opportunity to provide financial support. A suggestion to raise money in the parishes was rejected when everyone voted against it except for the proposer and the seconder.[4]

At this point, Edward Eyre asked to be authorised by the committee "to draw up the necessary appeals," and they granted him the authority.[5] He set up the "Sutherland-Waring Appeal Fund" and issued a leaflet: *The Moral Problem of To-Day*. In May 1924, *The Tablet* and *The Universe* appealed for funds. The editorial of the latter said:

"The Nation is being swept by a powerful and insidious campaign to encourage the artificial limitation of the family. It was a campaign designed to reach the masses, and it was reaching them. So successful was it that 'birth control' became a normal topic of conversation. From a national point of view it was a dangerous campaign. For the nation needs children. A nation with empty cradles is a nation with a black tomorrow..."[6]

The next part was set-in upper-case text:

"An action for libel, taken out by Dr Marie Stopes, Ph.D, went in favour of the defendants... the Court of Appeal reversed the decision and left the Catholic champions responsible for heavy legal costs. The case must not be allowed to end there..."[7]

The following month, Stopes took legal action for contempt of court against *The Tablet* and *The Universe* on the grounds that the matter was sub judice (in other words, before the court). Both publications were bound to not make mention of the matter until the appeal had been heard in the House of Lords.

Despite these setbacks, the funds were raised. Eyre wrote to Monsignor Jackman enclosing a cheque to repay Cardinal Bourne for the earlier loan of £400 that he had made before the High Court trial. Bourne instructed Jackman to return the cheque uncashed as a gift to the fighting fund.[8]

At this point, Braby went abroad, fell ill, and died. According to Maude's biography *Marie Stopes: Her Work and Play*:

"Her solicitor, the late Mr Percy Braby, felt confident of winning the appeal, being prepared to take the unusual steps to present the evidence of members of the jury to show what their intention had been, but he went for a short holiday abroad before dealing with the important data, some of which he alone knew, and a few days later he died after an operation, in Finland."[9]

In November, the case was heard in the House of Lords.

"The five law Lords hearing the appeal in the House of Lords on 21st November 1924, were Viscount Cave, the Lord Chancellor, Viscount Finley, Lord Shaw of Dunfermline, Lord Wrenbury and Lord Carson who held that: "(1) Judgement should be entered for the defendants on the ground that there was no evidence to support the finding that the comments were unfair; and by Lord Shaw of Dunfermline and Lord Carson on the further grounds that the finding of the jury on the plea of Justification afforded a complete answer to the action.
"(2) That a new trial ought not to be granted on the ground of misdirection, as no substantial miscarriage had been occasioned by the misdirection, if any. Lord Wrenbury dissented on both points.
"Decision of Court of Appeal reversed."[10]

Lord Wrenbury's dissent was on the grounds that, to him, it was clear the jury had found that "the libel of victimisation of poor and helpless persons and of criminal action" was not justified.[11] In other words, Sutherland's implied statement that Stopes was committing crimes and making victims of the poor was not true in substance and in fact.

Stopes was ordered to repay to the defendants the £100 damages that she had been awarded in the Court of Appeal, and to pay their legal costs in the High Court, the Court of Appeal and the House of Lords.

The Law Lords had made their final verdict and that was the end of the matter.

Stopes, however, was not to be denied the victory that she thought was rightfully hers, and she wrote to the Lord Chancellor:

"My Lord,
"May I humbly petition your Lordship's consideration. Now that my case (Stopes v Sutherland) is concluded by a majority of your Lordships allowing the Appeal from a Judgement of the Court of Appeal in my favour, I desire respectfully to draw your Lordship's attention to the very grave injustice done me in a judgement founded on the erroneous suppositions that the jury meant certain things by the answers left to them by the

Lord Chief Justice at the original trial. The position is perhaps without precedent in English law and merits your Lordship's careful attention.

"The Lord Chief Justice dismissed the jury the day before giving his judgement and thus they were deprived of the power exercisable by juries of then and there correcting any misunderstanding of their meaning and seeing that judgement is given in accordance with the intention of their verdict.

"That the attitude of the jury has been gravely misinterpreted I have conclusive reason to know, as more than one member of the jury approached my solicitor (the late Mr. Percy Braby) and informed him that the intention of the jury was throughout in my favour and they were much concerned with the legal construction placed upon their answers, with the resulting consequence to me.

"Although informing me of this, my solicitor did not use this fact in the Court of Appeal, as he was so confident that I should win there, and I did win. Thereafter, just before the hearing in your Lordship's house he died suddenly and unexpectedly and I was left solely aware of his intention to use this fact if necessary before your Lordships. I was most anxious that this matter of grave importance should have been made known to your Lordships had I not been restrained on the grounds that it was not regular for me to interpose, much as I wished to do so. Your Lordships were not acquainted as you should have been with the fact that the main stings of the libel (viz., the very serious charges that the methods used at my clinic are harmful and that my propaganda is criminal) were not considered by the jury as being matters of fact, but as among the matters of opinion for which damages were awarded to me: the true facts in the libel that I did found a Clinic and did there give information to the poor.

"I realise that your lordships would not willingly do me an injustice: hence I desire to make the strongest protest in my power against the serious injury done to me by a conclusion founded on wrong premises; and therefore even if it be without precedent, I pray your Lordship to

open a reconsideration of the Appeal by the House of Lords itself so that legal subtleties based on misapprehensions may not rob me of my victory.
"I am, My Lord, Your Lordship's faithful and obedient servant."[12]

The Lord Chancellor's response is not known.

The legal process is elegant and robust, imperfect and unpredictable. Overall, nine judges had been involved in the matter. Six of these had ruled in favour of the defendants, and three had ruled in favour of the plaintiff. Sutherland and Harding & More had won, and the costs for Stopes were vast, at around £12,000. [13]

The day after the decision, Cardinal Bourne told his congregation: "… a really great victory has been gained for the cause of morality… it seems to me there is a particular significance in the fact that this very far-reaching decision was arrived at on the Feast of the Presentation of Our Lady."[14]

---

[1] Letter from Charles Russell to Monsignor Jackman dated 7th August 1923. Westminster Archdiocese Archive. BO5/59 Birth Control 1921-26.
[2] Letter from Edward Eyre to Monsignor Jackman dated 3rd October 1923. Westminster Archdiocese Archive. BO5/59 Birth Control 1921-26.
[3] Letter from G.L. Smith to Monsignor Jackman dated 21st November 1923. Westminster Archdiocese Archive. BO5/59 Birth Control 1921-26.
[4] *Ibid.*
[5] *Ibid.*
[6] Hall, R. (1977). *Passionate Crusader: The Life of Marie Stopes*. New York: Harcourt Brace Jovanovich. Page 250-1.
[7] *Ibid.*, page 251.
[8] Letter from Edward Eyre to Monsignor Jackman dated 20th March 1924. Westminster Archdiocese Archive. BO5/59 Birth Control 1921-26. Cardinal Bourne contributed £500 in total.
[9] Maude, A. (1933). *Marie Stopes: Her Work and Play*. (2nd ed.). Covent Garden: Williams & Norgate. Page 202. Retrieved April 2017, 17, from https://archive.org/details/in.ernet.dli.2015.176142.
[10] Femina Books. (1967). *The Trial of Marie Stopes*. (M. Box, Ed.) London: Femina Books Ltd. Page 390.
[11] *Ibid.*, page 391.
[12] Copy of Petition sent 1st December 1924 to the Right Honourable, The Lord High Chancellor. Wellcome Library. PP/MCS/H/4a:Box72.
[13] Hall, R. (1977). *Passionate Crusader: The Life of Marie Stopes*. New York: Harcourt Brace Jovanovich. Page 240.
[14] *Ibid.*

Chapter 46

What Happened Next

Following the trial, Dr Sutherland continued to campaign against birth control. In 1924 he warned that the:

"... campaign in favour of birth control was a national danger. They could not point to any nation in the whole history of the world who adopted this vice and did not perish. The advocates of artificial birth control were clever people, well organised, well financed, and by every art — pictured, screened, staged and spoken — they were deliberately making an appeal to the lowest qualities in a nation weakened by war... The wildest Communist on the Clyde had done less to sow the seeds of revolution than had these Hedonists."[1]

In his 1925 book, *Birth Control Exposed*, he wrote:

"If a wave of madness passed over our country, and this eugenic nightmare came true, we might very well ask what tribunal is to decide as to which of us is unfit. About you who are reading this book, I know nothing whatever, but I have a shrewd suspicion that the neo-malthusians have already decided about me. The point is that when these people discuss sterilization, they picture themselves sitting round a table and ordering other people to be sterilized. In the same way Communists, when they talk about the bloody revolution, always picture themselves knocking other people on the head, and indeed they become very angry when I tell them that the other people will retaliate. And thus do all enemies of freedom."[2]

These words are a jarring reminder that the eugenic question had not been resolved when Sutherland wrote them. They were written three years before the Eugenics Society drafted the *Sterilization Bill*,[3] and six years before Archibald Church MP sought to introduce it into Parliament.[4]

For his part, Dr Sutherland was under no illusions as to what the "eugenic nightmare" would entail. In 1922 he wrote in the *Westminster Gazette*:

"Even if a Super-Eugenist, greatly daring, were to slay every consumptive in the land tonight, we should breed the disease afresh before tomorrow's morn."[5]

He referred to the lethal chamber again in *Birth Control Exposed* (1925)[6] and even featured one in his 1936 short story, *The Perfect Eugenic State*.[7]

In 1933, Dr Sutherland achieved international success with his autobiographical book, *Arches of the Years*. It made the *Publishers' Weekly* list for that year,[8] and was translated into eight languages.[9] Another autobiographical work, *A Time to Keep*, followed in 1934 which prompted this accolade from G.K. Chesterton:

"Dr. Halliday Sutherland is a born writer, especially a born story-teller. Dr. Sutherland, who is distinguished in medicine, is an amateur in the sense that he only writes when he has nothing better to do. But when he does, it could hardly be done better."[10]

One further autobiographical book, *In My Path* (1936), was followed by accounts of his travels: *Lapland Journey* (1938); *Hebridean Journey* (1939); *Southward Journey* (1942); *Spanish Journey* (1948) and *Irish Journey* (1956). Nonetheless, he continued to write about moral issues in *Laws of Life* (1935) and *Control of Life* (1944).

Given the ready availability of contraceptive devices today and the efforts to educate people in their use, one might be forgiven for thinking that Dr Sutherland lost the historical argument. If he did, he at least had the consolation of being right when, in 1922, he predicted the outcome of Stopes' experiment:

"Our declining birth-rate is a fact of the utmost gravity, and a more serious position has never confronted the British people. Here in the midst of a great nation, at the end of a victorious war, the law of decline is working, and by that law the greatest empires in the world have perished. In comparison with that single fact all other dangers, be they war, of politics, or of disease, are of little moment. Attempts have already been made to avert the consequences by partial endowment of motherhood and by saving infant life. Physiologists are now seeking the endocrinous glands and the vitamins for a substance to assist procreation. 'Where are my children?' was the question shouted yesterday from the cinemas.[11] 'Let us have children, children at any price,' will be the cry of tomorrow.

"And all these thoughts were once in the mind of Augustus, Emperor of the world from the Atlantic to the Euphrates, from Mount Atlas to the Danube and the Rhine. The Catholic Church has never taught that 'an avalanche of children' should be brought into the world regardless of consequences. God is not mocked; as men sow, so shall they reap, and against a law of nature both the transient amelioration wrought by philanthropists and the subtle expediences of scientific politicians are alike futile. If our civilisation is to survive we must abandon those ideals that lead to decline. There is only one civilisation immune from decay, and that civilisation endures on the practical eugenics once taught by a united Christendom and now expounded almost solely by the Catholic Church."[12]

And not just in relation to Britain:

"The cataclysm which may end the eighth known epoch in civilisation may be a lack of European children."[13]

[1] *"Dangers of Birth Control"*. Weekly Freeman's Journal, 24 May 1924. Page 7.

[2] Sutherland, H. (1925). *Birth Control Exposed*. Cecil Palmer, London. Page 219.

[3] *Sterilization Bill*. Eugenics Review. 1928 Oct; 20(3): 166–168.

[4] House of Commons Debate 21 July 1931 vol 255 cc1249-57. Strictly speaking the measure was to allow for the sterilisation of mental defectives, not for their compulsory sterilisation. That said, Church stated it was "… merely a first step in order that the community as a whole should be able to make an experiment on a small scale so that later on we may have the benefit of the results and experience gained in order to come to conclusions before bringing in a Bill for the compulsory sterilisation of the unfit." See: https://api.parliament.uk/historic-hansard/commons/1931/jul/21/sterilization retrieved August 1, 2020. For more information see *The Voluntary Sterelization Campaign in Britain 1918-39* by John Macnicol.

[5] Sutherland, H. (1922, May 19). *Heredity & Consumption: Marriage Problem - A Challenge To The Eugenists*. Westminster Gazette. Sutherland family archive.

[6] Sutherland, H. (1925). *Birth Control Exposed*. Cecil Palmer, London. Page 218.

[7] Sutherland, H. (1934). *A Time to Keep*. Geoffrey Bles.

[8] Korda, M. (2001). *Making the list: a cultural history of the American bestseller, 1900-1999*. New York: Barnes & Noble Publishing Inc.

[9] British Medical Journal. (1960, April 30). *Obituary Dr Halliday G. Sutherland*, M.D. , 1368-9 Retrieved January 29, 2019 from https://www.ncbi.nlm.nih.gov/pmc/articles/PMC1967536.

[10] Chesterton, G. K. *Documents of the Twentieth Century*. "The Listener" 12 December 1934.

[11] *Where Are My Children?* was a 1916 movie starring Tyrone Power and Helen Riaume which dealt with the themes of abortion, birth control and Malthusianism. One key scene is the trial of a birth-controller. Stopes was aware of the film (she mentioned it in her speech to the Voluntary Parenthood League on 27th October 1921) and, while she did not like it, it may have given her the idea of a courtroom drama to achieve publicity for her cause.

[12] Sutherland, H. (1922). *Birth Control: A Statement of Christian Doctrine Against the Neo-Malthusians*. London: Harding & More. Pages 155-6.

[13] *Uxbridge and West Drayton Gazette*. Friday 27th September 1929. Page 21.

Chapter 47

Everything Changed so that Everything Could Stay the Same

"The superficially sympathetic man flings a coin to the beggar; the more deeply sympathetic man builds an almshouse for him so that he need no longer beg; but perhaps the most radically sympathetic of all is the man who arranges that the beggar shall not be born."
— *Havelock Ellis, The Task of Social Hygiene (1912).*[1]

Stopes' name lives on today through Marie Stopes International (MSI), an organisation that provides contraception, sterilisation and abortion in 37 countries (including in many third world countries). In 2018, MSI received donations of £158 million and facilitated 4.8 million abortions.[2]

At first sight, there is little resemblance between MSI and the clinic opened by Stopes and Roe at 61 Marlborough Road, Holloway on 17th March 1921. The logo of the lantern has gone and "Babies in the right place" has been replaced with "Children by choice, not chance". There are connections though, most obviously the name, and the fact that MSI still retain Stopes' second clinic, established at 108 Whitfield Street, Fitzrovia in 1926.

◆　　◆　　◆

In 2015, while beginning the research for this book in London, I met Ann Farmer whose books (*By Their Fruits* and *Prophets and Priests*) concerned aspects of Dr Sutherland's work. We discussed the eugenists of one-hundred years ago and compared them to their modern equivalents. Ann said that she would rather deal with the eugenists back then than with the ones today. Given the vile language used to describe those they considered inferior — Stopes' "spawn of drunkards"[3] remark came to mind — this surprised me, so I asked her why. She replied that the eugenists of 100 years ago openly stated their aims whereas the eugenists of today conceal their hand.[4] Indeed, the concealment has been so successful that many people are under the impression that eugenics somehow ceased to exist after 1945.

◆　　◆　　◆

In 1958 Dr Marie Stopes died. She bequeathed the freehold of the building housing her clinic at 108 Whitfield Street to the Eugenics Society (formerly known as the Eugenics Education Society). Her intention was that it would be maintained as an independent unit. Marie Stopes Memorial Foundation Limited, a limited company ultimately controlled by the Council of the Eugenics Society, was established to receive and manage her bequest. Funds from the Foundation were allocated to the general purposes of the Eugenics Society and to research projects.

In 1960, the assets of the unincorporated Society for Constructive Birth Control and Racial Progress were legally transferred to the Marie Stopes Memorial Foundation.

At around that time, the Eugenics Society was at a crossroads. Recruitment programs had failed to abate the fall in membership from 768 in 1932 to 456 in 1956. The Honorary Secretary of the Society, Dr C.P. Blacker wrote a memorandum, *The Eugenics Society's Future*, in which he outlined the issues and recommended the way forward.

One of his suggestions was: "That the Society should pursue eugenic ends by less obvious means, that is by a policy of crypto-eugenics, which was apparently proving successful with the US Eugenics Society"[5]

It may be splitting hairs, but "crypto" is the Greek for "secret", not "less obvious". In February 1960, senior members of the Council presented recommendations for the re-orientation and reform of the Society, and they decided that: "The Society's activities in crypto-eugenics should be pursued vigorously, and specifically that the Society should increase its monetary support of the FPA [Family Planning Association] and the IPPF [International Planned Parenthood Federation]… "[6]

In addition, they decided: "The Society should change its name to The Galton Society."

Subsequent changes were in accordance with this policy. In 1968, the Society ceased publication of the *Eugenics Review* and replaced it with the *Journal of Biosocial Science*. In 1975, the Society sold the Whitfield Street clinic to Dr Tim Black, founder of MSI[7] and, in 1989, the Eugenics Society changed its name to The Galton Institute.[8]

MSI's website outlines how the organisation came to be established:

"In November 1975, [Dr Tim Black] learnt that the historic Marie Stopes clinic was closing. Together with his wife Jean Black and Phil Harvey, Tim took on the lease, founded Marie Stopes International and reopened Marie Stopes House in January 1976. They set about rebuilding its finances and reputation as a family planning services provider."[9]

Prior to that, in the 1960s, Tim Black had been working as a doctor in New Guinea. He returned to Britain and subsequently accepted a Ford fellowship to study Population Dynamics at the University of North Carolina.[10] It was here that he met Phil Harvey with whom he was to set up MSI.[11]

MSI's website includes the life-changing event that led Black from his career as a medical doctor to become a birth-controller:

"In the late 1960s, Tim Black was working as a district health officer in the Sepik district of New Guinea, and it was around that time that he began to reassess his focus on trying to cure or save lives as a matter of course. After saving the life of a three-month old girl, he was shocked that her widowed mother — who already had five children and no steady income — didn't want her to survive.

"'My shock was absolute. My immediate reaction was one of utter indignation. The gulf separating my life experience and that of this poor woman was complete. She had wanted the baby to die — not live — during the operation.

"'I suddenly realised that I had presented her, not only with her baby, but with another mouth to feed, another dependent human being to whom she could offer nothing: no father, no education, no future.

"'It was at that point that I began to realise that preventing a birth could be as important as saving a life.'"

Black's words bring to mind the words of Havelock Ellis in his 1912 book, *The Task of Social Hygiene*, quoted at the beginning of this chapter. Black and Ellis made essentially the same point.

The adoption of crypto-eugenics by the Eugenics Society enabled it to continue its program essentially unnoticed and avoiding controversy. Because everything changed, everything could remain the same — we have come full circle.

---

[1] Ellis, H. (1912). *The Task of Social Hygiene*, Houghton Mifflin Company, Boston and New York.

[2] "Providing access to safe abortion and post-abortion care is at the core of our mission. In 2018, MSI provided more than 4.8 million services to women and girls who turned to us for safe abortion and post-abortion care services." Source: https://mariestopes.org/media/3567/financial-statement-and-annual-report-2018.pdf viewed on 7 November 2019. Pages 14 and 50.

[3] "From the point of view of the economics of the nation, it is racial madness to rifle the pockets of the thrifty and intelligent who are struggling to do their best for their own families of one and two and squander the money on low grade mental deficient, the spawn of drunkards, the puny families of women so feckless and deadened that they apathetically breed like rabbits." Dr Marie Stopes, *John Bull*, 2nd February 1924.

[4] In *By Their Fruits: Eugenics, Population Control, and the Abortion Industry*, Farmer shows how many of the advocates for abortion reform in post-war Britain were eugenists.

[5] Schenk, Faith and Parkes F.A. (1968, September). *Activities of the Eugenics Society. The Eugenics Review*, 142-161. Retrieved May 27, 2019, from https://www.ncbi.nlm.nih.gov/pmc/articles/PMC2906074/pdf/eugenrev00 003-0012.pdf.

[6] *Ibid.*

[7] Dr Tim Black C.B.E. was the nephew of the great-grandson of Charles Darwin, traced as follows: (1) Tim Black was the son of Stephen Black. (2) Stephen Black's sister was Brigit Ursula Hope Black, who married Erasmus Darwin Barlow 1915-2005. (3) Erasmus was the son of Sir J.A.N. Barlow and Nora Barlow (nee Darwin). (4) Nora was the daughter of Horace Darwin. (5) Horace was the son of Charles Darwin. A list of members of the Eugenics Society (https://www.scribd.com/doc/97123506/Eugenics-Society-Members-A-Z-2012 Retrieved June 21, 2019) shows that Erasmus Barlow, his father (Sir J.A.N. Barlow) and his grandfather (Horace Darwin) were all members of the Eugenics Society.

[8] The Galton Institute. (2019, October 30). History / Archives. Retrieved from The Galton Institute: Exploring Human Heredity: http://www.galtoninstitute.org.uk/history/archives/.

[9] Marie Stopes International. About. Retrieved October 30, 2019 from https://mariestopes.org/about-us/our-history.

[10] Gulland, A. (2015, February 2). *Obituaries: Tim Black*. Retrieved November 12, 2019, from The BMJ: https://doi.org/10.1136/bmj.h459.

[11] Phil Harvey's book *The Government vs Erotica: The Siege of Adam & Eve*. Prometheus Books, 2001 included a detailed description of his meeting Dr Black and the establishment of their lifelong business partnership.

Chapter 48

Epilogue

In the preface, I cited the BBC's online history as a proxy for the accepted view of the Stopes v Sutherland libel trial:

"In 1921, Stopes opened a family planning clinic in Holloway, north London, the first in the country. It offered a free service to married women... The Catholic church was Stopes's fiercest critic. In 1923, Stopes sued Catholic doctor Halliday Sutherland for libel."

This book has presented evidence that the accepted view of the Stopes v Sutherland libel trial is false. Stopes' clinic was part of a eugenic program and the aims of the CBC were wider than what we would understand as "family planning". While Catholics were her fiercest opponents, the failure to mention the racial hygiene and eugenic aspects of her program, means that much of what it was that they opposed is excised. The history is reduced to a simplistic "Catholics against contraceptives" meme.

In 2014, I contacted the BBC to ask them to amend their article, and I gave the reasons. Following an exchange of e-mails, I was informed that the online history page had been "archived".

Now, if you think (as I did) that "archived" meant that the article would be removed from public view, you are wrong (as I was). In this case, "archived" meant that a notice had been placed at the top of the page stating: "This page has been archived and is no longer updated." The article remains online, readily accessible by Internet search engines, and it perpetuates what I would argue are significant errors.

In fairness, the BBC could claim that their article was based on the biographies of Stopes and so they are not to blame.

Were they to do so, I would accept their claim. For too long, the biographies of Stopes have failed to properly grasp the nettle of her eugenic agenda. It is time that the biographers of Stopes wrote about her agenda as it was, rather than as they would have liked it to have been.

One consequence is that the reputations of her opponents have been unfairly sullied. Here I am talking not just about Dr Sutherland, but Professor Louise McIlroy (and others) as well. Likewise, the same biographers should not repeat Stopes' false assertion that McIlroy was a hypocrite for using the cervical cap (See Appendix 4), not least because the memory of Professor McIlroy deserves far better.

These closing words are not just a gripe about a failed attempt to get the BBC to amend a webpage. They seek to address the inertia that leaves the accepted (but false) narrative in place, and the inability of those who call themselves historians to change their minds, despite the evidence.

It is vitally important that the events covered in this book are known because, contrary to the popular impression that eugenics stopped after 1945, it is still with us today. The fact is that eugenics never really went away, so much as to undergo a makeover and assume a new disguise.

The harsh words of the eugenists of one-hundred years ago (for instance, Stopes' reference to "an imbecile or monster or degenerate or diseased child" in the High Court) have been replaced with the innocuous language of medicine (for instance, the Nuchal Translucency Procedure for Downs Syndrome). While the language has changed, the moral issues have not.

We would do well to remember the words of Dr Halliday Sutherland in *Birth Control*:

"Moral catastrophes inevitably lead to physical catastrophes."

The Sutherland family in the early 1920s. From left
to right: Dr Sutherland, [nurse, name not known]
holding Jane Sutherland, Janie and Muriel Sutherland.

Jane, eldest daughter of Halliday and Muriel
Sutherland, with Muriel in the early 1920s.

The gravestone of Dr Sutherland in the Logie Easter
Graveyard, near Invergordon, Scotland.

"In memory of Halliday Gibson Sutherland (Edin) physician
and author. 24 June 1882 –19th Apr 1960 and of his 3rd son
Vincent Joseph Sutherland R.A.F.V.R. killed in action over
Germany 19 March 1945.

"This is the day which the Lord hath made,
let us be glad and rejoice therein.

May they rest in peace."

PART 4

GLOSSARY & APPENDICES

Glossary

A1. Used by military recruitment to designate recruits of the highest calibre. The letters designated the degree of utility ('A' meant fit for general service, 'B' meant fit for service abroad in a support capacity, and 'C' meant fit for service at home only).

Ab initio. Latin meaning "from the beginning".

Abortifacient. A device that destroys, or provides the means to destroy, the products of conception.

Aetiology. An enquiry into the causes or origins of a disease.

Antisepsis. Destruction or exclusion of disease-causing germs.

Asepsis. Absence of living germs of disease.

BMA. British Medical Association.

BMJ / British Medical Journal. The journal of the British Medical Association.

Bacillus Tuberculosis. Latin name for the germs that cause tuberculosis.

Barrister. A legal advocate who represents a party to a legal action in court. They present the case in court, liaise with and follow the directions of the judge, examine and cross-examine witnesses and make legal arguments in court. A barrister is an officer of the court and he or she is bound to act in accordance with the highest standards of the profession.

Besant, Annie. See: Bradlaugh, Charles.

Biometrics. The statistical study of biological phenomena.

Birth rate. The statistical measure of the number of live births in a population.

Bona fide. Latin meaning "in good faith".

Bradlaugh, Charles. A Member of Parliament who, with Annie Besant, published a Malthusian birth-control tract *The Fruits of Philosophy*. They were tried for criminal obscenity in 1877. For Dr Sutherland's account of their trial, see Appendix 3.

Burden of proof. The obligation to prove that something is true. The law specifies which parties to a legal action have the burden of proof. For instance, if the defence of "Justification" is used to defend an action for defamation, the law specifies that it is for the defendant to prove that the assertion was true, not for the plaintiff to prove that it was false.

C3. Used by military recruitment to designate recruits who were unfit to serve. See also: A1.

CBC. The Society for Constructive Birth Control and Racial Progress, founded in 1921 to support the Mothers' Clinic.

Cervical cap. A contraceptive device that adheres to the cervix and covers the *os* (the entrance to the womb). In the High Court trial, it was frequently referred to as the "check pessary".

Charwoman. Cleaning lady.

Consumption. Tuberculosis of the lungs.

Cross-examine. The cross-examination takes place when one of the parties to the action (or their witnesses) are questioned by the barrister representing their opponent. The person being cross-examined gives their testimony in the witness box and they take a solemn oath to tell the truth.

Defamation. The act of harming another person's reputation without good cause or justification. The act might be a permanent statement (such as a written statement in a book) in which case it is a libel, or impermanent (such as a spoken statement) in which case it is a slander.

Defendant. The person in a legal dispute who is accused of breaking the law.

Degeneration. Gradual deterioration.

Diaphragm. In the context of the book, a barrier contraceptive. The difference between a diaphragm and a cervical cap is explained in the chapter entitled "Stopes visits McIlroy".

Diathesis. A hereditary disposition to a disease or medical condition.

Differential birth rate. In the context of this book, the observation that poorer families produced more children than those who were well-off.

Dysgenic. The opposite of eugenic.

EES. Eugenics Education Society. In 1926 the EES changed its name to the Eugenics Society.

Edinburgh System. Also known as the "Edinburgh Anti-Tuberculosis Scheme". A coordinated program for the prevention, identification and treatment of tuberculosis developed in Edinburgh by Sir Robert Phillip.

Eugenics. Defined by its founder, Sir Francis Galton, as "the "study of agencies under social control that may improve or impair the racial qualities of future generations either physically or mentally." Eugenic measures are sometimes referred to as "positive" (in the sense of promoting or encouraging a particular outcome) and "negative" (in the sense of prohibiting or preventing a particular outcome).

Examination / examination in chief. The examination takes place when one of the parties to the action (or their witnesses) are questioned by the barrister representing them (or the party they are supporting) in court.

Fair Comment. A defence to an action for defamation. As a contemporary expert of defamation, W. Blake Odgers KC put it: "The plaintiff's reputation must not be injured [and] the defendant's freedom of speech must not be restricted." The defendant had an "undoubted right to criticise and comment on the public acts of a public man", but not to "unnecessarily impute dishonourable motives, or maliciously pry into his private concerns". The defence applies if the allegedly defamatory statement "… is a fair comment on a matter which is of public interest or is submitted to public criticism".

Feeble-minded. According to Daniel J. Kevles (in *In the Name of Eugenics*), a term used to denote a wide range of mental deficiencies and tendencies towards socially deviant behaviour.

French Letter. Slang term for a condom.

Gold Pin / Gold Spring. Intra-uterine contraceptive device.

Guinea. In pre-decimal currency, twenty-one shillings.

Hearsay. A statement made out of court that is offered as evidence in a trial. It is not allowed as evidence on the basis that it is unverified. For instance, when Hastings asked Sir William Arbuthnot Lane if he knew what Lord Dawson's view was, Lane could answer "yes" or "no", but Lane's statement as to what Dawson's view actually was is inadmissible on the grounds that it is hearsay.

Intra-Uterine Stem. A medical device that is inserted into the uterus.

Idiot. According to Daniel J. Kevles (in *In the Name of Eugenics*), a category of feeblemindedness devised by American psychologist Henry H. Goddard. An idiot was a feebleminded person with a mental age of one or two.

Imbecile. See "idiot". According to Goddard, a feebleminded person whose mental age ranged from three to seven.

Justification. A defence in a suit for defamation that claims that the defamatory statement was true in substance and in fact. It is a complete answer to the action, in other words, once the statement was found to be true then that is the end of the matter. The reason is that if you make a true statement about a person, they should not be able to recover damages for any harm to their reputation.

Libel. See "defamation".

Maintenance (also known as "unlawful maintenance"). The act of funding litigation that does not concern you.

Malthusian / Malthusianism. An adherent of / the theories relating to population first posited by T.R. Malthus (1766-1834) in *An Essay on the Principle of Population*. In a nutshell, Malthusianism posits that population will increase to the point at which it leads to war (from competition for scarce resources), disease (from over-crowding) and famine (from there being insufficient food to feed the increased population). Malthus himself thought that if people were to abstain from sex, the problem of over-population could be avoided.

Monsignor. Honorary title granted by the Pope to a small number of priests to recognise their valuable service to the Catholic Church.

Neo-Malthusian. A Malthusian who supports the use of contraceptives in order to limit the population, in contrast with T.R. Malthus who thought that the limitation of population should be achieved by abstinence from sex.

Occlude. To cover, shut or close.

Os. A mouth or opening. In the context of this book, the *os* is the opening to the womb.

Paleobotanist. A botanist who studies plant fossils and ancient vegetation.

Panegyric. An uncritical work or performance that formally and elaborately praises its subject.

Perjury. The intentional act of swearing a false oath or falsifying an affirmation to tell the truth.

Pasteurisation. The heat-treatment of milk to kill bacteria that may be present in it.

Pessary. A device that worn in the vagina, for example, a contraceptive diaphragm.

Phthisis. A medical condition characterised by wasting away (pronounced "thigh-sis").

Picture Palace. Old-fashioned British term for a cinema.

Plaintiff. The person who initiates a legal action in civil law.

Pro tanto. Latin term meaning "only to that extent".

Race suicide. The death of a race of people brought on (in the context of this book) by dysgenic breeding.

Racial stocks. The quality and calibre of a nation's citizens.

Rubber shop. A shop that sold rubber goods, though its colloquial meaning was a place where rubber contraceptives were sold.

Sanatorium. A residential medical institution for the supervision and treatment of disease.

Sepsis. A life-threatening condition caused by infection that leads to systemic organ failure.

Shorthand writer, also known as a stenographer. A person who transcribed spoken words, such as in a meeting or in court proceedings. Shorthand refers to the system of symbols used to facilitate the transcription of the spoken words.

Slander. See "defamation".

Solicitor. A legal advisor who prepares a case for trial, including drawing up and registration of legal documents, gathering evidence, arranging for the appearance of witnesses and liaising with the solicitor for the opposing party. A solicitor is an officer of the court and he or she is bound to act in accordance with the highest standards of the profession.

Statement of claim. The statement of claim is one of the first legal documents in a legal dispute in civil law. The statement is issued by the plaintiff to the defendant and it sets out the legal wrongs that the defendant is alleged to have committed as well as the legal remedies that the plaintiff seeks. Like other documents in a legal dispute, the statement of claim is registered with the Court.

Stenographer. See shorthand writer.

Sterilisation. In the context of this book, the means by which a person is rendered incapable of reproducing.

Subpoena. A court order compelling someone to attend the court, usually to testify in a case.

Tubercle Bacillus. Latin name for the bacteria that causes tuberculosis.

Tuberculosis. Disease caused by the *tubercle bacillus*.

Undesirables. Persons who eugenists did not want, owing to their inferior mental and physical qualities.

Unfit. A person who is not well adapted to their environment and who finds it difficult to survive as a result. It derives from Herbert Spencer's concept of "the survival of the fittest".

Uterus. also known as the womb. A muscular organ found in female mammals in which offspring are developed prior to birth.

Venereologist. A doctor who specialises in sexually transmitted diseases.

Writ. A written order of the court which issues a command to the person to whom it is addressed.

Appendix 1

The Tenets of the CBC

The tenets of the Society for Constructive Birth Control and Racial Progress was published in an appendix in *The Authorized Life of Marie C. Stopes* by Aylmer Maude.[1]

THE TENETS OF THE CBC

The objects for which the CBC was founded are as follows:— The objects of the Society are (a) to bring home to all the fundamental nature of the reforms of the conscious and constructive control of conception and the illumination of sex life as a basis of racial progress: (b) to consider the individual, national, international, racial, political, economic, scientific, spiritual and other aspects of the theme, for which purpose meetings will be held, publications issued, Research Committees, Commissions of Enquiry and other activities will be organized from time to time as circumstances require and facilities offer; (c) to supply all who still need it with the full knowledge of sound physiological methods of control.

As these objects indicate, the scope of the Society is very wide, its interests far-reaching, and its possibilities of future development very elastic. Even to-day the tenets which appear fundamental to different members of the Society will naturally vary, hence no one of the following is binding on an individual member. General agreement with the objects of the Society suffices for membership.

Nonetheless, it has been felt that it would be useful explicitly to state in concise form what may be described as the bedrock of general agreement of the Society. This is as follows:—

1.—The hygiene of sex is as suitable and proper a subject for scientific and serious study as the hygiene of nutrition, locomotion, or any other human function.

2. — Owing to the shamefaced attitude which has until recently characterized our dealings with the subject, all the manifold data involved in the different aspects of sex life have not had the direct scientific and physiological handling they deserve and require. We deplore this and shall endeavour to remedy it.

3. — We maintain that the highest spiritual development, the noblest intellectual illumination, and the sweetest romantic possibilities of individual sex experience, are not damaged by sound scientific knowledge, but contrariwise, are enhanced and elevated.

4. — We consider that in relation to the procreation of additional members of the community, the best possible knowledge of scientific and technical details should be available to those undertaking this important social duty.

5. — We believe that the haphazard production of children by ignorant, coerced, or diseased mothers is profoundly detrimental to the race. We believe, therefore, that parenthood should no longer be the result of ignorance or accident, but should be a power used voluntarily and with knowledge.

6. — We maintain that to achieve this result a knowledge of the simple hygiene of contraception is essential.

7. — We advocate that no individual contraceptive measure as final or fundamental, but maintain that the best measures available at any time should be taught and known by the people.

8. — We desire to keep constantly in touch with all advances in science which may have a bearing on the practical details of contraceptive measures, and for this purpose we have organized a Medical Research Committee to keep our Society informed as to the current scientific position of the hygiene of contraception.

9. — AS REGARDS THE POPULATION AT PRESENT. We say that there are unfortunately many men and women who should be prevented from procreating children at all, because of their individual ill-health, or the diseased and degenerate nature of the offspring that they may be expected to produce. These considerations would not apply to a better and healthier world.

10. — There are many women unfortunately so constructed — suffering from weakness of certain organs — that

they would risk death if they were to attempt to bear children, and who, therefore, should not bear them.

11.—There are unfortunately many couples so ill-provided with this world's goods, or with means to acquire them, that they cannot support further children, and therefore should not bear them. Women, owing their own or their husband's incapacity to be self-supporting, may be permanently or temporarily in such a position owing to disaster or unemployment. The following Resolution was passed by our Society: Resolution passed at General Meeting November 22nd, 1921: "Both to spare your own personal distress and to avoid bringing a weakly child into the world, it is important that all should realize that no one should conceive in times of individual misery or ill-health. Of course wherever a child is already on the way, the best must be made of it. But sound and wholesome methods of Birth Control (Control of Conception) are known, and advice will be given free by a qualified nurse to all unemployed married persons who present this slip at the Mothers' Clinic, 61 Marlborough Road, Holloway, London, N.19."

12.—The Society approves and welcomes the work done by the first British Birth Control Clinic (The Mother's Clinic, 61 Marlborough Road, Holloway, London, N.19.), where the very poor and ignorant receive personal instruction; but we consider that this public service should not be left to private enterprise to maintain, and hence the Ministry of Health should supply suitable help and contraceptive instruction to working-class women at the many Ante-natal Clinics, Welfare Centres, etc., already in existence all over the country.

13.—We maintain that science has already made available contraceptive measure as safe and as simple to use as any other hygienic measures widely known and practised, such as brushing ones's teeth, or the removal daily of a dental plate by one who has artificial teeth. We, therefore, maintain that knowledge and instruction in these matters for the normal and healthy is an hygienic and not a medical matter. The problem of controlling conception on the part of those who are diseased, abnormal and unhealthy is on the other hand a purely medical matter and may involve measures which this Society would not advocate for general use.

14.—We as a Society are at present working for the dissemination of the best possible hygienic knowledge to all who are intelligent enough to be capable of using it, but we recognize the grave National problem raised by the fertility of those too degenerate or too careless to be capable of using any form of contraceptive.

15.—We are convinced that children spaced by voluntary means have a less mortality, and that the mother of such children has time to recover her health and attend to the young children in a better way, than if the pregnancies follow rapidly one after the other, and we are therefore in favour of voluntarily spacing all the desired children of even the healthiest woman.

16.—In short, we are profoundly and fundamentally a pro-baby organisation, in favour of producing the largest possible of healthy, happy children without detriment to the mother, and with the minimum wastage of infants by premature deaths. In this connection our motto has been "Babies in the right place," and it is just as much the aim of Constructive Birth Control to secure conception to those married people who are healthy, childless, and desire children, as it is to furnish security from conception to those who are racially diseased, already overburdened with children, or in any specific way unfitted for parenthood.

17.—We hold no fixed opinions concerning the total numbers wither of individual families or of populations, desiring only that the optimum shall be obtained. Passed by the Executive Committee, CBC March 1923.

Everyone who is interested in securing the best future for our Race should join the Society for Constructive Birth Control and Racial Progress. Apply for membership forms to the Hon. Secretary, CBC, 4-5, Adam St., Adelphi, London, W.C.2. Gerrard 4431.

---

[1] *The Authorized Life of Marie C. Stopes*. Covent Garden: Williams & Norgate Ltd. Appendix C on pages 222-226. Retrieved October 6, 2019, from https://archive.org/details/b29977587/page/n9.

Appendix 2

Lambert, Stopes and 61 Marlborough Road

In Birth Control Nursing in Marie Stopes Mothers' Clinics 1921-1931, Dr Pauline Brand discussed the acquisition and sale of 61 Marlborough Road, Holloway, the site of Stopes' first clinic.[1] In doing so, Brand revealed the close business relationship between Lambert and Stopes.

As mentioned elsewhere in this book, Lambert had met Stopes in 1920 and by 1921 they had informal arrangements in place (for instance, Lambert would send women to Dr Hawthorne to be fitted with a Gold Pin,[2] or that women who could afford to buy contraceptives would be sent to Lamberts in Dalston).[3] Lamberts donated 144 cervical caps to the Mothers' Clinic shortly before it opened, presumably because they valued the relationship with Stopes.

By 1925, the year Stopes moved to new premises in Whitfield Street Fitzrovia, the relationship had grown. In July of that year, Lamberts acquired the freehold for 61 Marlborough Road, where they opened a commercial birth control clinic which they subsequently named the "Birth Control Advisory Bureau".[4]

Lamberts paid Stopes £3,000 (or £3,800) for the title deeds,[5] over five (or six) times the £575 she paid in 1920.[6] Lamberts agreed to certain other conditions, such as agreeing to disassociate the Lambert clinic from the CBC and to ongoing arrangements to hire staff from Stopes as well as supplying them to her.[7] At some point the "Prorace" brand name was transferred to Lamberts and the firm became Lamberts Prorace Limited.[8]

Exterminating Poverty

Brand remarked that these arrangements have received little attention despite the vast historiography surrounding Stopes,[9] a view with which this author would concur.

---

[1] Brand, P. (2007). *Birth Control Nursing in the Marie Stopes Mothers' Clinics 1921 to 1931.* De Montfort University. Page 165.

[2] Letter from Stopes to Lambert dated 21st January 1921. British Library: Western Manuscripts MS58638 Vol.CXCII. 1920-1929.

[3] Letter from Stopes to Lambert dated 15th March 1921. British Library: Western Manuscripts MS58638 Vol.CXCII. 1920-1929.

[4] Lamberts Prorace Limited. (Circa. 1941). *Catalogue: Latest Price List of Approved Contraceptive Appliances.* Dalston: Lamberts Prorace Limited. Retrieved December 4, 2019, from https://muvs.org/en/bib/document/details/a1849.

[5] Brand, P. (2007). *Birth Control Nursing in the Marie Stopes Mothers' Clinics 1921 to 1931.* De Montfort University. Page 165.

[6] UK Land Registry. (n.d.). *UK Land Registry enquiry on Title No. 244758 (61 Marlborough Road, North Holloway, London N19 4PA).* Retrieved from https://www.gov.uk/government/organisations/land-registry.

[7] Brand, P. (2007). *Birth Control Nursing in the Marie Stopes Mothers' Clinics 1921 to 1931.* De Montfort University. Page 166.

[8] Lamberts Prorace Limited. (Circa. 1941). *Catalogue: Latest Price List of Approved Contraceptive Appliances.* Dalston: Lamberts Prorace Limited. Retrieved December 4, 2019, from https://muvs.org/en/bib/document/details/a1849.

[9] Brand, P. (2007). *Birth Control Nursing in the Marie Stopes Mothers' Clinics 1921 to 1931.* De Montfort University. Page 163.

Appendix 3

The Bradlaugh and Besant Trial

This account of the Bradlaugh and Besant trial was written by Dr Halliday Sutherland and was published in *Laws of Life*.[1]

Early in the nineteenth century there was published in Boston, Mass., a small book entitled *Fruits of Philosophy: An Essay on the Population Question* by Charles Knowlton, M.D., a well-qualified physician. This book is a popular treatise in favour of artificial birth control, and describes the physiology of generation, and certain methods of contraception. Although unnecessary details are given, the tone of the book is cold in comparison with the erotic productions of our own time. In America it circulated amongst Free Thinkers, and was first published in London about 1833. From that time the book was freely sold at Free Thought depots, until on December 23rd, 1876, a Bristol bookseller named Cook, who had interleaved the pages with indecent plates, was convicted. On January 10th, 1877, the London publisher was charged at the Guildhall with publishing an indecent book. He pleaded guilty, and the book was seized by the police. Charles Bradlaugh and Annie Besant, "honestly believing that on all questions affecting the happiness of the people" the "fullest right of free discussion ought to be maintained at all hazards," reprinted *Fruits of Philosophy*, and on March 23rd, 1877, intimated to the magistrates and to the police that it was once more on sale. Arrested on April 5th, they were charged at the Guildhall on April 16th, and remanded on bail. Further police court proceedings were taken on April 18th, and on April 20th, when the late Dr G. R. Drysdale, founder of the Malthusian League, gave evidence for the defence. Defendants then obtained an order transferring the proceedings into the High Court. So great was the public interest that 20,000 people are said to have assembled outside the Guildhall. The trial [1] before Lord Justice Cockburn and a Special Jury commenced on June 18th, 1877 and lasted five days. The Solicitor-General, Sir Harding Giffard, Mr. Douglas Straight, and Mr. Mead appeared for the prosecution.

Charles Bradlaugh and Annie Besant appeared in person, and were indicted for having published an obscene libel, this being the form of indictment adopted by the English Criminal Courts for preventing the dissemination of any matter which is calculated to destroy or corrupt the morals of the people. The defendants argued that the book itself was not obscene, and that the practices therein advocated were in the best interest of humanity. So wide was the scope of their defence that it included every single argument that has ever been advanced, even up to our own time, in favour of artificial birth control. Their defence was also remarkable by reason of the forensic ability of Bradlaugh and the eloquence of Mrs. Besant. Her opening speech included the following passage:

"I find my clients among the little children. Gentlemen, do you know the fate of so many of these children? The little ones half-starved because there is food enough for two but not enough for twelve; half-clothed because the mother, no matter what her skill and care, cannot clothe them with the money brought home by the bread-winner of the family; brought up in ignorance, and ignorance means pauperism and crime. Gentlemen, your happier circumstances have raised you above this suffering, but on you also this question presses; for those over-large families mean also increased poor rates, which are growing heavier year by year. These poor are my clients, and if I weary you by length of speech, as I fear I may, I do so because I think of them even more than I think of your time and trouble. You must remember that those for whom I speak are watching throughout England, Scotland and Ireland for the verdict you will give. Do you wonder I call them my clients, these poor, for whom I plead? They cannot bring the fee of gold such as is received by the learned gentlemen who are briefed against me here; but they bring what is better than gold; they send up a few pence week by week out of their scanty wage for as long as the trial lasts; they send up kindly thoughts and words of cheer and of encouragement; mothers who beg me to persist in the course on which I have entered, and at any hazard to myself, at any cost and any risk, they plead to me to save their daughters from the misery they have themselves passed through during the course of their married lives."

The case for the prosecution was twofold: First, that the book was obscene in itself; and secondly, that it tended to corrupt public morals because not only the married, but also the unmarried, and any boy or girl, could buy it for sixpence, and thereby learn how they might give way to passion without fear of results.

Lord Chief Justice Cockburn, in summing up, drew the jury's attention to two aspects of the criminal law. "In the first place, are there in this publication details inconsistent with decency, details calculated to enkindle the passions and desires of lust, and excite libidinous thoughts in the minds of the readers? Even if that should not be the case, the second point is whether the purpose advocated in the work, and the purpose and effect of the details, so elaborately given, is a purpose inconsistent with the morals of society. If so, the work is an illegal work, and the offence with which the defendants were charged, is made out."

On June 22nd, 1877, the jury brought in the following verdict: —

The Clerk: "Do you find the defendants guilty or not guilty of this charge?"

The Foreman: "We are unanimously of opinion [sic] that the book in question is calculated to deprave public morals, but at the same time we entirely exonerate the defendants from any corrupt motives in publishing it."

The Lord Chief Justice: "I am afraid, gentlemen, I must direct you, on that finding, to return a verdict of guilty under the indictment against the defendants."

Thereafter His Lordship postponed sentence until June 28th.

On June 28th, before the Lord Chief Justice and Mr. Justice Mellor, the defendants moved first to quash the indictment on the ground that the whole libel should have been set out thereon; and secondly, to arrest judgment on the same ground. These applications were refused. The defendants then asked for a new trial by reason of a contradiction in the finding of the jury. In refusing that application, the Court held that in a criminal trial the verdict must be either guilty or not guilty, and that the jury, by finding the book was calculated to deprave public morals, had returned a verdict of guilty, although the want of evil intention might be considered in the punishment. The Solicitor-General then produced two affidavits showing that the defendants, on the night of June 24th, had addressed a public meeting where *Fruits of Philosophy* was sold by the hundred to young women and lads. The Lord Chief Justice said that if the defendants had openly admitted their error and undertaken to do everything in their power to prevent the further circulation of a book which the jury found was calculated to deprave public morals, he would have been prepared to discharge them on their own recognizances to be of good behaviour in the future. But the case had now assumed the form of a most grave and aggravated offence. The sentence was that each of the defendants be imprisoned for six months, fined £200, and enter into recognizances in a sum of £500 each to be of good behaviour for the term of two years. The defendants then applied to stay execution of the sentence, and gave a pledge to stop the circulation of the book pending the result of an appeal. Leave to appeal was then granted, the defendants being discharged on their own recognizances for £100. In the Court of Appeal the sentence was quashed on the ground of serious omission in the indictment. It is right to add that Mrs. Besant, on becoming a Theosophist, renounced her approval of contraceptives.

[1] *Trial of C. Bradlaugh and A. Besant*. Published by A. & H. Bradlaugh Bonner, 1 Took's Court, London, E.C.

---

[1] Sutherland, H. (1936). *Laws of Life*. New York: Sheed & Ward. Pages 21-27.

Appendix 4

Stopes Visits McIlroy

Some years after the trial, Dr Stopes visited Professor McIlroy at her clinic in the Royal Free Hospital. Stopes' biographers commonly include this episode and falsely assert that despite her damaging testimony in the High Court, McIlroy was herself dispensing the cervical cap.

While the accounts of the encounter differ in the details, all are agreed that Stopes was disguised as a grimy charwoman, that she did not see McIlroy immediately, that McIlroy did not recognise Stopes and that McIlroy fitted a contraceptive device in Stopes.

The key difference in the accounts is whether McIlroy fitted a cervical cap or a diaphragm.[1] Establishing which account is the correct one is important, because if McIlroy fitted a cervical cap to Stopes — a device that she had attacked so publicly — it would have been the height of hypocrisy.

Below are four accounts of the encounter by Ruth Hall in 1977, June Rose in 1992, Clare Debenham in 2018 and Peter Neushul in 1998

In *Passionate Crusader* Ruth Hall wrote:

"A few years later, Marie claimed a moral revenge. Hearing that Professor McIlroy was now fitting women with pessaries, she disguised herself as a very dirty charwoman and went along to the clinic: 'After I was arranged on the examination couch underneath a coverlet, Professor McIlroy approached me wearing a rubber glove and told me to move my legs apart, pushing my legs in the desired direction through the coverlet. Before actually fitting the cap she did not even glance at organs or, even by a momentary view, examine the labia or vaginal orifice for discharge. She made no examination for venereal or other germs... A nurse supplied Dr McIlroy with a graded series of vaginal rubber caps, thrust the cap in, and almost immediately withdrew it, saying 'Yes, that is your size!' While the cap was being inserted, I felt extreme discomfort amounting to pain sufficiently acute to make it a great strain not to cry out or wince...

"Marie wrote to the Royal Free Hospital, demanding an apology and a retraction from Professor McIlroy for her earlier statements about the pessary. The secretary of the hospital wrote back: "Dear Madam, I am directed to acknowledge receipt of your letter of the 10th inst, which has been considered by the Weekly Board. They are much surprised that you should have abused the privileges of the Hospital by obtaining advice under such circumstances. They are not concerned with the dispute to which you refer and as you make no complaint regarding your treatment, my Board see no object in continuing the correspondence."[2]

In Marie Stopes and the Sexual Revolution, June Rose wrote:

"... to Marie, Professor McIlroy's attacks rankled. When she heard, four years later, that at the Royal Free Hospital Dr McIlroy herself was inserting the very vaginal caps she professed to find so harmful, Marie determined to find out. She first disguised herself as a 'work-grimed charwoman', then went along to the out-patients' clinic. 'When Professor McIlroy examined the grimy Marie Stopes, she did not even glance at the sex organs or, even by a momentary view, examine the labia or vaginal orifice for discharge. She made no examination for venereal or other germs...' Marie left the clinic with a cap and later wrote to the Royal Free Hospital demanding an apology and a retraction from Dr McIlroy. The Secretary relied stiffly that that Hospital had considered her letter and believed her to have abused the privileged of the Hospital by obtaining advice under false pretences. She received no apology."[3]

In Marie Stopes' Sexual Revolution and the Birth Control Movement, Clare Debenham wrote:

"Under cross-examination by Patrick Hastings the Professor admitted that she had never witnessed any woman using a rubber check diaphragm. After the end of the trial Marie took her revenge on Professor McIlroy who she heard was fitting this contraceptive device at the Royal Free Hospital. In her book *Ten Thousand Patients* Marie describes how theatrically she disguised herself as a work-grimed charwoman and after a wait of three hours was conveniently fitted with the rubber check pessary by the same Professor McIlroy."[4]

The source for the Hall and Rose accounts was an "autobiographical fragment" dated 13th December 1927, held in the British Library's Stopes Collection, and Debenham stated that she based her account on Stopes' book: *Ten Thousand Patients*. The element common to all three is that Stopes was fitted with a cervical cap, Hall and Rose concur that McIlroy did not examine Stopes for disease prior to fitting it and Debenham mentions a three hour wait.

Hall, Rose and Debenham's books are published "landmark" biographies by recognised scholars that are readily accessible to researchers, students and to the general reader.

The fourth account of the visit is given in *The Popularization of Birth Control Technology* by Peter Neushul. It was published in *Technology and Culture*. He wrote:

Disguising herself as a charwoman, Stopes made it through the reception room by insisting "in a hoarse cockney voice that I had been told to see Professor McIlroy herself." She used the name Marian Parker, age fifty-seven, of 17 Hill Road, Penge, S.E., and was told to see Professor McIlroy.

After a five to ten minute wait, Stopes met with McIlroy and informed her that "I had had a 'Sessarean' section and I was not very strong. My first baby had died; I had

320

been pregnant two other times and could not have any more. My husband was a van driver and after the 'Sessarean' section it took me nearly six months to get about again, and I could not have any more babies."

Throughout the meeting with McIlroy, Stopes spoke in a "slightly husky cockney voice and dropping aspirates." Stopes recalled that "her face was close to mine, within three or four inches, but there was not the slightest wavering of recognition or doubt to who she was looking at appeared to cross her face." When McIlroy tried to get Stopes to convince her husband to use a condom, Stopes replied, "Well, I got one of my kids that way one broke — and besides my husband does not like them." McIlroy then examined Stopes by "merely putting her finger in the vagina and estimating the size." Shortly thereafter McIlroy called for a box of diaphragms ("Fetch the sizes"), selected one, thrust it in, concluded that it was her size, and gave her an identical dry one. McIlroy said, "You see, what you do is to scrunch it up in your hand, and then slip it in as far as it will go using the centre finger. Leave it in all night and you ought to douche before taking it out next morning."

In an obvious effort to get McIlroy to prescribe a cervical cap, Stopes retorted, "[T]hat is awfully big, ain't it. The Nurse showed me something, but hers was less than half this size."

Professor McIlroy pinched the cap together in her hand, reducing it to about the size of a cervical cap and said, "I suppose you mean one like that." Stopes responded, "That's more like it; this looks so big." McIlroy replied, "Oh that kind, you cannot use that because it is very troublesome; you see it has to be fitted very time by a Nurse or Doctor, whereas this one you can fit yourself." Stopes concluded, "I said: 'Oh, all right, where do I pay'."

After her visit Stopes wrote a speech condemning McIlroy for going back on her word. In her notes, Stopes conceded that "she may reply that the cap she fitted is not exactly identical to ours". She also noted that "to emphasise the difference is but splitting hairs in the face of the photograph showing the extreme degree of similarity."

In fact, there was a big difference between the diaphragm and the cervical cap, one that Stopes sought to gloss over when she blasted McIlroy for prescribing the very "rubber cap" that she had testified about at the trial. Stopes' written account, published in the CBC newsletter, also criticised McIlroy for not taking "anything like the same care and precautions in the insertion of the cap that are the routine at our Birth Control Clinic; that she made no effort whatever to detect infection or venereal disease in the critical regions."[5]

Stopes' photograph to which Neushul referred was reproduced in Alymer Maude's *Marie Stopes: Her Work and Her Play*:[6]

There is a degree of similarity between the diaphragm ("B" in the centre) and the cervical caps ("A" and "C"), after all, they are all dome-shaped rubber devices. To say that they are the same, however, ignores the sleight-of-hand enabled by a still photograph of only one part of the fit. The difference between the devices is the dynamic of the fit: the cervical caps at "A" and "C" press inwards around the cervix while the diaphragm at "B" presses outwards against the walls of the vagina.

Neushul concluded:

"Unfortunately Stopes' calculated effort to smear McIlroy is perpetuated by her biographers, including the most recent, who repeats the propaganda that

McIlroy was "inserting the very vaginal caps she professed to find so harmful."[7]

In defence of Hall, Rose and Debenham, the Stopes' papers are voluminous — according to Rose a three-ton lorry was required to transport them from Stopes' home in Surrey to the British Museum when she died in 1958 — so they may not have been aware of the document on which Neushul based his paper. On the other hand, contraceptives played a major part in Stopes' life, so it is surprising that the terms used by her biographers are, at times, more confusing than those used by the male lawyers in the 1923 libel trial.[8]

Professor Louise McIlroy was a female pioneer who made an enormous contribution to medicine in Britain and to the Royal Free Hospital for Women. Stopes' false account unfairly tarnished her memory and the biographers of Stopes should not repeat the spiteful attack.

---

[1] The visit was discussed in greater detail in the article *The Trap* on hallidaysutherland.com. In particular, it shows the consistency between McIlroy's statements to Stopes in person and her testimony under oath in the High Court. See: https://hallidaysutherland.com/2019/06/01/stopes-visits-mcilroy/

[2] Hall, R. (1977). *Passionate Crusader: The Life of Marie Stopes*. New York: Harcourt Brace Jovanovich. Page 232.

[3] Rose, J. (1992). *Marie Stopes and the Sexual Revolution*. London: Faber and Faber Limited. Pages 170-1.

[4] Debenham, C. (2018). Marie Stopes' Sexual Revolution and the Birth Control Movement. Palgrave Pivot. Page 111.

[5] Neushul, P. (1998). *Marie C. Stopes and the Popularization of Birth Control Technology*. Technology and Culture, 39(2 (April 1998)), 245-272.

[6] This photo engraving shown from Maude's biography is an accurate representation of Stopes' photograph in the Wellcome Library. Maude, A. (1933). *Marie Stopes: Her Work and Play*. (2nd ed.). Covent Garden: Williams & Norgate. Page 277. Retrieved April 2017, 17, from https://archive.org/details/in.ernet.dli.2015.176142/page/n285.

[7] Neushul, P. (1998). *Marie C. Stopes and the Popularization of Birth Control Technology*. Technology and Culture, 39(2 April 1998)), 245-272.

[8] Hall referred to "pessaries", "vaginal rubber caps", "cap" and "cap". Rose used the terms: "the very vaginal caps she professed to find so harmful" and "cap" and Debenham used "rubber check diaphragm", "this contraceptive device" and "rubber check pessary".

Works Cited

Anglican Communion Office. (n.d.). *www.anglicancommunion.org/media*. Retrieved August 28, 2019, from Anglican Communion: https://www.anglicancommunion.org/media/127731/1920.pdf

Barr, Sir James (1911). *The Aim and Scope of Eugenics*. Edinburgh: Neill & Co., Ltd. Retrieved January 6, 2019, from https://archive.org/details/b30617030

Barr, Sir James (1912, July 27). *President's Address Delivered at the Eightieth Annual Meeting of the British Medical Association*. British Medical Journal, 157-163. Retrieved January 6, 2019, from https://www.ncbi.nlm.nih.gov/pmc/articles/PMC2334152

Barr, Sir James (1918, September 21). *The future of the medical profession*. British Medical Journal, 218-321. Retrieved July 16, 2018, from https://www.ncbi.nlm.nih.gov/pmc/articles/PMC2341835

Belloc, H . (1912). *The Servile State*. T.N. Foulis Limited, London and Edinburgh.

Brand, P. (2007). *Birth Control Nursing in the Marie Stopes Mothers' Clinics 1921 to 1931*. De Montfort University.

Brand, R. A. (2009). *Sir William Arbuthnot Lane, 1856–1943. Clinical Orthopaedics and Related Research*, 467(8). Retrieved September 23, 2019, from https://www.ncbi.nlm.nih.gov/pmc/articles/PMC2706364

British Broadcasting Corporation. (2018, December 28). *History. Marie Stopes (1880-1958)*. Retrieved from http://www.bbc.co.uk/history/historic_figures/stopes_marie_carmichael.shtml

British Medical Journal. (1924, September 13). *Obituary: Sir William Bayliss*.

British Medical Journal. (1930, November 29). *Obituary of Dame Mary Scharlieb*. British Medical Journal, 935-937. Retrieved January 29, 2019, from https://www.ncbi.nlm.nih.gov/pmc/articles/PMC2451802/?page=1

British Medical Journal. (1938, November 26). *Obituary Sir James Barr, M.D., F.R.C.P.*

British Medical Journal. (1945, March 17). *Obituary Viscount Dawson of Penn*. British Medical Journal, 389-392.

British Medical Journal. (1960, April 30). *Obituary Dr Halliday G. Sutherland, M.D.* , 1368-9 Retrieved January 29, 2019 from https://www.ncbi.nlm.nih.gov/pmc/articles/PMC1967536

British Medical Journal. (1968, February 17). *Obituary Notice Louise McIlroy D.B.E.* British Medical Journal, 451.

Chesterton, G. (1922). *Eugenics and Other Evils*. London, New York, Toronto and Melbourne: Cassell and Company, Limited.

Cohen, D. (1993). *Private Lives in Public Spaces: Marie Stopes: the Mothers' Clinics and the Practice of Contraception*. History Workshop (No.35 (Spring 1993)), 95-116.

Debenham, C. (2018). *Marie Stopes' Sexual Revolution and the Birth Control Movement*. Palgrave Pivot.

Debenham, C. (2018, March 23). *Married Love: the 1918 book by Marie Stopes that helped launch the birth control movement*. Retrieved November 14, 2019, from theconversation.com: https://theconversation.com/married-love-the-1918-book-by-marie-stopes-that-helped-launch-the-birth-control-movement-93108

Debenham, M. C. (2018, April 3). *Married Love: the 1918 book by Marie Stopes that helped launch the birth control movement*. Retrieved November 7, 2019, from The Independent: https://www.independent.co.uk/arts-entertainment/books/marie-stopes-birth-control-married-love-book-sex-eugenics-a8274036.html

Drapers' Company Research Memoirs. (1908). *A Second Study of the Statistics of Pulmonary Tuberculosis: Marital Infection*. London: Dulau and Co. Retrieved January 4, 2019, from https://archive.org/details/b22419123/page/n1

Elderton, E. (1915). *The Relative Strength of Nurture and Nature*. London: Cambridge University Press. Retrieved August 20, 2019, from https://archive.org/stream/relativestrength00eldeiala#page/n1/mode/2up

Ellis, H. (1912). *The Task of Social Hygiene*, Houghton Mifflin Company, Boston and New York.

Eugenics Education Society. (1912). *Programme and Time Table*, First International Eugenics Congress. Beverley: Minster Press.

Eyler, J. M. (1997). *Sir Arthur Newsholme and State Medicine, 1885-1935*. Cambridge, U.K.: Cambridge University Press.

Farmer, A. (2008). *By Their Fruits: Eugenics, Population Control, and the Abortion Campaign*. Washington D.C.: The Catholic University of America Press.

Femina Books. (1967). *The Trial of Marie Stopes*. (M. Box, Ed.) London: Femina Books Ltd.

Fraser, S. H. (1898). *A Compendium of the Law of Torts*. London: Sweet and Maxwell. Retrieved March 28, 2019, from https://archive.org/details/compendiumoflawo00fras/page/n3

Galton, F. (1873). *Hereditary Improvement*. Fraser's Magazine, 116-130.

Galton, F. (1904). *Eugenics: Its Definition Scope and Aims*. Nature (70), 82. Retrieved January 4, 2019, from http://galton.org/essays/1900-1911/galton-1904-am-journ-soc-eugenics-scope-aims.htm

Galton, S. F. (1904) *Eugenics: Its Definition, Scope and Aims*. The American Journal of Sociology, X (Number 1).

Goring, C. (1913). *The English Convict: A Statistical Study*. London: His Majesty's Stationery Office. Retrieved January 7, 2019, from https://archive.org/details/englishconvictst00goriuoft/page/n3

Greer, G. (1985). *Sex and Destiny: The Politics of Human Fertility*. London: Picador (in association with Martin Secker & Warburg Limited).

Gulland, A. (2015, February 2). *Obituary: Tim Black*. Retrieved November 12, 2019, from The BMJ: https://doi.org/10.1136/bmj.h459

Hall, L. (2015). *"The Subject is Obscene: No Lady Would Dream of Alluding to It": Marie Stopes and her courtroom dramas*. In S. R. Katie Barclay (Ed.), Performing the Self: Women's Lives in Historical Perspective. London and New York: Routledge.

Hall, L. (n.d.). *Book Review, June Rose "Marie Stopes and the Sexual Revolution"*. Retrieved 2019, from Leslie Hall's Web Pages: https://www.lesleyahall.net/jrose.htm

Hall, L. (n.d.). *Situating Stopes: or, putting Marie in her proper place*. Retrieved January 17, 2019, from http://www.lesleyahall.net/: https://www.lesleyahall.net/stopes.htm

Hall, R. (1977). *Passionate Crusader: The Life of Marie Stopes*. New York: Harcourt Brace Jovanovich.

Haycraft, J. B. (1895). *Darwinism and Race Progress*. London: Swan Sonnenschein & Co. Retrieved January 4, 2019, from https://archive.org/details/darwinismandrac01haycgoog/page/n6

Hunter, D. (1912, November 30). *Letter*. British Medical Journal, 1578-1579. Retrieved January 7, 2019, from https://www.ncbi.nlm.nih.gov/pmc/articles/PMC2334872

Kevles, D. J. (2004). *In the Name of Eugenics: Genetics and the Uses of Human Heredity* (5th Printing ed.). Cambridge, Massachusetts: Harvard University Press.

Kingston University. (n.d.). *Sir William Arbuthnot Lane (1856 - 1943)*. Retrieved September 23, 2019, from HHARP: Historic Hospital Admissions Records Project: http://www.hharp.org/library/gosh/doctors/william-arbuthnot-lane.html

Korda, M. (2001). *Making the list: a cultural history of the American bestseller, 1900-1999*. New York: Barnes & Noble Publishing Inc.

Lamberts Prorace Limited. (Circa. 1941). *Catalogue: Latest Price List of Approved Contraceptive Appliances*. Dalston: Lamberts Prorace Limited. Retrieved December 4, 2019, from https://muvs.org/en/bib/document/details/a1849

Ludovici, A. M. (1925). *Lysistrata or Woman's Future and Future Woman*. London: Kegan Paul, Trench, Trubner & Co., Ltd. Retrieved September 30, 2019, from https://archive.org/stream/lysistrataorwoma00ludouoft#page/6/mode/2up

Malthusian League. (1922). *The Fifth International Neo-Malthusian and Birth Control Conference*. In R. Pierpoint (Ed.), Report of the Fifth International Neo-Malthusian and Birth Control Conference. London: William Heinemann (Medical Books) Ltd. Retrieved October 21, 2017, from https://archive.org/details/reportoffifthint00inteuoft

Marie Stopes International. (2019, October 6). *About*. Retrieved from Marie Stopes International: https://mariestopes.org/about-us/our-history

Maude, A. (1924). *The Authorized Life of Marie C. Stopes*. Covent Garden: Williams & Norgate Ltd. Retrieved October 6, 2019, from https://archive.org/details/b29977587/page/n9

Maude, A. (1933). *Marie Stopes: Her Work and Play*. London: John Bale, Sons & Danielsson, Ltd. Retrieved April 2017, 17, from https://archive.org/details/in.ernet.dli.2015.176142

McCrystal, C. (1992, August 23). *Notebook: The monster and the master race: She altered women's lives for ever. But a new book reveals that Marie

Stopes's motives were distinctly dubious. The Independent. Retrieved May 23, 2019, from https://www.independent.co.uk/voices/notebook-the-monster-and-the-master-race-she-altered-womens-lives-for-ever-but-a-new-book-reveals-1541975.html

National Birth Rate Commission. (1920). *Problems of Population and Parenthood. Being the Second Report of and the chief evidence taken by the National Birth-rate Commission, 1918-1920*. London: Chapman and Hall, Ltd. Retrieved January 28, 2019, from https://archive.org/details/problemsofpopula00natiuoft/page/n8

Neushul, P. (1998). *Marie C. Stopes and the Popularization of Birth Control Technology*. Technology and Culture, 39(2 (April 1998)), 245-272.

Newsholme, A. (1908). *The Prevention of Tuberculosis*. London: Methuen & Co.

Odgers, W. (1897). *An Outline of the Law of Libel: Six lectures delivered in the Middle Temple Hall during Michaelmas Term 1896*. Macmillan and Co., Limited.

Pearson, E. (1938). *Karl Pearson: An Appreciation of Some Aspects of His Life and Work*. Cambridge: Cambridge University Press.

Pearson, K. (1907). *A First Study of the Statistics of Pulmonary Tuberculosis*. London: Dulau and Co.

Pearson, K. (1910, April 28,). *Nature and Nurture: The Problem of the Future*. A Presidential Address at the Annual General Meeting of the Social and Political Education League.

Pearson, K. (1912). *Treasury of Human Inheritance (Vol. 1)*. London: Dulau and Co. Ltd. Retrieved January 7, 2019, from https://archive.org/details/treasuryofhumani01bull/page/n5

Pearson, K. (1912). *Tuberculosis, Heredity and Environment: Being a Lecture Delivered at the Galton Laboratory for National Eugenics*. London: Dulau and Co., Ltd.

Peel, J. (1963, November). *The Manufacture and Retailing of Contraceptives in England*. Population Studies, 17(2), 113-125. Retrieved April 22, 2018, from http://www.jstor.org/stable/2172841

Penn, L. D. (1921). *Love-Marriage-Birth Control: Being a Speech delivered at the Church Congress at Birmingham, October 1921*. London: Nisbet & Co. Ltd. 22 Berners Street, W.1. Retrieved March 25, 2019, from https://archive.org/details/lovemarriagebirt00dawsrich/page/n5

Rose, J. (1992). *Marie Stopes and the Sexual Revolution*. London: Faber and Faber Limited.

Salmond, J. W. (1916). *The Law of Torts: A Treatise on the English Law of Liability for Civil Injuries (Fourth ed.)*. Temple Bar: Stevens and Haynes. Retrieved January 18, 2019, from https://archive.org/details/cu31924022354173/page/n5

Searle, G. (1976). *Eugenic and Politics in Britain 1900-1914*. Leyden: Noordhoff International Publishing.

Shaw, G. (1921, August 4). *Postcard to Halliday Sutherland*. Personal papers of Dr Halliday Sutherland.

Schenk, Faith and Parkes F.A. (1968, September). *Activities of the Eugenics Society*. The Eugenics Review, 142-161. Retrieved May 27, 2019, from

https://www.ncbi.nlm.nih.gov/pmc/articles/PMC2906074/p
df/eugenrev00003-0012.pdf

Soloway, R. (1997). *The Galton Lecture 1996: Marie Stopes, Eugenics and the Birth
Control Movement*. In R. Peel (Ed.), Marie Stopes Eugenics and
the English Birth Control Movement (p. 113). London: The
Galton Institute.

Soloway, R. A. (1990). *Demography and Degeneration: Eugenics and the Declining
Birthrate in Twentieth Century Britain* (Digital Edition ed.).
Chapel Hill: University of North Carolina Press.

Southern Cross. (1939, October 20). *Echoes of Famous Law Case, A.R.P. At Sea*.
Southern Cross, p. 9. Retrieved January 20, 2019, from
https://trove.nla.gov.au/newspaper/article/167762630

Souvenir of the Marriage of Mr Halliday Sutherland M.D. with Muriel
Fitzpatrick. (1920). London.

St Marylebone Dispensary for the Prevention of Consumption. (1911). *First
Annual Report*. London: Martin & Son, The Harewood Press, 18
Lisson Grove, Marylebone, N.W.

Stopes, M. (1920). *Radiant Motherhood: A Book for Those who are Creating the
Future*. London: G.P. Putnam's Sons Limited. Retrieved August
24, 2019, from
https://archive.org/details/radiantmotherhoo00stopiala/page/n5

Stopes, M. (1921). *Queen's Hall Meeting on Constructive Birth Control: Speeches
and Impressions*. London: G.P. Putnam's Sons Ltd.

Stopes, M. (1921). *Verbatim Report of the Town Hall Meeting under the Auspices of
the Voluntary Parenthood League*. New York: Voluntary
Parenthood League. Retrieved January 14, 2019, from
https://archive.org/details/101553806.nlm.nih.gov

Stopes, M. C. (1918). *Married Love (6th ed.)*. London: A.C. Fifield. Retrieved
August 28, 2019, from
https://archive.org/details/married_love/page/n1

Stopes, M. C. (1920). *Wise Parenthood: A Practical Sequel to Married Love (6th ed.)*.
London: G.P. Putnam's Sons Ltd, London. Retrieved January 3,
2019, from https://archive.org/details/cihm_990552/page/n7

Stopes, M. C. (1923). *Contraception (Birth Control): Its Theory, History and
Practice*. London: John Bale, Sons & Danielsson, Limited.
Retrieved March 28, 2019, from
https://archive.org/stream/in.ernet.dli.2015.94163/2015.94163.
Contraception#page/n5/mode/2up/search/sutherland

Sullivan, A. (1952). *The Last Serjeant: The Memoirs of Serjeant A.M. Sullivan*.
London: Macdonald.

Sutherland, H. (Director). (1911). *The Story of John M'Neil* [Motion Picture].
Retrieved January 4, 2019, from
https://player.bfi.org.uk/free/film/watch-the-story-of-john-
mneil-1911-online

Sutherland, H. (1912, November 23). *The Soil and the Seed in Tuberculosis*.
British Medical Journal, 2(2708), 1434-1437. Retrieved January 5,
2019, from
https://www.ncbi.nlm.nih.gov/pmc/articles/PMC2334807

Sutherland, H. (1917). *Consumption: Its Cause and Cure*. London: Red Triangle
Press.

Sutherland, H. (1922). *Birth Control: A Statement of Christian Doctrine Against the Neo-Malthusians*. London: Harding & More.

Sutherland, H. (1922, May 19). *Heredity & Consumption: Marriage Problem - A Challenge to The Eugenists*. Westminster Gazette.

Sutherland, H. (1933). *Arches of the Years*. Geoffrey Bles.

Sutherland, H. (1934). *A Time to Keep*. Geoffrey Bles.

Sutherland, H. (1936). *In My Path*. Geoffrey Bles.

Sutherland, H. (1936). *Laws of Life*. New York: Sheed & Ward.

Sutherland, H. (1944). *Control of Life*. London: Burns, Oates and Washbourne, Ltd.

Sutherland, H. (1956). *Irish Journey*. London: Geoffrey Bles.

Sutherland, H., & (Editor). (1911). *The Control and Eradication of Tuberculosis*. London and Edinburgh: William Green and Son.

The Air Ministry and Royal Air Force Service Records. (n.d.). *The National Archives*. Retrieved January 17, 2019, from http://discovery.nationalarchives.gov.uk: http://discovery.nationalarchives.gov.uk/results/r?_q=hallida y+sutherland

The Galton Institute. (2019, October 30). *History / Archives*. Retrieved from The Galton Institute: Exploring Human Heredity: http://www.galtoninstitute.org.uk/history/archives/

The Linnean Society. (2019, September 17). Retrieved from The Linnean Society of London: https://www.linnean.org/the-society

The Royal Courts of Justice. (2019, September 12). *History*. Retrieved September 12, 2019, from The Royal Courts of Justice: https://theroyalcourtsofjustice.com/

The University of Manchester. (2016, June 22). *Who was the real Marie Stopes?* Retrieved November 7, 2019, from The University of Manchester: https://www.manchester.ac.uk/discover/news/who-was-the-real-marie-stopes/

UK Land Registry. (n.d.). *UK Land Registry enquiry on Title No. 244758 (61 Marlborough Road, North Holloway, London N19 4PA)*. Retrieved from https://www.gov.uk/government/organisations/land-registry

Vickers, M. (2013). *By the Thames Divided: Cardinal Bourne in Southwark and Westminster*. Gracewing Publishing.

Williams, Z. (2011, February 2). *Marie Stopes: a turbo-Darwinist ranter, but right about birth control*. The Guardian. Retrieved December 29, 2018, from https://www.theguardian.com/theguardian/2011/sep/02/ma rie-stopes-right-birth-control

Winter, J. (1980, April). *Military Fitness and Civilian Health in Britain during the First World War*. Journal of Contemporary History, 15(2), 211-244.

Wyndham, D. (1996). *Striving for National Fitness: Eugenics In Australia 1910 To 1930s*. Sydney: Department of History, University of Sydney. Retrieved November 6, 2019, from http://www.kooriweb.org/foley/resources/AEK1201/eugenic s/eugenics1.pdf

Wyndham, D. (2012). *Norman Haire and the Study of Sex*. Sydney: Sydney University Press.

About the authors

Mark Sutherland is a trainer, facilitator and executive coach who lives with his wife and son in Sydney. A graduate of the Australian Graduate School of Management (MBA), he has worked in banking, financial services and investment in Britain and Australia. Mark was born in Singapore and spent his childhood in Brunei, HongKong, Malaysia, the Philippine Islands and Yorkshire. He served in the Honourable Artillery Company. Mark's articles have been published in the *Catholic World Report* and *One Peter Five* websites. He curates and writes articles for hallidaysutherland.com a website celebrating the life and work of Dr Halliday Sutherland. *Exterminating Poverty* is his first book.

Neil Sutherland is an Independent Financial Adviser who owns and manages his company, Sutherland IFA, a business that specialises in investment. He lives with his wife and two children on the edge of the New Forest in Whiteparish, Wiltshire.

To contact the authors, use the form on the "contact" page at:

ExterminatingPovertyBook.com

Index

Printed in Great Britain
by Amazon